A COMMENTARY OF THE CODE OF CANON LAW

A Commentary on the Code of Canon Law

IN THE LIGHT OF VATICAN II AND THE ECUMENICAL AGE

Marriage TODAY

Bernard Andrew Siegle, T.O.R., J.C.D.

SECOND EDITION

ALBA · HOUSE NEW · YORK

SOCIETY OF ST. PAUL, 2187 VICTORY BLVD., STATEN ISLAND, NEW YORK 10314

Ex Parte Ordinis
Nihil Obstat: Christian Oravec, T.O.R., Censor Librorum
Imprimi Potest: Columba Devlin, T.O.R., Minister
Provincial

Library of Congress Cataloging in Publication Data

Siegle, Bernard Andrew.
Marriage today.

Bibliography: p. 339
1. Marriage (Canon law)   I. Title.
LAW   262.9'33   72-4055
ISBN 0-8189-0253-1

Nihil Obstat:
Robert Senetsky, J.C.D.

Imprimatur:
Michael J. Dudick, D.D.
Bishop of Passaic Diocese
March 28, 1972

*The Nihil Obstat and Imprimatur
are a declaration that a book or pamphlet is considered
to be free from doctrinal or moral error. It is not implied that those
who have granted the Nihil Obstat and Imprimatur agree with the contents,
opinions or statements expressed.*

*Designed, printed and bound in the United States of America by the Fathers
and Brothers of the Society of St. Paul, 2187 Victory Boulevard,
Staten Island, New York 10314, as part of their
communications apostolate.*

2 3 4 5 6 7 8 9 (Current Printing: first digit).

FOREWORD

While marriage is divine in its origin, it is natural in its purpose. It is a sacred institution through which the Author of life permits His creatures to share in the act of creation. Yet, marriage is a contract that must be lived by frail humans in an ever-changing and often confusing world.

The fundamental importance of marriage to society can never be over-emphasized. St. Augustine said that, "the first natural tie of human society is man and wife," and other great minds have never ceased to worry and warn about the close relation between the stability of marriage and the stability of the nation. Yet, one-third of all marriages in the United States ends in divorce—and Catholics are not entirely strangers to this tragedy.

Immense and heroic efforts are now being made to halt the deterioration of modern marriages. Cana and pre-Cana conferences are given; marriage and psychological counseling are offered; splendid doctrinal, moral and spiritual treatises are being attractively published, as well as handbooks for the married and those contemplating marriage.

Excellent though these books and services are, there has long been a breach in the defenses against the dangers to modern marriage. There has been an inadequate supply of practical, up-to-date manuals of principles and procedures in matrimonial matters for those who need them most—the parish priests, chancery and tribunal officials, missionaries and those who are preparing for the priesthood.

Marriage Today was written to fill this gap and it does it well. Father Bernard Siegle, eminently qualified by training and experience to write this book, deserves the gratitude of all who wrestle with the complexities of today's marriage problems and who seek guidance and help in their extremely complicated and delicate work.

May *Marriage Today* help to fulfill the fifth century prayer read in the Nuptial Mass:

"Graciously hear our petition, Lord, and in Your loving kindness further Your own design for the continuance of mankind. Let the union made by Your warrant be preserved by Your help."

Richard Cardinal Cushing

"For this cause a man shall leave father and mother and cleave to his wife, and the two shall become one flesh. Therefore now they are no longer two, but one flesh."

Mark 10:7-8

FOREWORD

TO THE 2ND EDITION

Numerous marriages between members of the Roman rite and the faithful of Eastern rite Churches occur annually in our country. More often than not, Catholics of different rites encounter difficulties when they intend to marry each other because one or both lack knowledge of Church legislation concerning inter-ritual marriages. Since all rites possess their own spiritual heritage and canonical discipline, difficulties and problems do arise. For this reason, it is necessary to be knowledgeable or have some understanding regarding ecclesiastical marriage legislation in both the Western and Eastern Churches. Because few books are available which deal with laws involving the various rites of the Catholic Church, I am pleased an updated second edition of *Marriage Today* is being published.

The first edition of *Marriage Today* by the Reverend Bernard Siegle, T.O.R., has proven to be a well written, informative and helpful book. We look forward to the same success for the second edition. Father Siegle's experience as a professor of Canon Law for more than twenty-five years in both Roman and Byzantine rite seminaries and his continued interest in inter-ritual affairs have given him a deep insight into today's modern marriage problems, which many unfortunately encounter. His aim is to help avoid needless pitfalls. His many years of Tribunal practice, together with the experience derived from his present office as Officialis of the Tribunal of the Metropolitan-Archdiocese of Munhall, Pennsylvania, qualify him to speak with firsthand knowledge on this subject. As an author, he deserves the gratitude of the clergy, seminarians and laity of all rites.

Since the Commission for the Revision of the Code of Canon Law, which has been working for several years in Rome on a new codification of ecclesiastical legislation, will not be ready with a revision for several years, *Marriage Today* remains relevant to our time and needs. It should continue to serve as an invaluable aid to those interested in the complexities of today's marriage problems and for those who look for guidance in their present difficulties.

Most Reverend Michael J. Dudick, D.D.
Bishop of Passaic

PREFACE

Canon Law is a universal law binding both Catholics of the Latin rite and Catholics of the Oriental rite. It is necessary to state that law in general is divided into two categories, namely, (1) Divine Law and (2) Human Law. Divine Law is subdivided into (a) Divine Natural Law which is the participation of the Eternal Law of God, placed in the very nature of things when by God; and (b) Divine Positive Law which is made known by God himself through divine revelation. (2) Human Law is subdivided into Ecclesiastical Law and Civil Law.

The Church teaches that all authority comes from God because in God's plan we find an orderly government of the world. The Church upholds that God delegated his authority to two perfect sovereign societies independently and exclusively competent to regulate the affairs of mankind within its own sphere. These two societies we call the Church and the State. The Church was established by God for the spiritual welfare of man in the world to help him attain his salvation. The State, on the other hand, was established by God for the temporal welfare of mankind.

Within the Church's exclusive realm of jurisdiction come the seven Sacraments instituted by Christ. Moreover, the Roman Catholic Church considers itself as divinely appointed guardian and interpreter of the Divine Positive and Natural Law. It considers the State the legitimate civil authority which God grants the authority to make laws, carry them out and pass judgment upon all things which pertain to the temporal welfare of mankind.

Since marriage is the foundation stone of human society, the Church considers this institution most sacred because it was instituted by God not man.

God made certain positive regulations concerning marriage, but all the other important detail requirements and restrictions follow from the very nature of marriage itself for the benefit of mankind. All marriages should be governed by the precepts of divine-positive and natural laws, regardless of the tenets or belief of the individuals contracting marriage.

Marriage is a contract between a man and a woman, who are juridically capable of contracting marriage, by which each gives and accepts the perpetual and exclusive rights to acts suitable for the generation of offspring. This definition pertains to all marriages, regardless of the subjective beliefs, or the lack of belief, of the parties who contract marriage. Therefore, all persons, regardless of their religious belief, who are not juridically capable, who do not give and accept the rights to acts suitable for generation, or who do not give and accept the right perpetually and exclusively, do not make a valid contract. Therefore, unity and indissolubility are the essential qualities of every true marriage by the Natural Law and by the very definition and nature of marriage. Because of this, a valid marriage contract is much different from every other contract; the marriage contract results in a bond and relationship sealed by God, who instituted it, between the two parties.

Therefore, the marriage contract cannot be broken by mutual agreement of both parties; although the two made the mutual contract, they cannot undo or break this bond since this contract is governed by Divine Law. It is principally with this end in view that this work has been written, and now revised as the second edition, in order to bring up-to-date all the new legislation according to the recommendations of Vatican Council II, the Synod of Bishops, and the Ecumenical Age. This work is intended for every priest and clergyman, as well as the teacher, lawyer and other members of the laity to whom it may concern who wish to be more knowledgeable about the marriage regulations in this modern age.

CONTENTS

CHAPTER III

IMPEDIMENTS IN GENERAL   73

CHAPTER IV

PROHIBITIVE IMPEDIMENTS   97

Contents   13

CHAPTER V

DIRIMENT IMPEDIMENTS   113

CHAPTER VI

MATRIMONIAL CONSENT   169

CHAPTER VII

FORM OF MARRIAGE   197

CHAPTER VIII

CONSEQUENCES OF MARRIAGE   231

CHAPTER IX

SEPARATION OF MARRIED PERSONS   249

CHAPTER X

CONVALIDATION OF MARRIAGE   257

APPENDIX

A COMMENTARY OF THE CODE OF CANON LAW

CHAPTER I

GENERAL PRINCIPLES

NATURE OF MARRIAGE

Canon 1012: 1. CHRIST OUR LORD ELEVATED THE MAT-
RIMONIAL CONTRACT BETWEEN TWO
BAPTIZED PERSONS TO THE DIGNITY OF
A SACRAMENT.

2. THEREFORE, EVERY VALID MARRIAGE
CONTRACTED BETWEEN BAPTIZED PER-
SONS IS BY THAT VERY FACT A SACRA-
MENT.

Canon 1012 is a dogmatic theological law stating that marriage between Christians is not only a contract but also a sacrament.

1. *Marriage as a Sacrament*: It is a visible sign instituted by
Christ to give sacramental grace; this he did by making the
contract the instrument by which sacramental grace is conveyed
to the parties. The sign consists of *matter* and *form*: "The mutual
and lawful surrender of the bodies indicated by *words* or *signs*
expressing the interior consent which is the *matter* of the sacra-

ment while the mutual lawful acceptance of the bodies is its *form*" (Pope Benedict XIV).[1]

The matter, then, is the mutual offer made by the words or signs expressing genuine internal consent to the contract, while the form is the mutual acceptance expressed in a similar manner. For a valid contract, consent must be both interiorly genuine and mutually expressed externally.

The sacred quality of any marriage is emphasized by Pope Pius XI when he said: "The light of reason alone—above all, if we study the ancient records of history, if we question the unchanging conscience of peoples, if we examine the institutions and moral codes of nations—is enough to establish that there is in marriage itself a sacred and religious quality" (*Casti Connubii*). Even Pope Innocent III and Pope Honorius III "felt able to affirm without rashness and with good reason that the sacrament of marriage exists among believers and unbelievers," says Pope Leo XIII. What he means is that the act of marriage itself is holy as a fact of nature willed by God.

Pope Pius XI continues: "The sacred character of marriage, intimately linked to the order of religion and of holy things, is the effective result of its divine origin and also of its purpose which is to bring children to birth and to form them for God, and at the same time to bind husband and wife to God in Christian love and mutual help; and finally it is the result of the duty which is mutual to married union itself, instituted as it is by the all-wise providence of God the Creator, the duty to serve as a sort of medium for the transmission of life, by which parents become as it were the instruments of the almighty power of God." To emphasize still further that the sacred character of marriage is inherent in its nature Pius XII reminds us that "even among those who are not baptized, legitimately contracted marriage is, in the natural order, a sacred thing" (Allocution to the Sacred Roman Rota, Oct. 6, 1946).

The grace of the sacrament of matrimony corresponds to

1. Benedict XIV, *Paucis Abbino*, March 19, 1758.

the threefold effects it has upon marriage, namely, (1) sacramental effect which is potential indissolubility (*bonum sacramenti*); (2) the fidelity to one another (*bonum fidei*); and (3) the welfare of the offspring (*bonum prolis*).

2. *Marriage as a Contract*: Marriage is by its nature a contract. This does not mean that it is a mere civil contract, neither is it a civil transaction, even though it takes place before a civil magistrate. Marriage, for all human beings, is by its very nature, a sacred contract as emphasized by many of the pontiffs. The marriage of two pagans—two unbaptized—is a sacred contract. To be a sacramental marriage, however, two parties must be validly baptized. It makes no difference if the parties are baptized in the Catholic or Protestant Church. Two questions arise: (1) Is a marriage between a baptized person and a non-baptized person a sacrament? This marriage is not sacramental. It could not be; we have no such thing as half a sacrament. The Holy Office refers to such a marriage as a "natural bond" [2] (S. C.S. Office, Nov. 5, 1924); (2) Does the marriage of two pagans become a sacramental marriage, if both receive baptism? The answer is affirmative. Their marriage becomes a sacramental marriage without renewing their consent.

PURPOSE OF MARRIAGE

Canon 1013: 1: The Primary end of marriage is the procreation and education of children; the secondary end is mutual support and allaying of concupiscence.

2: The essential properties of marriage are unity and indissolubility, which give stability to a Christian marriage by virtue of the sacrament.

---

2. S.C.S. Office, Nov. 5, 1924. / Wm. W. Bassett, *The Bond of Marriage*, Univ. of Notre Dame Press, 1968. The chapter "The Marriage of Christians — Valid Contract, Valid Sacrament?," pp. 117-179. An excellent treatise on marriage as a sacrament and a contract.

Comment: This canon as stated is the traditional teaching of the Church. If this canon had been studied in depth during the codification of the law (1904-1912), the result might have been different because over the years there has been very much controversial discussion over this teaching, namely, the primary and secondary ends of marriage. Canonists and theologians find it difficult to provide an adequate explanation of the nature of marriage; these experts claim that if the term "primary" is retained, then there is more than one primary end of marriage as will be illustrated.

The secondary end of marriage, says the canon, is mutual support and allaying of concupiscence. This also is the traditional teaching of the Church. However, this secondary end of marriage known as the "remedy of concupiscence" is, to say the least (in its terminology), very misleading and offensive. It gives one the impression that God instituted marriage to remedy concupiscence. The notion which *remedium concupiscentiae* conveys is offensive because it gives the idea that marriage is a permission to engage in activities which are shameful, sinful and improper. This concept of *remedium* arises in part from the historical and cultural background of theologians who fostered this idea from a failure to appreciate the insights of modern psychology which sees this in a different light. The desire for marital relations is fully normal and good. Yet, to speak of it as "concupiscence" or a desire in need of a remedy, namely marriage, is to imply that it is a human weakness, or that something is lacking, or that something is defective in man.

Therefore to answer the question: what are the ends of marriage? we put aside the traditional answer and state that there are many subjective ends of marriage: such as companionship, security, love, etc.; there are also objective ends which flow from the marital act itself: namely procreation, mutual love and education of the offspring.

Vatican Council II deliberately left out the terminology of primary and secondary ends of marriage because of the mistaken notion it once conveyed. In the pastoral Constitution of the

Church in the Modern World we find the following: "Marriage to be sure is not instituted solely for procreation; rather, its very nature as an unbreakable compact between persons, and the welfare of children, both demand that the mutual love of the spouses be embodied in a rightly ordered manner, that it grow and ripen. Therefore, marriage persists as a whole manner and communion of life, and maintains its value and indissolubility, even when despite the often intense desire of the couple, offspring is lacking." With this we can discard the traditional expression of "primary" and "secondary" ends of marriage and simply state that the ends of marriage are the procreation and education of offspring and mutual love between the spouses.

ESSENTIAL PROPERTIES

Unity and Indissolubility

Unity: This is one of the essential characteristics of every marriage whether Christian or non-Christian. By unity is meant oneness. A husband has only one wife; a wife has only one husband. In other words unity means that marriage can take place only between one man and one woman. Another word for unity would be monogamy. The opposite is polygamy which is twofold: (a) polyandry—which exists when one woman has several husbands; (b) polygeny—which exists when one man has several wives. Polyandry is opposed to the primary concept of natural law; it is also opposed to the primary ends of marriage since it not only interferes with the love and companionship of the spouse, but is also the potential cause of sterility. If there are children, the paternity is doubtful in which case the education of children is uncertain.

Indissolubility: This is the second essential characteristic of marriage which means that the contract of marriage cannot be dissolved at will or with the consent of the contracting parties but only through death of one of the parties.

MARRIAGE FAVORED BY LAW

Canon 1014: Marriage enjoys the favor of the law; hence in case
of doubt the validity of the marriage is to be upheld until the contrary is proved, without prejudice to the prescription of Canon 1127.

I. Whenever a doubt arises concerning the validity of a
marriage that was certainly celebrated, the marriage is considered valid until the contrary is proved with moral certainty.
If there is a doubt of fact that the marriage was celebrated
but the parties are in possession of decent public reputation as
a married couple, the marriage is considered valid until it is
proven otherwise. In all cases the presumption is in favor of
marriage both in the internal and external forum. Since every
presumption is a probable conjecture in an uncertain matter,
the presumption holds whether the marriage is valid or invalid
until proven definitely. This theory is based on the fact that one
would take the risk of violating the natural law by making either
decision. In the case of marriage, the Code Commission gave a
decision in such cases that the presumption of the validity of a
first marriage (in which a doubt arose) is sufficient to justify
a declaration of nullity of a subsequent marriage, provided the
case is being handled according to the ordinary course of law.
This canon is applicable especially in the U.S.A. in the ligamen
or bigamy cases.

Exception: The exception in this canon is provided for in
Canon 1127. In case of doubt, the privilege of the faith enjoys
the favor of the law. In other words, the presumption of Canon
1127 takes precedence over the presumption of Canon 1014 because the privilege of the faith enjoys the favor of the law, when
there is doubt as to the validity of a marriage contracted by the
non-baptized; in other words, the doubt is to be resolved in
favor of the faith, or in favor of the convert.

II. In his talk at the meeting of the Canon Law Society of
America in Denver, 1967, Monsignor Stephan Kelleher, J.C.D.

brought to light some interesting facts about Canon 1014 which are worthy of consideration. He says: "The canon goes on to state that in case of doubt a marriage is to be considered valid unless the contrary is proved. This is the heart of our subject. When there are strong reasons favoring the invalidity of a marriage, must its validity be upheld because there is a probability that it may be valid? It is with this question that we are primarily concerned . . . Granted that marriage enjoys the favor of the law, what action may a person take to try to free himself from the bond of an unhappy marriage? What steps can be taken so that the force of presumption of Canon 1014 may be reduced? Can steps be taken so that, where the presumption stands, marriages may be dissolved? These answers are offered: (a) a revised judicial procedure whereby a judicial official grants annulments; (b) a judicial or administrative procedure whereby an ecclesiastical official grants a divorce; (c) a personal decision by a party, or parties, to a marriage that the marriage is null.

". . . It is probable that in half of the dioceses and arch-dioceses of the United States functioning tribunals do not exist; that is, the tribunals . . . do not process cases in formal trial. These tribunals exist in name only. The Defender of the Bond in one such diocese thought this was an honorary title. They do not render decisions at all. In a quarter of the dioceses one or two cases are processed annually in formal trial. In the remaining quarter—thirty-six dioceses out of 144 in the country—from five to twenty cases are processed annually. However, even in these latter dioceses a person seeking an annulment will not be declared free to marry (with a rare exception) in less than two years, and then only if he is so fortunate as to receive affirmative decisions in two instances. These facts constitute an appalling injustice. The injustice is the result of inefficiency on the part of those responsible for applying the law as well as the result of defects in the law."

Some of the complaints (which are justified) of Monsignor Kelleher were against our judicial process of three judges and the mandatory appeal. This fortunately has been simplified through the new provisional faculties granted for three years by the Holy See, through the Canon Law Society of America.

"However, the question is asked: 'Can there be a judicial or administrative procedure whereby the Church will grant divorces, including divorces in sacramental, consummated marriages?' The answer to this question lies with the teaching authority of the Catholic Church, guided, in large part, by scripture scholars and theologians. The ideal of the indissolubility of marriage is not at stake. Every divorce has elements of tragedy. There is a potential tragedy in any marriage if the parties do not initially intend a permanent marriage. . . . Granted the validity of the ideal of the indissolubility of every marriage, is every marriage an ideal marriage? Given the fact that divorce is, in fact, almost as common among Catholics as among non-Catholics, does the present teaching of the Church contribute to the common good? My response to these questions inclines to the negative. In view of the number of persons who cannot go to the sacraments, does our present teaching derogate from the common good and adversely affect the spiritual lives of many individual persons? If the Church permitted divorce, would Catholics be in a more realistically effective position to influence civil legislation to sustain individual rights and to foster the common good? My response to these questions inclines to the affirmative.

"Canon 1014 states that, for the welfare of the community, the stability of the institution of marriage is to take precedence over the rights of individual persons. In our culture there is a fundamental error in a juridical system which is more concerned with protecting what it conceives to be the stability of a given institution than the safeguarding of rights of the human persons involved in that institution.

"The present law looks upon marriage as a 'thing,' a sacred 'thing,' but nevertheless, a 'thing.' This concept is in opposition to contemporary theological thought which looks upon the sacrament as a personal relationship . . . . Canon 1014 is concerned primarily with marriages whose validity is in some way doubt-ful. There is an inconsistency between what this canon requires of Christian souls and what we have consistently been taught to require of souls in other moral situations. For example, when the Church recognizes the moral system of probabilism to be used in the sacrament of Penance, it is saying that we have no right to impose the more strict obligation upon a Christian soul when there is a reasonable doubt concerning the immorality of a certain action. In such matters the Church does not look primarily to the protection of the institution; she looks primarily to safeguarding the basic right of the Christian to be free from obligations other than those that are certain.

"Consistent logic, as well as the present conciliar teaching on the meaning of Christian freedom and responsibility, call for change in our outlook concerning doubtfully valid mar-riages. It would be well if we adopt the principle that where there is a preponderance of evidence that marriage is invalid, or where there is solidly probable evidence that marriage is not viable the individual who so desires could be declared free of such a marriage.

"The objection may be raised that this solution is too sub-jective. In this context, I suggest a note which would pervade our ideas concerning a rethinking of the law in this and other areas. Only God is sovereign, supreme, absolute, and objective. It would be preferable if we used these words only when we speak of God. The best of men, whether this phrase applies to official status or personal competency, can give only a subjective approximation of what is objective.

"In conclusion, I offer these thoughts. The present judicial system for the processing of marriage cases appears to be based upon the premise that when a man seeks an annulment of his marriage two presumptions are to be made: (1) he was in the state of original justice at the time he marries; (2) upon pres-entation of a petition for nullity of a marriage, he is saturated with the effects of original sin. It may be that in an attempt to eliminate each of these presumptions the proponents of the personal-responsibility decision place too much expression on the immediate perfectibility of the responsible individual.

"In the light of Vatican Council II on personal freedom and responsibility, the teaching of the Church may address itself to this latter question . . . . It is my opinion that the extension of divorce to sacramental, consummated marriages would serve well the mission of the Church. If the personal-responsibility theory is not acceptable, it is hoped that in annulment and divorce proceedings, a presumption of respect for the freedom, credibility, responsibility, and dignity of the individual person will be given a secure place."

KINDS OF MARRIAGE

Canon 1015: 1. A valid marriage of baptized persons is called *ratum* if it is not yet completed by consummation. Matrimonium *ratum et consummatum*, if there has taken place between the parties the conjugal act to which the marriage contract is by nature ordained and by which the parties become one flesh.

2. After the celebration of marriage, if the parties have lived together, the consummation of the marriage is presumed until the contrary is proved.

3. A marriage celebrated validly between unbaptized persons is called *legitimate*.

4. An invalid marriage which has been celebrated in good faith on the part of at least one of the parties is called *putative*, until both parties become certain of nullity.

This canon gives the legal terms which are constantly used when discussing the question of marriage.

1. *Ratum*: A *ratum* marriage is sacramental marriage which takes place between two validly baptized persons (Catholics as well as Protestants) but which has not been consummated by the conjugal act.

2. *Ratum et Consummatum*: This is a marriage which is both sacramental and consummated by the conjugal act. A marriage is not considered consummated by sexual intercourse which may have occurred prior to a valid marriage. Neither is onanistic intercourse a complete act.

3. *Consummatum et Ratum*: Whenever two unbaptized persons enter into matrimony and later, after their marriage is consummated, they receive baptism together, it is considered in the *consummatum et ratum* category.

4. *Legitimum*: This is a marriage between two non-baptized individuals.

5. *Naturale*: This is a marriage between a baptized and an unbaptized person. This is not used by the Code but by the Holy Office in one of its decisions (S.C.S. Office, Nov. 5, 1924). This is not a sacramental marriage because the sacrament cannot exist in one party and not in the other.

6. *Putativum*: This is an invalid marriage which was contracted in good faith by at least one of the parties, and it remains putative until the parties become aware of its invalidity. Children born of a putative marriage are considered legitimate. This is due to the principle that because of the ignorance of one or both parties regarding an impediment which invalidated the marriage, and because of the absence of malice on the part of the parties. It is this which makes the putative marriage differ from the ordinary invalid marriage. The Code Commission was asked whether the word *celebratum* of Canon 1015:4 is to be understood only by a marriage celebrated before the Church. The reply was:

In the affirmative. Jan. 26, 1949.[3] Therefore, a marriage of a Catholic and a non-Catholic contracted outside the Church, though the Catholic was in good faith, cannot be called putative.

7. *Attempted Marriage*: This is an invalid marriage, strictly speaking, when the contract is made whereby at least one of them is cognizant of an invalidating impediment, e.g., ligamen, or a marriage takes place without the proper form according to Canon 1094.

8. *Public Marriage*: This is a marriage celebrated in the external form or in some public way and recognized by the Church as valid.

9. *Clandestine Marriage*: This is a marriage that is contracted without the presence of the pastor and two witnesses.

10. *Secret Marriage*, also called *Marriage of Conscience*: This is a marriage which is contracted before the pastor and two witnesses *secretly*, for some very grave reason. These marriages are not entered into the regular matrimonial register in the parish but entered in the secret archives in the Chancery (C. 1107). One must have special permission to perform such a secret marriage (C. 1104).

LAWS GOVERNING MARRIAGE

Canon 1016: The marriage of baptized persons is governed not only by Divine Law, but also by Canon Law, without prejudice to the competency of the civil power in regard to the civil effects of such a marriage.

I. *Divine Law*: Whatever is required by the natural law for all marriage contracts is also necessary for a Christian marriage. All marriages are governed by the natural and divine posi-

3. AAS 41-158.

tive law. Moreover, it must be remembered that marriage was restored to its pristine category (unity and indissolubility) by Christ not only for all Christians but for all men.[4]

II. *Canon Law*: *Marriage is a sacrament.* Because of this the Church claims independent and exclusive right over marriages of all that are baptized validly, Catholics as well as Protestants. This power of authority has been given to the Church by Christ (Leo XIII, Encycl. Arcanum). The Church as such is the official custodian and interpreter of laws governing marriage. This jurisdiction—legislative, judicial, and coercive—includes all marriages in which at least one of the parties is baptized. It has the power to establish both diriment and prohibitive impediments. It is competent to render decisions on matrimonial cases within the limits of the natural and the divine laws.

Although the Church does not legislate directly for the unbaptized persons (c. 12), nevertheless, whenever one of the parties is Catholic it claims direct jurisdiction over the entire contract of marriage and, as such, indirectly over the unbaptized.

The question is disputed, however. Whether such a marriage would be valid is argued from the fact that the contract which is indivisible must be governed by the one power or another, namely, the Church or the State. *According to jurisprudence, the right of the Church is upheld.*[5] The reason is that the contract is considered indivisible. Canon Law concerns itself with marriage under both aspects as a contract and as a sacrament.

The contract and sacrament cannot be separated; they are one and the same. The priest present at the marriage does not contribute anything to the matter and form of the sacrament. The bodies of the spouses constitute the MATTER of the sacrament, the words they express represent the FORM. The matter and form are found in the natural contract itself. Christ added

4. Joyce, George, *Christian Marriage,* Sheed & Ward, N.Y. 1933. (Mostly historical and doctrinal).

5. Bouscaren, T. Lincoln, S.J., *Canon Law,* Bruce, 1957, p. 455.

nothing external to that contract. He merely raised the natural contract to the dignity of a sacrament.

III. *Civil Law*: According to this canon the civil power has jurisdiction over the mere civil effects of marriage, but not over the bond itself, or what is essential to marriage. The civil effects are those which are separable from the substance of the marriage contract, e.g., a dowry, the tenure of property, the right of succession, the right of the wife to use the husband's name (Vidal No. 10). If there is no infringement upon divine or canon law, the civil power may prescribe regulations which safeguard health and public order, just as it requires a license or the registration of marriage. As in all legislation, the civil law affecting marriage must always be just and reasonable.[6]

IV. *Form of Marriage for the Unbaptized*: Since the Church does not claim the right over the non-baptized, they must be subject to some authority; otherwise it would be detrimental to peace and public order. The good of the family and of society would suffer. Therefore, within the realm of the natural law, the state can determine the form of marriage for the unbaptized for the valid marriage contract.

V. *Orientals*: The Oriental or Eastern Church is governed by the motu proprio, *Crebrae Allatae* of Pope Pius XII, 22 Feb. 1949, regarding its marriage legislation. This codification went into effect May 2, 1949. All marriages celebrated on or after this date are governed by *Crebrae Allatae*. All marriages celebrated before that date are governed by the Latin Code when the legislation is derived from divine law and the particular discipline in force in the rites to which the parties belonged. For example, some Maronites would come under the Synod of Lebanon, while others would not, after May 2, 1949.

6. Goldsmith, J. W., *The Competence of Church and State over Marriage*, Catholic Univ. Press, 1944.

VI. *Oriental Dissidents*: The Orthodox faithful are not subject to *Crebrae Allatae*, (even though there are authors who think otherwise—Coussa, Pospishil, Herman, etc.). The Orthodox Church is not bound by *Crebrae Allatae* because 1) there are no conciliar or papal statements extant denying the Orthodox hierarchy the authority to make or change their disciplinary legislation. As a matter of fact, there are innumerable statements to the effect that the Latin Church is committed to uphold the laws, rites, and customs of the Oriental Churches. 2) Clement Pujol, of the Oriental Institute, who studied the preparatory acts and the motu proprio, *Crebrae Allatae,* concluded that it was not the intention of Pope Pius XII to legislate for the Orthodox. Motivated by the pleas of Catholic bishops, the Pope promulgated the new legislation in 1949 *only for those Orientals in union with the Holy See*. To legislate for the Orthodox would have separated the Catholic Church even more than it is at present. Pujol holds that the technical term: *"christifideles"* refers only to Catholics—the same term that was used in other previous documents with this same meaning. (Moreover, *leges quae . . . liberum iurium exercitium coarctant . . . strictae subsunt interpretationi*.) It is a general principle of the Roman Church not to legislate for the Orthodox Church.

CHAPTER II

PRELIMINARIES TO MARRIAGE

THE ENGAGEMENT CONTRACT

Canon 1017:
1. A promise of marriage, whether it is unilateral or bilateral which is called an engagement, is null for both the internal and external forum, unless it is made in writing signed by the parties and by either the pastor or Ordinary of the place or at least two witnesses.

2. In case both parties, or either party have never learned to write, or cannot write, it is required for validity that this fact be noted in the writing itself, and that an additional witness sign the document with the pastor or Ordinary of the place or with the two witnesses mentioned in § 1.

3. From a promise of marriage, even if it be valid and there be no just cause excusing from its fulfillment, there arises no right of action to compel the celebration of the marriage; but there is a right of action for damages, if any are due.

No. 1: An engagement is a contract whereby two persons mutually promise to marry each other in the future. They must be capable of making this contract; for example, an engagement by minors would be valid but illicit. It is possible to have a conditional engagement.[1]

No. 2: *Form of Engagement*

1. The promise of marriage must be (a) in writing, (b) signed by the parties, (c) signed by the pastor or local Ordinary or two witnesses, in order to be valid.

2. If either or both parties are unable to write, an additional witness must sign the above-mentioned document for validity.

3. This contract may be made by proxy.

4. All parties involved must sign in each other's presence.

No. 3: *Binding Force of Engagement*

1. The parties involved have a grave obligation in justice to fulfill the terms of the contract; e.g., to marry at the time specified in the contract.

2. An obligation of fidelity to one another arises to the exclusion of any third party; i.e., fornication with a third party would be unjust.

3. Although the engagement contract is valid, it does not give rise to the right of legal action in compelling the celebration of the marriage.

4. If one of the parties suffers harm, financial or any other, by the breaking of this contract, he may sue for damages.

No. 4: *Dissolution of the Contract*

The Contract can be dissolved by:

(a) mutual consent of the contracting parties,
(b) papal dispensation,
(c) a subsequent invalidating impediment which cannot be dispensed,
(d) entrance into a religious institute,
(e) reception of Sacred Orders,
(f) inability to change the object of the contract; i.e., one becomes a heretic, an alcoholic, mentally ill, or mutilated.

Introduction: 1. With almost 1 out of 3 marriages ending in di-

1. Mathis & Meyer, S.J., *The Pastoral Companion*, Chicago, 1961, p. 170.

vorce in the United States, many priests have successfully initiated a program to reduce the number of divorces in this country by using the protective Canon 1017 regarding the solemn engagement. Although this Canon has been with us since 1918, it has so seldom been used that priests who have been approached by prospective couples have turned them away because he was not acquainted with the betrothal contract and ceremony. This laudable ceremony which is sanctioned by the Church should be introduced into our pastoral work and employed for all couples contemplating future marriage. Since it is found in every Canon Law and Moral Theology book, much emphasis has been placed on this ceremony in an attempt to help cut down the leakage in the field of marriage in the United States.

2. Historically, formal engagements were considered a "promise of future marriage" by Roman law and the Roman Pontiffs. St. Thomas referred to this engagement contract as a "quasi-sacramental." The Code of 1918 treats engagements as either bilateral or unilateral contracts; i.e., when the contract is made and accepted by both parties, it is *bilateral;* when made by only one party and accepted by the other, it is called *unilateral.*

3. *The pastor is not bound to insist on a formal engagement contract, but with so many attempted divorces in the Church today, use of the solemn engagement contract may serve to help correct this abuse. If canonical betrothals were more common during the period of the Second World War, we would have had fewer divorces, broken homes, so-called parentless children (from divorced parents); we would have fewer regrets, heartaches, and nervous breakdowns.*

4. *The betrothal contract is a safety measure which provides an excellent opportunity for proper preparation and anticipation of many obligations, cares, and responsibilities which every marriage presents to those entering this particular state of life.*

5. It must be understood that the Natural Law requires no special formality, but that such a special formality or solemnity is required by the positive law found in Canon 1017. For this solemnity and for validity, the several conditions specified must be observed; it must be signed by both parties and by either the

pastor or the local Ordinary or at least two witnesses, i.e., women, non-Catholics, and even children with the use of reason can act as witnesses. The contract should be dated, and the place should also be indicated; this is not necessary, however, for validity.

ORIENTAL LAW

Unlike the Latin Church, the Oriental Church has retained the ordinary practice of formal engagement for centuries as far as the contract and ceremony are concerned. The new Oriental Code specifically treats of this solemn engagement in Canons six and seven:

Canon 6: 1. The promise of marriage, even though bilateral, or in the nature of a mutual espousal, is null in both forms, unless made before the pastor of the local hierarch, or before a priest to whom the faculty of assisting has been given by either of these.

2. #1 - The same pastor or local hierarch or priest designated by either, can validly assist at a promise of marriage, who, by prescription of Canons 86 and 87, can validly assist at the marriage.
#2 - He who assists at a promise of marriage is by obligation bound to see to it that the celebration is entered into his book of espousals.

3. However, from the promise of marriage, no judicial action is made available for seeking the celebration of marriage; such action is granted for the repairing of damages if any be due.

Canon 7: The priest assisting at the promise of marriage must not neglect to impart to the Catholic parties the blessing prescribed by the liturgical books, if particular law provides for this.

This canon is practically the same as in the Latin Code, except that it need not be made in writing. If a couple belonged to different rites, either pastor may have a choice in the matter.

However, it may be more advantageous for the pastor who will eventually assist at the marriage to handle this matter.

SUGGESTIONS FOR THE LATIN RITE CEREMONY

An engagement ceremony may take place as follows:

1. A brief talk can be given by a priest who is dressed in surplice and stole, standing at the altar rail, telling the couple that the promise they will make to each other does not bind under sin. It is well that they come to make it publicly and to ask the Church's blessing on such an important occasion in preparation for the great sacrament of matrimony. The priest can also tell them that an individual who enters a religious community prepares for his life by a novitiate. Candidates for the Priesthood spend many years in study and prayer. So also Matrimony should be entered into with great care and consideration. Some instructions could be given regarding their sincerity and devotion to one another.

2. *The Reading of the Formula of Engagement*: Kneeling at the communion rail or at the altar of the Blessed Virgin, they should listen attentively to the words of the priest. Then standing they read the document together aloud and then sign it. The priest adds his own signature, stating that he has been witness to this proposal and declares them engaged in the name of the Father, of the Son and of the Holy Spirit. And then he should sprinkle them with holy water.

3. *The Blessing of the Engagement Ring*: The formula: *Our help is in the name of the Lord/Who made heaven and earth. The Lord be with you/And with your spirit. Let us pray: Bless, O Lord, this ring which we bless in thy name, that she who will wear it, keeping full faith with her betrothed, may abide in thy peace and in thy will, through Christ our Lord. Amen.* He then sprinkles it with holy water. The man then takes the ring and puts it on the ring finger of the woman with the words: *"In the name of the Father, and of the Son, and of the Holy*

Spirit." If it is a double ring ceremony, the woman does the same thing to the man.

4. If further solemnity is desired, the priest may read the Gospel of St. John, 15, while all stand. This may be followed by an appropriate hymn sung by the assembled attendants of the couple.

5. Then the engaged couple kneel before the priest who places his stole over their clasped hands and says: "*May God bless your bodies and your souls. May he send His blessing upon you as He blessed Abraham, Isaac, and Jacob. May our blessed Mother keep you in her motherly care. May the Guardian Angel protect you from all harm and lead you on to the path of holiness. Go in peace in the name of Christ. Amen.*"

ENGAGEMENT CONTRACT

We, the undersigned, being of sound mind and understanding full well the obligations to be assumed, do hereby freely and mutually promise to enter into Matrimony on the day _____ Month _____, 19 __.

In testimony whereof, we affix our signature on this _____ day ____ Month _____, 19 __.

Signature of Man _____
Signature of Woman _____
Signature of Pastor _____

(Church Seal)

INSTRUCTION OF THE PASTOR

Canon 1018: The pastor must not fail prudently to instruct the people regarding the Sacrament of Matrimony and its impediments.

1. Every pastor is a teacher—he must instruct. Therefore, he must have the right knowledge and understanding of the principles of Christian marriage, since the general morality and the common good depends on this.

2. Today, when pornography and sex information of all kinds is being freely distributed to the young, the proper approach to instruction in sexual matters is different from what it was in past generations. Again, with almost one out of three marriages ending in divorce in the United States, a definite stand must be taken by pastors to counteract this deluge of bad information which is distributed daily.

3. This canon uses the word *prudenter*, which cautions the pastor to avoid abruptness or embarrassing situations. There are various means and techniques of dealing with such a delicate subject. The priest instructor should first acquaint himself with the person to be instructed and proceed according to the circumstances; e.g., a different approach would be required in the case of a nurse, or an ordinary layman, or that of an illiterate person, even though the same essential doctrine must be given to each. This is stressed here because unfortunate mistakes have been made in the past in this regard.

4. Every priest has had sufficient training to use good common sense and good judgment. He must face facts; he must explain the principles of marriage and the responsibility married people have to society. He must stress the fact that marriage is not a private matter; that the common good plays an important role in this particular phase of life.

5. Pope Pius XI [2] recommends the study of the encyclical *Casti Connubii*, which deals with the nature and dignity of marriage; and it is imperative that a thorough course in this matter be given in high schools as well as colleges. By all means it should be given to high school students; they are certainly not too young for this instruction, and many of them will not go on to college to be exposed to this at a more mature age. Many modern philosophies, false as they are, are diabolical in their tendency to undermine the good of society. It is the pastor's duty to offset this by insisting on the proper instruction both to the young as well as to those about to be married. It should be

2. Pius XI, *Casti Connubii* (Christian Marriage), 1930, America Press, N.Y.

noted that there are many books and pamphlets published today on this matter, one of which is outstanding, viz., *Modern Youth and Chastity* by Father Kelly, S.J.[3] This pamphlet, complete and very successful in its treatment, was written by the collaboration of two Jesuit Fathers who have had many years of experience in working with youth.

Canon 1018 obliges the pastor to give proper instruction to the parties wishing to enter marriage. In other words, he is to lay the foundation for their future happiness and keep in mind that society is plagued by too many invalid marriages today, and that "an ounce of prevention is worth a pound of cure." Many failures in marriage have been traced to priests who have been a failure in counselling, or have been disinterested, or gave no counsel at all. It would be well if all priests encouraged young people to seek counsel and help before deciding to get married.

As a guide for counselling, the priest could use the highly recommended course offered by *Novalis,* St. Paul University, 1 Stewart Street, Ottawa, Canada, called *MOSAIC*—which is a marriage preparation course, in nine illustrated booklets, to confront engaged couples with the realities of their future life in marriage. It deals with communication, psychology, sex and sexuality, maturity, establishing a home, celebrating marriage, parenthood, the community, and the law on marriage.

This series was prepared by professional men and women along with engaged and married couples, to inspire engaged couples, to spell out the ideals of Christian marriage, and to help make good marriages. The Handbook for the Organizer or priest instructor provides important aids for setting up a discussion group:—how to contact resource people; where to hold group discussions; choice of leaders and their training; advertising to attract engaged couples; special speakers and selected reading lists.

The method of using *Mosaic* is through study sessions and group discussions in homes, high schools, churches, colleges and

3. Kelly, G., S.J., *Modern Youth and Chastity,* Queen's Work, St. Louis, Mo.

community centers. *Mosaic* may also be used for personal private instructions as well as through correspondence courses where engaged couples are mailed the booklets regularly and questionnaires are completed and returned for evaluation.

LIST OF SUBJECTS TREATED

1. *The Present Situation with regard to Marriage.* What some people think of it. The Christian ideal of marriage. How to prepare for it.
2. *The Ideal Husband — The Ideal Wife.* The qualities to look for in your future partner. Defects to be avoided. The correction of faults.
3. *Love and Happiness in Marriage.* Love. Its elements. True love and sham love. True happiness in marriage. Differences in conjugal love.
4. *Courtship and Engagement.* The nature, purpose, qualities, place of courtship. Subjects to be discussed and settled during courtship. Engagements.
5. *Masculine and Feminine Psychology.* Mutual understanding. Various temperaments. Man's vocation; woman's vocation. Physical, intellectual and emotional differences.
6. *Economic Preparation.* Nature and importance of economic preparation for marriage. Economic organization of family: the budget, management of the home. Benefits of economy.
7. *The Spirituality of Marriage.* The vocation. The Sacrament. The purposes and qualities of marriage. God's call within marriage. Sacramental grace. The model for Christian couples.
8. *Church Law concerning Marriage.* Nature of the contract; the consent to marriage. Impediments to marriage. The pre-nuptial inquiry. Publication of banns. "Form of the marriage."
9. *Civil Law concerning Marriage.* Legal formalities, marriage license. Civil impediments. Property rights. Declaration of nullity, separation, divorce. Invalid marriage. Last will and testament.
10. *The Marriage Ceremony.* Liturgical explanation. Events before and after the ceremony. Showers, parties, receptions. Wedding clothes. The Nuptial Mass and Blessing. Special blessings.
11. *Masculine and Feminine Anatomy and Physiology.* God's Plan. Reproductive organs of the female; the menstrual cycle. Reproductive organs of the male. Puberty. Personal and social purity.
12. *Relations between Husband and Wife, Pregnancy, Birth, Nursing.* The mystery of the transmission of life. Pre-natal care. Childbirth. Care of mother and child.
13. *Physical and Emotional Health; Personal and Conjugal Hygiene.* Good health habits. Preventing disease. Mental and emotional health. Safety

for adults, children. Personal and conjugal hygiene.
14. *What is Allowed, and What is Forbidden in Marriage.* The moral aspect. Duties of marriage. Birth prevention. The Rhythm System.
15. *The First Months of Marriage.* Honeymoon. First relations. Physical, social, intellectual and moral adaptation. Parenthood. Summing up.[4]

THE PRENUPTIAL INVESTIGATION

Canon 1019: 1. Before a marriage is celebrated, it must be certain that nothing stands in the way of its valid and licit celebration.

2. In danger of death, if other proofs cannot be had, and there are no indications to the contrary, the sworn testimony of the contracting parties that they have been baptized and are under no impediment, is sufficient.

1. *The Prenuptial Investigation*
   (a) examination of each party privately
   (b) publication of the banns

After giving the parties the proper instructions (cf. C. 1018), the pastor will interrogate privately each party carefully after which he will publish the banns. The reason for such a thorough investigation is to prevent an invalid marriage as well as to show respect for the sacrament of matrimony in the interest of the family and society (cf. Inst. 1941).[5]

2. In danger of death, the law is not so strict for the parties. They merely declare under oath that they are baptized and that they are not under any impediment of marriage. Should there be any impediments, Canons 1043-44-45 should be invoked.

Canon 1020: 1. The pastor who has the right to assist at a marriage shall inquire diligently at an opportune time beforehand whether there is an obstacle to the celebration of marriage.

4. With permission of The Catholic Centre, Univ. of Ottawa, Canada.
5. S. C. of the Sacraments: Instruction on Canonical Investigation, June 29, 1941. AAS 33-297.

2. He must interrogate both the bridegroom and the bride, even separately and carefully, whether they are under any impediment, whether they are giving their consent freely, and whether they are sufficiently instructed in Christian doctrine, unless in view of the quality of the persons this last question should seem unnecessary.

3. The local ordinary has the right to establish specific norms for this investigation by the pastor.

Introduction: Too many marriages have failed in our generation due to the negligence of pastors in making the proper investigation before marriage. These findings are prevalent in so many instances when a search is made in parochial files. Some cases reveal that the pastor had no time to be bothered. Yet, if he had taken the time out to check each couple according to this canon, he would have discovered that they were either not sufficiently instructed, or did not have the proper intention.

1. All pastors have the very grave responsibility to make the proper investigation, even though someone else performs the marriage through his delegation.

2. If the party or parties involved are living away from the parish, the pastor of their residence will investigate the matter and send all his findings to the pastor who will assist at the marriage. Sometimes this is feasible because of the distance and inconvenience.

3. Each party should be interrogated separately. Many things are revealed when they are free to talk. (This is true also when a married couple is having trouble.) Separate investigations are invaluable. We must be prudent in making the investigation, especially when we are dealing with non-Catholics. Priests should be open-minded, discreet and tactful.

4. Historically speaking, the Holy See has tried to impress pastors of this great responsibility.

In 1670, the Holy Office gave definite instructions regarding prenuptial investigations; they were to check carefully to see if there were any impediments and to determine whether they are entering the marriage freely; this question must be directed to the woman especially. It further demanded that priests and bishops comply with this regulation strictly.

In 1911, the Sacred Congregation of the Sacraments again issued a decree regarding this matter and spoke out against careless pastors in this regard. In 1921, a few years after the promulgation of the Code, pastors again were reminded of the evils connected with poor and improper investigations; they were also reprimanded for this laxity. The decree contained the following items of importance:

(1) Ordinaries were instructed to remind all pastors to refrain from assisting at marriages unless they had *satisfactory proof* of the freedom of the parties to marry according to Canons 1020, 1097: 1, n.1, and above all, to demand certificates of baptism of both if they were baptized in another parish.

(2) The pastor who assisted at the marriage must *promptly* inform the pastor of baptism of this marriage (c. 1103: 2).

(3) For security sake and expediting the matter better, pastors were exhorted to send all necessary documents through their respective chanceries.

(4) Pastors were to consult the Ordinary regarding vagi and immigrants, and migrant workers, except in case of necessity, or danger of death.

(5) If the pastor of baptism received a notice of marriage to be entered into the record and found that the party was married before, he is to consult the Ordinary immediately.

(6) Ordinaries were instructed to impose the necessary canonical sanction on those pastors that were negligent in making the proper prenuptial investigations.

(7) Later in 1941, the Sacred Congregation of the Sacraments sent out detailed instructions on how the pastor was

to conduct the prenuptial investigation of the parties; it also gave the form to be used.

From the instructions given above, it is obvious that the Church is concerned about this grave obligation. Negligent pastors had to be reminded from time to time.

Suppose one of the parties or both were totally ignorant of the principles of Christian doctrine, should the pastor delay the marriage until they are sufficiently instructed? The Code Commission answered by saying that the pastor should give them as much instructions as is possible under the circumstances, but if they refuse to come for instructions, the marriage should not be delayed. Because many difficulties do arise after marriage, chanceries are using special forms to cover any and all possibilities.

The Sacred Congregation of the Sacraments, on June 29, 1941, issued an Instruction on the manner of making this investigation. In summary, it indicated that (1) the pastor of the bride has the right and grave duty to investigate whether there are any obstacles to the marriage; he may conduct the inquiry regarding the groom or request the groom's pastor to do so; (2) when the parties are from different dioceses, the documents of investigation should be transmitted through the groom's diocesan chancery to the pastor of the bride, or if the marriage is to take place in the domicile of the groom, then the documents should be sent in the same manner to the groom's pastor. It is also suggested that the *nihil obstat* be obtained by the chancery of the place of marriage. Many chanceries have drawn up their matrimonial forms according to this Instruction.

A GUIDE TO THE USE OF THE INSTRUCTION OF THE SACRED CONGREGATION OF THE SACRAMENTS

NORMS TO BE OBSERVED BY PASTORS IN PRENUPTIAL INVESTIGATIONS [6]
June 29, 1941

O. M. CLORAN, S.J. S.T.D., J.C.D.
SAINT MARY OF THE LAKE SEMINARY
MUNDELEIN, ILLINOIS

SOURCES	SUMMARY OF THE INSTRUCTION

I. INSTRUCTION,
   nn. 1-3

1. PREAMBLE: SANCTITY OF MATRIMONY

NOTE: INSTRUCTION ARABIC NUMERALS IN LEFT COLUMN CORRESPOND TO THE NUMBERS OF THE MAIN PARAGRAPHS IN THE INSTRUCTION.

Canons 1012, 1033
Arcanum,
Leo XIII, Feb. 10, 1880
C.I.C. Fontes, III,
   n. 580
Casti connubii,
Pius XI, Dec. 31, 1930
A.A.S., XXII, p. 539

1. In her solicitude at all times to safeguard the sanctity and dignity of Christian marriage, the Church has ordained suitable precautions to protect matrimony from irreverence and nullity. The pre-eminent sacredness and dignity of this divine institution are manifest from the Encyclical *Casti connubii* of Pope Pius XI, which delineates the true nature, the noble prerogatives, and the high purposes of the marriage state.

Canon 1036
Canon 1019
Conc. Trident. Sess.
   XXIV
C. 3, X, IV, 3

2. Grave sin is involved in the disregard of the laws which the Church has enacted to the end that Christian marriage may be celebrated licitly and validly; and this guilt is shared by ministers who are gravely remiss in observing the prenuptial require-

---

6. By request of His Excellency, the Most Rev. Samuel A. Stritch, this outline study of the recent Instruction of the Sacred Congregation of the Sacraments was given at a Quarterly Conference of the Clergy of the Archdiocese of Chicago. Later, requests from other dioceses necessitated the printing of the outline. The summary form is designed to facilitate a mastery of the requirements of the Instruction, not merely for ready use in pastoral work but also for teaching purposes in seminary classes.

ments, even though their neglect of duty results merely from inconsideration.

Canons 1058-1080
Canons 1081-1093
Canons 1094-1103

3. The causes of invalid or illicit marriages are reducible to three heads, namely:

    a) matrimonial impediments in the strict sense;

    b) vitiated consent;

    c) defect of canonical form.

CANON 1020, §1. The Pastor whose right it is to assist at the marriage shall in due time beforehand carefully investigate whether there is any obstacle to the marriage.

II. INSTRUCTION,
n. 4

II. GENERAL PROVISIONS REGARDING THE INVESTIGATION

4. These concern:

Rituale Romanum
Tit. VII, c. I, nn. 1-20

Canons 1097, §2, 94

    a) PASTORS: 1° The responsibility for the pre-nuptial investigation rests with the pastor of the parish where the marriage lawfully takes place,—which is regularly the parish of the bride. The groom's pastor, however, *may* of his own accord and *shall* at the instance of the groom or of the bride's pastor, conduct the inquiry to determine the groom's freedom to marry. In these cases he shall forward at once to the bride's pastor the duly executed and signed questionnaire together with the baptismal certificate and other necessary documents which are in his parish records. Similarly, the bride's pastor shall conduct the investigation when requested to do so, if for some reason the marriage is to take place in another parish church.

Canon 1029

S.C.Sacr., July 4, 1921
A.A.S., XIII, p. 348

2° When the pastors are of *different dioceses* and the bride's pastor is to assist at the marriage, the matrimonial documents should be transmitted to the bride's pastor through the *groom's* diocesan Chancery; and a testimonial from this Chancery should indorse the groom's freedom to marry. If, on the other hand, the groom's pastor is to assist at the marriage, the documents are to be sent to him through the *bride's* diocesan Chancery together with its testimonial of her freedom to marry.

(Note: Translations of
documents cited from the
Acta Apostolicae Sedis
may be found in the
CANON LAW DIGEST,
by the Rev. T. L.
Bouscaren, S.J.)

3° Moreover, when the pastors are of *different dioceses, it is prescribed* that the pastor who is to assist at the marriage receive the authorization of his

own Chancery, known as the *nihil obstat*. Even when the parties belong to different parishes within the same diocese, the *nihil obstat is desirable*.
[Note: When the bride and groom reside in *different parishes* of the *same diocese*, the pre-nuptial documents need not be referred to the Chancery, but may be exchanged directly between the pastors unless the Ordinary has *prescribed* that the *nihil obstat* be obtained in this case also.]

4° The pastor who is to receive the *nihil obstat* should send to his Chancery in due time beforehand the properly executed questionnaires of both parties and the other pre-nuptial documents, together with a *transcript* giving the summary information outlined in Questionnaire V. This *transcript*, as its terms indicate, is to be used by the Chancery in issuing the *nihil obstat*, and by the pastor when a marriage is to be contracted outside his parish, in granting permission (canon 1097, §1, 3°) to a priest otherwise invested with ordinary power (canon 1095) or delegation (canon 1096) to assist. The authenticated *transcript* together with the other marriage documents is to be kept in the files of the parish where the marriage takes place.

5° The duty of investigation binds the pastor *sub gravi* even though he is morally certain that there is no obstacle to a valid and licit marriage. The examination must be made by the *pastor in person*, unless there is some reasonable excuse.

b) TIME: The investigation should be made before the banns or during their publication. If the marriage is to take place in another parish, the questionnaires properly executed and all other pertinent documents duly authenticated, should be delivered to the pastor of that parish at least three days before the date set for the marriage.

c) SCOPE: 1° Documentary proof of baptism and confirmation. The baptismal certificate must be recent,—issued within six months of the date set for the marriage, so as to provide if need be the items prescribed by canon 470, §2 (confirmation, marriage, subdiaconate, solemn religious profession) and by Article 225 (declaration of nullity and prohi-

Romana et aliarum, XI
S.C.C., Feb. 1, 1908
C.I.C. Fontes, VI,
n. 4344

Canons 1095-1097

Canons 21, 1019

Canons 1029, 1030

Canon 1021

Canon 470, §2

S.C.Sacr., Aug. 15,
1936, §225

A.A.S., XXVIII, p. 313

Canon 90

Canons 94, 1022, 1103, §2
Canons 88, §1, 1034

Canons 1094, 1099

Canon 1069
S.C.Sacr., Mar. 12, 1910
A.A.S., II, p. 196
S.C.S. Off., An. 1868
A.A.S., II, p. 199
Ne temere, V.
S.C.C., Apr. 19, 1908
C.I.C. Fontes, VI, n. 4340

Nimiam licentiam,
Bened. XIV, May 18, 1743
C.I.C. Fontes, I, n. 337

bition of future marriage), of the Instruction of this Sacred Congregation, August 15, 1936. Sworn affirmation of non-baptism should be investigated even to the extent of inquiry from the pastor of the place of origin (canon 90) whether the baptismal registry there reveals the contrary, unless the pastor knows with certainty of the non-baptism from other sources.

2° Parishes to which notice of the marriage should be sent.

3° Whether the parties are twenty-one years of age or not.

4° Whether both are catholics, or one or both non-catholics but bound to observe the canonical form, according to canon 1099.

5° Legal proof of death of a former spouse, or of a decree of nullity, or of a dispensation from non-consummated marriage, if the case demands such.

[Note: For further references to sources, see below, numbers 6 and 11. Cf. especially Articles 220, 221, §3, and 225, of the Instruction of the Sacred Congregation of the Sacraments, August 15, 1936 (A.A.S., XXVIII p. 313).]

6° Proof of free state of parties. See below, 6. (Note: A certified photograph should be demanded to establish the identity of a party who is unknown to the pastor.)

d) METHOD: The parties should be examined separately and with due prudence and caution, especially as regards impediments or circumstances that might occasion embarrassment.

(Note: Another prudent person, but not the father or mother of either party, may be allowed to be present at this inquiry.)

CANON 1020, §2. The Pastor shall ask the groom and bride, separately and prudently, whether they are under any impediment, whether they are giving their consent freely, especially the woman, and whether they are sufficiently instructed in Christian doctrine unless the quality of the persons makes this question unnecessary.

III. SPECIFIC PROVISIONS REGARDING THE INVESTIGATION

5. These concern:
   a) ABSENCE OF IMPEDIMENTS:
      1) Inquiry about impedient and diriment impediments.
      2) Special directions for consanguinity and affinity:

Canons 1058-1080
C. 3, X, IV, 3
C. 17, X, IV, 1
Canons 96, 1076
Canons 97, 1077
Canon 1031, §1, 1°
S. Paen. Apos., Sept. 5, 1899
C.I.C. Fontes, VIII, n. 6446

1° If there is suspicion of concealed relationship, reliable witnesses should be questioned under oath.

2° To prevent errors which sometimes occur in dispensations sought from the Apostolic See, a *genealogical tree* should be included with the petition.

Canons 1042, 1054

3° Equivocal description of impediments should be avoided, such as would occur, for example, if parties under a *double* impediment of consanguinity in the collateral line,—namely, one in the *second* degree (a *major* impediment), the other in the *third* degree (a *minor* impediment),—were represented without further explanation as being under the impediment of consanguinity "in the second-third" or "in the second and third" degree: for such a formula can denote an impediment of the "second degree mixed with the third," which is only *one* impediment and that a *minor* one: and so a dispensation obtained perhaps in this way, might be invalid.

Canon 1052

[Note: If two brothers marry two first cousins in another family, and descendants of these separate marriages wish to marry, a *double* impediment of consanguinity exists,—one in the *second* degree and the other in the *third degree*, of the collateral line.

If a man wishes to marry the daughter of his first cousin, a *single* impediment exists,—namely, consanguinity in the *third* degree of the collateral line mixed with the *second* (a *minor* impediment).]

3) Other directions:

S.C. Prop. Fid., May 9, 1877
Collectanea, II, n. 1470

4° For the validity of a dispensation from a *major* impediment (canon 1042) there is required a canonical cause actually existing and proportioned to the gravity of the impediment. If a dispensation is given *in forma commissoria* (that is, not directly to

Canons 1042, 1054

Canons 38, 40, 41

Canon 2361

the petitioner but through an agent), *before execution of the rescript* it must be *certain* that the reason actually exists; otherwise the dispensation may be invalid (canons 38, 41). If, for example, the Ordinary obtains from the Holy See a dispensation for an uncle-niece marriage, the alleged cause must exist at the moment the Ordinary executes the rescript.

[Note: Dispensations granted by Ordinaries in virtue of their Quinquennial Faculties are usually given *in forma gratiosa* (that is, without using an executor or agent), and these are effective if the alleged cause exists when the document is signed in the Chancery.]

5° For *aetas superadulta*, a reason often advanced in behalf of a woman *who is not a widow*, the *twenty-fourth year must have been completed*.

Besides, the *age* of the parties derived from the baptismal certificate must always be stated in the testimonial letters.

Canon 1018
S.C.Sacr., Aug. 1, 1931
A.A.S., XXIII, p. 413
Conc. Plen. Balt. III
Acta et Decreta, nn.
125-134

6° Pastors should instruct the faithful regarding marriage impediments; and should urge them to avoid marriages within the forbidden degrees, or to petition a dispensation when there are special reasons for such unions; and they should inform them that the tax for a dispensation is moderate, and in the case of the poor, even negligible.

Canon 1056

Canons 1069, 1987

Canons 1990-1992

S.C.Sacr., Aug. 15, 1936
A.A.S., XXVIII, p. 313

Canons 1022-1028

6.   4) Special directions for ligamen:
1° The invalidity of a previous marriage must be established according to canonical procedure alone, observing the judicial process until a declaration of nullity is confirmed in a second concordant decision from which no appeal is made by the defender of the bond (canon 1987); or in the documentary cases (canons 1990-1992), observing the rules stated in Articles 226-231 of the Instruction of this Sacred Congregation, August 15, 1936.

2° If after puberty the parties have resided elsewhere for six months, the Ordinary may require that the banns be published there or that other evidence of freedom to marry be collected (canon 1023, §2). Even in case of shorter residence, similar proofs must be sought if there are positive reasons for suspecting that an impediment was incurred (canon 1023, §3).

Cod. Com., June 3, 1918
A.A.S., X, p. 345

[Note: Whether, if residence after puberty was in far-distant places, it is sufficient to accept the oath of the party that he is free to marry, together with the testimony of two other persons,—or if that be impossible, at least of one other person who was with him in those places,—is left to the prudent judgment of the Ordinary, who may according to canon 1023, §2, require other proofs, not excluding the suppletory oath (Code Commission, June 3, 1918).]

C. 3, X, IV, 3

Canons 1829, 1830

The banns should not be dispensed from except for a legitimate and established cause; nor, to the neglect of the other methods of proof, should recourse be had easily to the suppletory oath of the parties. The difficulty experienced at times in seeking documentary proof of freedom to marry is met usually by applying for the documents through the diocesan Chanceries of the parties; and these Chanceries will reduce the customary fee (canon 1507, §1) if that presents a further hindrance.

Canons 1056, 1507, §1

Canons 90-95, 1032
Conc. Trident., Sess.
  XXIV
de ref matrim., c. 7
S.C.Sacr., July 4, 1921
A.A.S., XIII, p. 348

S.C.Sacr., Mar. 6, 1911
A.A.S., III, p. 102

S.C. Prop. Fid., Sept.
  21, 1840
Collectanea, I, n. 913, §4

    3° Special care is necessary in the case of those who have nowhere a domicile or quasi-domicile (canon 91), and of those who after puberty have moved from their place of origin (canon 90) to a distant locality and wish to contract marriage there: in these cases, the Instruction of this Sacred Congregation, July 4, 1921, should be observed strictly, and hence the Ordinary should be consulted; moreover, if the pastor of baptism, upon receiving notice of the marriage, finds that either party is already bound by another marriage, he shall notify at once, through the Chancery, the pastor of the unlawfully attempted marriage.

Canons 1081-1087
C. 14, 29, X, IV. 1
Conc. Trident., Sess.
  XXIV
de ref. matrim., c. 9

b) FREEDOM OF CONSENT:

7. The pastor must be assured that the parties, and particularly the bride, are marrying of their own free will, especially where the marriage seems to be an escape from some civil penalty. One of the foremost causes of invalid marriages is force and fear.

Cod. Com., June 3, 1918
A.A.S., X, p. 345
Etsi minime. §11
Bened. XIV, Feb. 7,
  1742

C.I.C. Fontes, I, n. 324

c) SUFFICIENT KNOWLEDGE
OF CHRISTIAN DOCTRINE

8. If the pastor finds that the parties are ignorant of Christian doctrine, he should instruct them; but if they refuse to accept instruction, they are not to be deterred from the marriage.

Cum religiosi, §4
Bened. XIV, June 26, 1754
C.I.C. Fontes, II, n. 429
S.C.S. Off. (Kentucky), May 9, 1821
C.I.C. Fontes, IV, n. 861

[Note: The instruction referred to here should not be confused with that prescribed in canon 1033. This latter is concerned with the *sanctity* and *obligations of matrimony*, and this instruction should be given to *all who are entering marriage*. The instruction required by canon 1033 is set forth admirably in an excellent little book, *Marriage*, by Von Streng-Bruehl.]

Canon 1092

d) CONDITIONED CONSENT:

9. If the parties are entering marriage with an *illicit* condition, or if the condition is *licit* but the *means of verifying it* are *unlawful*, the pastor should insist that the condition be retracted, or else forbid the marriage. Retraction of an *illicit* condition should be noted in the record of the case. If the condition is *licit*, the pastor must consult the Ordinary and obey his decision.

Canons 1094-1103
Canons 465, §§4, 5; 1923, §2
Canons 472-476
Cod. Com., July 14, 1922
A.A.S., XIV, p. 527
Cod. Com., May 20, 1923
A.A.S., XVI, p. 114
Cod. Com., Dec. 28, 1927
A.A.S. XX, p. 61
Cod. Com., Jan. 31, 1942
A.A.S., XXXIV, p. 50

e) CANONICAL FORM:

10. To prevent invalid or illicit marriages arising from a defect in *witnesses* or in *legitimate delegation*, priests should be thoroughly familiar with the provisions of canons 1094-1103 and the replies of the Code Commission concerning assistance at marriages and delegation or subdelegation by:

a] administrators of vacant parishes (canons 472, 473);

b] vicar substitutes (canons 474, 465, §§4, 5, and 1923, §2);

c] vicar coadjutors (canon 475); and,

d] assistant pastors (canon 476).

CANON 1020, §3. It is the province of the local Ordinary to prescribe special rules for this investigation by the pastor.

IV. INSTRUCTION, nn. 11, 12

IV. SPECIAL NORMS FOR THE MOST REVEREND ORDINARIES

11. Ordinaries are directed to provide that:

1° The civil authority should be notified of a marriage when notice is required by Concordat law.

2° The officiating pastor, besides entering a marriage in his marriage register, should also record it in his baptismal registry: or notify *as soon as possible* the pastor of the place of baptism, and require him to remit a certified notice that the marriage has

Canons 470, §2; 1103, §2
Ne temere, IX
S.C.C., Apr. 19, 1908
C.I.C. Fontes, VI,

n. 4340
S.C.Sacr., Mar. 6, 1911
A.A.S., III, p. 102
S.C.Sacr., July 4, 1921
A.A.S., XIII, p. 348

Canon 1988

S.C.Sacr., Aug. 15, 1936,
§225
A.A.S., XXVIII, p. 313

Canon 90
Canon 777

Canon 2383

Firmandis, §10
Bened. XIV, Nov. 6,
1744
C.I.C. Fontes, I, n. 349
Canons 470, §4; 343, §1,
1094

Ne temere, X
S.C.C., Apr. 19, 1908
C.I.C. Fontes, VI, n.
4340

Canon 2222, §1
S.C.Sacr., Mar. 6, 1911
A.A.S., III, p. 102
S.C.Sacr., July 1, 1932
A.A.S., XXIV, p. 272

been entered in his baptismal register. This certification must be filed with the documents of the marriage.

3° A declaration of nullity or an apostolic dispensation from non-consummated marriage with any prohibition of future marriage decreed therein, should be sent as soon as possible to the pastor in whose register the marriage was entered, so that these may be inserted in the *marriage* and *baptismal* registers. If the baptisms were elsewhere, the same pastor must notify the pastor of the place of baptism, and inform his own Ordinary immediately that he has fulfilled these requirements.

4° Baptism should be recorded not only in the registry of the church of baptism but also in the parish register of the place of origin (canon 90), and hence the *pastor of the church of baptism* should send as soon as possible to the *pastor of the place of origin* all the items required by canon 777.

5° Remissness in fulfilling the requirements concerning parish records should be liable to the sanction of canon 2383.

6° Marriage and baptismal registers should be inspected every six months, or at least annually, by the Ordinary or his delegate, and each entry should be checked with some relevant mark. Where it appears that delegation was necessary (canon 1094), inquiry should be made whether the delegation was granted according to law.

12. Ordinaries shall enforce these safeguards, even with canonical penalties, according to canon 2222, §1; and shall record in the *Annual Report on Marriage Causes* their observance of this Instruction and refer, in particular, to the fact that the inspection of the marriage files was made as prescribed.

Imprimi potest: GULIELMUS M. MAGEE, S.J.,
    Praep. Prov. Chicagiensis
Nihil obstat: A. C. ELLIS, S.J. Censor deputatus
Imprimatur: ✠SAMUEL A. STRITCH,
    Archiepiscopus Chicagiensis, March 28, 1942

THE ESSENTIAL DOCUMENT- BAPTISMAL CERTIFICATE

Canon 1021: 1. Unless baptism was conferred in his own territory, the pastor shall require proof of baptism of both parties, or from the Catholic party only, if the marriage is to be contracted with a dispensation from the impediment of disparity of cult.

2. Catholics who have not yet received the sacrament of confirmation should first receive this sacrament before being married, if they can do so without grave inconvenience.

Proof of baptism is most essential in the prenuptial investigation. If the parties were baptized in the same church where the marriage will take place, the proof of baptism can be found in the parish baptismal record. The pastor usually checks the records. If the parties were baptized elsewhere, then they must secure proof of the baptism from the church of baptism. The certificate, will indicate whether the parties are free to marry. It will indicate whether the person was married before, received the order of subdeaconate or solemn religious vows.

Canon 470 obliges all pastors to record in the baptismal register of the parish all these important facts. For this reason Canon 1103 demands that pastors who assist at a marriage send a record of this marriage with the names, dates, witnesses, dispensations received, etc., to the church of baptism. Hence, a certificate of baptism will show whether there was a previous marriage, etc. Information of any marriages that have been declared null by the ecclesiastical court should also be included.

Sometimes we find that baptismal books have been destroyed by fire. One trustworthy witness would suffice to prove reception of baptism, e.g., the Godparent or the priest who baptized. In litigated cases, more proof is needed. *The pastor of a marriage must insist on a baptismal certificate which is issued at least within the past six months. Old certificates must never be accepted.*

Non-Catholics: Pastors must also demand a certificate of baptism from non-Catholics. This will determine just what type of dispensation is needed. If the parties were unbaptized it might be well to ask further questions. This information may prove valuable later on to some matrimonial tribunal.

PUBLICATION OF THE BANNS

Canon 1022: The pastor must announce publicly the names of those persons who are about to contract marriage.

1. In order to safeguard the marriage contract, every possible precaution must be taken. The Council of Trent laid down a law announcing the banns of marriage. The banns of marriage are to be published by the proper pastor of the parties. Although banns are not required for validity, the pastor should nevertheless in every case discharge this duty to be morally certain that there is no impediment to the marriage.[7]

Place of Publication

Canon 1023: 1. The banns of matrimony must be announced by the pastor of the parties.

2. If a party has lived in another locality for a period of six months since attaining puberty, the pastor shall consult his ordinary, who in his prudent discretion will either demand that the banns be announced in that place, or, other proofs of presumptive evidence regarding freedom of the party be gathered.

7. (a) Canon 21: Laws are made for the purpose of safeguarding against common danger, bind, even though in a particular case there is no danger. (b) In some dioceses faculties have been given whereby pastors may dispense from one, two or three banns. Cf. *Diocesan Faculties in the U.S.*, Woodstock College Press, Md., 1948, pp. 22-23.

3. If there is any suspicion that an impediment has been incurred, the pastor, even for the case of a briefer period of residence, should consult the ordinary who should not permit the marriage until the suspicion has been removed according to paragraph 2.

The pastor who is bound to publish the banns is the one in which the parties have their domicile or quasi-domicile (The Catholic acquires a proper parish and pastor either by domicile or quasi-domicile). A domicile is acquired by residence in any parish with the intention to stay there permanently unless something calls one away or one's residence must extend over a period of ten years. A quasi-domicile is acquired by residence in a parish with intention to stay there for the greater part of a year unless something calls the person away, or, by having actually lived there for the greater part of the year, at least more than six months. Canon 92: 2 states "If the parties have several domiciles or quasi-domiciles the publication of the banns should be made at the parish churches of each."

It is possible that one could have incurred an impediment or impediments in a place where he or she lived for six months. After reaching the age of puberty,[8] however, it is left to the local ordinary whether the banns should be published in all these places. A difficulty may arise when people have been moving about from place to place because of business or for other reasons and would not be known to the people there, in which case the announcement of the banns would be useless. In such a case the ordinary may demand testimony of a reliable witness or witnesses. In any case all necessary information regarding the parties should be obtained. Regarding a pending urgent marriage wherein there is not sufficient time to make the necessary investigation the pastor should consult the ordinary; the Code

8. Canon 88: 2. A boy is regarded as having reached the age of puberty when he completes his 14th year; a girl is regarded as having reached the age of puberty when she completes her 12th year.

Commission suggested that reliable witnesses and the parties should be questioned on the matter and have them take the suppletory oath (Canon 1829: "This is better than nothing at all.").

Time of Publication

Canon 1024: The publications are to be made on three successive Sundays or other days of obligation in the church during the solemnities of the Mass or during other divine services at which many people are in attendance.

The code does not specify the manner in which banns are to be published. One should follow the custom of the place. Publication should be made in the vernacular language and specifying the name or names and residences of the parties. The faithful should also be informed that they have a grave obligation to make known any impediment of the parties to the pastor if they know of any.

Form of Publication

Canon 1025: The ordinary may, for his own territory, substitute for the publications the public posting of the names of the parties on the doors of the church, or near the door of the parochial church or another church for at least eight days provided, however, that within this time two feast days of precept are included.

Although this is a new form of publication of the banns, historically we find it used in the case of necessity with special permission. The oral announcement was customary because many people could not read. The names must be posted at the door of the parish church or another church within the parish limits, e.g., a church of religious if there is one.

Publication for Mixed Marriages

Canon 1026:   Publications are not to be made for marriages which are contracted with a dispensation from the impediment of disparity of cult or mixed religion, unless the local ordinary in his prudent judgment, in the absence of scandal, deems it advisable to permit them, provided that the apostolic dispensation has been obtained previously and no mention is made of the religion of the non-Catholic party.

This prohibition is had because otherwise the publication might encourage others to mixed marriages. Here in the U.S. it has been the custom not to make such announcements. In one large city in the U.S. where there is a great non-Catholic population, out of 53 marriages that occurred, 50 were mixed marriages and announcement of banns was made only three times in that year. Publication of banns in mixed marriages is very seldom done although it is known that permission can be granted by Rome. The publication of banns is also prohibited in marriages of conscience and in marriages in danger of death.

Duty of The Faithful

Canon 1027:   All the faithful are bound to reveal to their pastor or local ordinary impediments, if they know of any, before the celebration of marriage.

This is a grave obligation on the part of the faithful stemming from the natural and divine law and for the benefit of the common good. No exception is made for a relative or friends. Only a grave reason would excuse them from divulging this information. Historically, in 1886, the Synod of Baltimore [9] inflicted excommunication on persons who neglected to reveal such impediments. This is an indication of the gravity of the matter. One would be excused from revealing this information if the information came from a sacramental confession. If the knowl-

9. Synodus Diocesan Baltimorensie 9, p. 51.

edge came through some particular profession as, for example, a doctor or a lawyer or a priest outside of confession, there is no need to reveal it because the common good may suffer or that particular profession might suffer because of this. Although some authors hold that if it is not revealed, harm would come to a third party.

Dispensations

Canon 1028:   1. The local ordinary of the parties can in his prudent judgment for a legitimate cause dispense from making the publications even in another diocese.

              2. If there are several proper ordinaries, that one has the right to dispense in whose diocese the marriage takes place; if the marriage takes place outside the parties' own diocese, then any ordinary of either party can dispense.

When we speak of legitimate reasons for the local ordinary to dispense his subjects in a strange diocese, we may enumerate among these: (a) danger of civil marriage; (b) fear of scandal; (c) a business trip; (d) transfer from one military post to another. Of course, it is presumed that freedom to marry has been established.

CASE

(Domiciles or Quasi-Domiciles) *A wishes to marry B in Washington, D.C.* A has a domicile in Boston and a quasi-domicile in Connecticut. B has a domicile in Reno and a quasi-domicile in Los Angeles. The ordinaries from any of these dioceses of the domiciles or quasi-domiciles can grant the dispensation. Since a pastor may marry parties who have stayed in his parish for at least one month without acquiring a domicile or quasi-domicile, it seems a fortiori (C. 1097: 1, n.3) that the pastor's ordinary would also have the right to dispense from the banns even though he is not mentioned among the ordinaries in this particular canon. Woywood is hesitant in admitting this.[10]

Canon 1029: If another pastor has conducted the investigation or the publications he must immediately by an authentic document send information as to the result of the same to the pastor who must assist at the marriage.

This sometimes happens when parties move about the country and belong to several dioceses. According to the instructions of 1941, the *nihil obstat* should be given by the respective chanceries.

After Publication

Canon 1030: 1. After the investigation and the publications the pastor shall not assist at the marriage, until he has received all the necessary documents, and unless a reasonable cause warrants it, not until *three days have elapsed* since the last publication.

2. If the marriage is not contracted within six months, the publications must be repeated unless the ordinary of the place decides otherwise.

The pastor must wait three days so that any documents, reports, dispensations, rescripts, that are necessary will be in his possession before the marriage takes place. For a serious reason of inconvenience, the pastor may go ahead with the marriage without consulting the ordinary to dispense with these three days.

Canon 1031: 1. If a doubt has arisen concerning the existence

10. Woywood, S., O.F.M., *A Practical Commentary on the Code of Canon Law*, Wagner, Inc., N.Y., p. 664.

of some impediment: (1) The pastor shall investigate the matter more thoroughly by questioning, under oath at least two trustworthy witnesses, unless the impediment is one which if known would injure the good reputation of the parties, and if necessary he shall also question the parties in the same way. (2) He shall make or finish the publication if a doubt arose before they have been begun or before they are finished; (3) If he prudently judges that the doubt still exists he must not assist at the marriage without consulting the ordinary.

2. If a certain impediment has been discovered: (1) If the impediment is occult, the pastor shall continue or complete the publications and refer the matter, without mentioning the names, to the local ordinary or to the Sacred Penitentiary; (2) If the impediment is public and is detected before the publications are begun, the pastor shall not proceed further until the impediment has been removed, even though he may know that a dispensation has been obtained in the forum of conscience alone, if it is detected after the first or second publication of banns, the pastor shall finish the publications and refer the matter to the local ordinary.

3. Finally, if no impediment has been detected, either doubtful or certain, the pastor, the publication having been completed, shall admit the parties to the celebration of marriage.

When marrying, the pastor encounters usually no difficulties such as are mentioned in this canon because he usually knows the individuals and their families. In some of our parishes when the pastor does not know the parties, he should proceed cautiously. He will, of course, have many investigations before publishing banns. The law states that if a doubt arises before the publication of the banns, he should endeavor to solve that doubt before beginning the publication. If the doubt cannot be solved, the law does not forbid him to go ahead with the announcement. Someone might be present who knows more about the parties and this impediment, and can inform the pastor if they are aware of this impediment. If the doubt arose just before the official announcement, the code specifies that he go ahead. If the doubt arose during the period of the time of the announcing of the banns, he must go ahead and complete them. Should the doubt still remain after the publication, the pastor should consult the Ordinary before proceeding with the marriage. The necessary precautions are taken here, otherwise, the sacrament of matrimony might be exposed to danger of nullity and lead the parties into a union which would be sinful. Every effort should be made to remove any doubts that might occur, in which case interrogation of the witnesses is in order. If the pastor finds that the impediment is occult, the publication of the banns continues and in the meantime the pastor should write for the proper dispensation. If the impediment happens to be public, nothing should be done without obtaining a dispensation.

VAGI

Canon 1032: Except in the case of necessity, the pastor should never assist at the marriage of vagi, as described in Canon 91, unless, after he has referred the case to the local ordinary or to the priest delegated by him, he has obtained permission to assist.

A vagus is one who has neither domicile or quasi-domicile (Canons 91 and 92). This is not an unusual occurrence but if it happens the pastor should consult the ordinary. In danger of death, an oath of their freedom to marry would suffice. Proper instructions for parties, according to the various needs of the individuals on the sanctity of the sacrament of matrimony, initial obligation and the obligation of parents toward their children should be given. The pastor shall earnestly exhort them before the marriage to make a good confession of their sins and to receive Holy Communion devoutly.

FORMULA IN ANNOUNCING THE BANNS OF MARRIAGE IN A PARISH

Banns of Marriage

Be it Known to All Here Present That the Following Parties, God Willing, Purpose to Marry. Therefore, We Advise Each and Everyone to Whom it Concerns That if Any Person Knows of Any Impediment of Consanguinity, Affinity, Spiritual Relationship, or Any Other Impediment, or Any Other Reason Which Would Prevent These Parties from Entering into the State of Matrimony, He is Hereby Bound to Advise the Pastor or Any Other Priest, of This Fact as Soon as Possible.

First Time: John A. Brown, son of Maurice C. Brown and Mary Baker of St. James Parish and *Anna M. Smith,* daughter of Michael Smith and Mary Jones, of St. Rita's Parish.
Second Time: ....
Third Time: ....

INSTRUCTIONS TO THE SPOUSES

Canon 1033:   The pastor must not omit, with due regard to the condition of the persons concerned, to instruct the parties on the sanctity of matrimony, their mutual obligations, the obligation of parents toward their children; he shall earnestly exhort them to make a careful confession of their sins and receive with devotion the Most Blessed Eucharist.

Through the investigation of marriage cases, it has been found that many couples have not been given the proper instruction by their pastors. Perhaps the instructions would have saved the marriage. If pastors would take this canon seriously, they would give all the instructions necessary. Every case is different. Some parties need more than other parties. Giving instructions to the people on Sunday is very good but this canon has reference to private instructions. This canon is connected with Canon 1018, and all the recommendations given there should be followed in such an instruction. (It would be well to review Canon 1018). To receive so great a sacrament as matrimony and to venture into a new profession for a lifetime, the parties need all the graces and blessings that are possible. Hence, this canon strongly exhorts the pastor to persuade the parties to make a good confession and to receive Holy Communion. Confession and Communion are not obliged by any law; it is highly recommended. To receive sacraments in mortal sin only aggravates the situation. It could result in sacrilege.

Revision of the Code

Cardinal Spellman of New York announced at the National Convention of the Canon Law Society of America in N. Y., September 18, 1963, that the Committee working on the revision of the Code in Rome, will consider the request of the American bishops that the *proclamation of banns be restricted* in such a way that it be left up to the pastor to determine whether the banns should be announced or not. The pastor knows his people and he is in the best position to determine that matter. This was the reason for offering such a change. In most of our parishes today, people do not know each other too well.

MARRIAGE OF MINORS: TEENAGERS

Canon 1034: The pastor must seriously exhort minors from contracting marriage without the knowledge or against the reasonable wishes of their parents; but if they refuse to obey, he should not assist at their marriage without having first consulted the local ordinary.

Rights and Duties of Minors

1. This law is based on the legislation of the Council of Trent and adopted by the codifiers who uphold the rights of minors to marry, but emphasize their duty to parents.

2. The implication is that minors can marry validly without their parents' consent; although they should consult their parents, it in no way gives them absolute right to command them in the choice of a partner. If the parents have a reasonable cause to oppose the marriage and they are insistant, the pastor should consult the ordinary of the diocese. Want of consent of the parents is in no way a prohibitive impediment. However, pastors and diocesan authorities are urged to give the matter utmost consideration because even though minors have a right, it is not always feasible to use this right for economical, psychological, and spiritual reasons. *The best answer to this situation is deferment.*

Teen-Age Marriage

3. Pastors, judges, lawyers, sociologists, psychiatrists, physicians, and all such professional people deplore the unhealthy situation of teen-age marriages in the U.S. According to a general survey, it is revealed that one third of all the divorces granted were for marriages that were contracted during the teen-age years of the couple. Today more and more pregnancies of teen-age girls are occurring in our high schools, public as well as the Catholic schools. Sometimes shame drives them to marriage; at times they get married just to give the child a name; or to avoid any court trials. Almost a quarter million illegitimate children were born in 1962 in the U.S.; one-third of these were from girls 13 to 17.

TEEN-AGE CASE

In one such case, we found that a girl, 16, who was pregnant wanted to marry the boy of 17. The girl's parents would not hear of it. The parents of the boy were in favor of it, because they knew many people who married at such an age with success; the couple presented a marriage license to the pastor and threatened to have a civil ceremony if he would not marry them. Although the couple were sixteen and seventeen, the license indicated that they were twenty-one. The pastor called the chancery and got the permission to marry them. The problem arose whereby the father of the girl was going to sue the pastor, for marrying the couple without the parent's consent. Could the pastor be sued even though he knew that they were not twenty-one? No. Because even though he knew this, the official civil license gave him the right to marry them. According to civil law, this judgment was passed by the civil official that they were of age; the pastor merely had a permission to marry them, not to investigate them. The father of the girl was informed that a perjury charge could be brought against his daughter. The case was dropped.

Today, with the difficulty of finding employment in the country, pastors must point out to all parents and teen-age individuals that venturing into the field of matrimony at this age, without any formal training makes it difficult to face the economic problems of providing a home, and to raise a family; one is trying to compete with many skilled professional men who are unemployed. After putting up with this situation for a time, the young couple becomes disgruntled and upset and eventually are seeking a way out of their marriage. The result of one third of the divorces stems from such a source.[11]

Due to the fact that 50% of all teen-age marriages end in divorce, California has introduced a state law (Nov. 1970), designed to make it more difficult for teenagers to marry:

"To marry, any boy or girl under 18 must get:

1) Superior Court's permission.
2) Permission from parents or guardians.
3) Premarital counseling can be required by the court (court permission was formerly required only for girls under 16)."

11. "Teenage Marriages," *The Jurist*, XXIII, Jan., 1963. Joyce, *Christian Marriage*, pp. 71-116. Augustino, P. Chas., *The New Code of Canon Law*, Vol. V, Herder, 1923, p. 79.

Canon 1034:

QUESTIONNAIRE FOR PARENTS OF PARTY UNDER
TWENTY-ONE YEARS OF AGE

(This deposition of parents or guardians must accompany each application for a dispensation in favor of parties under twenty-one years of age.)

Names: ....

....

Having reminded the witness of the sanctity of an oath and the severity of the punishment that perjurers are subject to, also of the solemnity of the act which he or she is about to perform, let the pastor address the witness.

Are you willing to invoke God's name in witness of the truth, while touching the Holy Gospels, in the following manner:

"I solemnly swear that I shall tell the truth, the whole truth, and nothing but the truth in answer to your questions. So help me God and these His Holy Gospels which I touch with my hand."

1. What is your full name?...
2. Where do you live?..
3. What religion do you profess?...
4. Are you a practical Catholic?..
5. How are you related to...............................? ....
   When was he (she) born?..
6. Are you aware of..
   intention to marry...............................? ....
7. How long has this couple known each other?.....................................
8. How long has this couple been keeping company with a view to marriage? ....

9. Have they perhaps contracted a civil marriage; if so, where and when and before whom did they attempt this civil marriage?..............................

....

City and State   Day, Month, and Year   Minister or Justice of the Peace

10. Is this the first marriage of..?
    If not, to whom was she married before?....................................

11. Is this the first marriage of..?
    If not, to whom was he married before?....................................

12. Is there any reason why..is being
    persuaded to marry at this time?...

13. Is..entering this marriage through fear of
    his parents, relatives, or any third party; is there any duress or undue
    persuasion; is there any reason whatsoever why.................................
    should feel compelled to enter this marriage?.......................................

....

(Pastor should prudently inquire concerning the physical condition of the girl.)

14. Do you know any reason why...should not
    enter this marriage?...

15. Do you fully approve of this marriage at the present time?....................

16. Are you willing to state that..is freely
    giving his (her) consent to this marriage?..................................

17. Have you anything to add concerning this marriage?................................

....

....

(Father)   (Mother)

Subscribed and sworn to in my presence this........day of....................,19........

(PARISH SEAL)   ....

(Pastor)   (Assistant)

Remarks: The priest who is to assist at the marriage should indicate
          whether or not he believes that the marriage should be per-
          formed at once; he should give his own personal opinion about
          the contracting parties, etc.:

....
....

JUSTICE OF THE PEACE AND MARRIAGE

QUESTION: Is a justice of the peace obligated to perform all marriage ceremonies that come to his attention?

A justice of the peace is not required by law to perform a marriage ceremony. *It is a privilege of his office to do so.* Most judges of our Common Pleas Court refuse to perform marriage ceremonies stating publicly that this is a matter peculiarly for a cleric. They too have the right to officiate at a wedding. A justice of the peace is not obliged to offer his services to all callers nor can he be required to perform a marriage ceremony against his will. Before performing a marriage ceremony, a justice of the peace is not required to make any investigation other than to be satisfied that the parties are of age and that a marriage license has been issued. Before a justice of the peace may perform a ceremony, the parties must present to him a marriage license which they have previously obtained from the marriage license clerk in the Orphan's Court Office. It is the duty of the license clerk to ascertain whether the parties are of age and otherwise free to marry, i.e., whether either party has a spouse in being from whom no divorce has been granted. A justice of the peace may marry anyone in his office who brings to him the marriage license regardless of whether the parties reside outside of the county or state. He himself can perform the ceremony any place within the Commonwealth.

A priest who also holds the office of Justice of the Peace can refuse, as a justice of the peace, to perform the ceremony. Indeed, it would be his duty to do so. The same holds true for a Catholic layman who holds the office of Justice of the Peace.[12]

---

12. Moore, Thos., Esq., Legal Reply, Luzerne County, Penna.

CHAPTER III

IMPEDIMENTS IN GENERAL

IMPEDIMENTS IN GENERAL

Canon 1035: All persons may contract marriage who are not
prohibited by law.

All persons have a natural right to marry. Natural society is
founded by God for the propagation of the race. Hence, this right
must be honored, unless there is some prohibition of the divine
or ecclesiastical law. Since marriage between the baptized is a
sacrament, the ecclesiastical authority must always safeguard
the sanctity of holy matrimony. Hence, the Church must determine how, when, and where the marriage will be celebrated.
The prohibition mentioned in this canon occurs when there is
some impediment which could render a marriage illicit or invalid.

KINDS OF IMPEDIMENTS

Canon 1036: 1. An impedient impediment contains a grave
prohibition a g a i n s t contracting marriage,
which, however, is not indeed invalid if it is
contracted notwithstanding the impediment.

2. A diriment impediment both gravely prohibits
the marriage and prevents it from being concluded validly.

3. Although an impediment exists only on the part of *one party*, nevertheless, the marriage is illicit or invalid.

---

1. Impeding Impediments: simple vows; mixed religion; relationship through adoption if forbidden by law.

2. Diriment Impediments: want of age; impotency; existing bond of previous marriage; disparity of cult; sacred orders; solemn religious vows; abduction; crime; consanguinity; affinity; public propriety; spiritual relationship; legal relationship through adoption, if according to the law of the states, it invalidates marriage.

3. Impediments are said to be absolute if they prohibit marriage with any person; they are said to be relative if they prohibit a marriage with some particular person only.

Canon 1036: 1, prohibits marriage; however, if it is contracted, it does not invalidate the marriage, that is, it forbids marriage under the pain of sin but does not invalidate it.

A diriment impediment is one which not only gravely prohibits any marriage contract but makes the marriage null and void.

Furthermore, the canon mentions that if an impediment exists in only one of the parties, it presents an obstacle because the marriage contract is indivisible. Consequently, if it is invalid for one, it is equally as invalid for the other to make the contract. An impediment could effect one or both parties: *one party*: impediment of age, impotency, ligamen or sacred orders. *Both parties*: consanguinity, affinity, adoption or spiritual relationship. In other words, both parties must be qualified to make the contract.

PUBLIC AND OCCULT IMPEDIMENTS

Canon 1037: An impediment is considered as public, if it can be proved in the external forum; otherwise it is occult.

A public impediment is one which can be proved in the external forum, that is, the circumstances from which it arises are public. Facts can be proved in the external forum in most cases either by authentic public documents (C. 1816) (e.g., sacred orders, religious vows, disparity of cult, consanguinity, affinity, etc.) OR, two trustworthy witnesses (C. 1791: 2) who can testify because of their personal knowledge, OR one exceptional witness with regard to official acts (C. 1791: 1).

The reason why we have a distinction between public and occult impediments, because (with the former) after a dispensation, this fact must be put in the public record. Confessors therefore should be very careful in dispensing from such impediments. A conflict may arise between the internal and the external forum. (An impediment *occult by nature* would be, e.g., a private vow, crime arising from adultery or conjugicide, occult consanguinity.) We have an *occult case* when an impediment is *public by nature and occult in fact*, e.g., consanguinity which is *public by nature but not known* in a new domicile - city or town.

Canon 1038:   1. The Supreme Authority of the Church has the sole right to declare authentically in what instances the divine law forbids or invalidates marriage.

2. The same Supreme Authority has the exclusive right of establishing impedient or diriment impediments for baptized persons either by universal or particular law.

MAJOR AND MINOR DEGREE

Canon 1039:   1. Local ordinaries can forbid marriage in a particular case, but only temporarily, for a just cause, and as long as the cause continues, to all persons actually sojourning in their territory, and to their subjects even outside their territory.

2. ONLY THE APOSTOLIC SEE CAN ADD AN INVALIDATING CLAUSE TO THE PROHIBITION.

The ordinary of the place may forbid a certain marriage only as long as the cause exists; for example, if there is danger of scandal, doubtful impediment, etc. *The ordinary cannot prohibit a marriage under pain of nullity.* If, for instance, an ordinary enacts a law that no marriage whatsoever can be celebrated in his diocese after 6:00 p.m., would the marriage be invalid if this law were disobeyed, viz., performing the marriage at 8:00 p.m.? *This canon forbids such a sanction,* therefore the marriage would be valid but illicit.

Canon 1040:   No one except the Roman Pontiff can abrogate or derogate impediments of ecclesiastical law whether they be impedient or diriment; nor dispense from the same unless this power has been granted either by the common law or by special indult from the Holy See.

This canon deals exclusively with ecclesiastical law for no human authority can abrogate or dispense from impediments of the divine law. The Holy Father can abrogate an impediment—take it out completely from the Code, or derogate it by taking out only part of the law as he did in 1949 regarding Canon 1099: 2.

Canon 1041:   A custom which introduces a new impediment or one which is contrary to an existing impediment is reprobated.

Canon 1042:   1. Some impediments are of minor, others of major grade.

2. Impediments of minor grade are:
   (1) *Consanguinity* in the third degree of the collateral line;
   (2) *Affinity* in the second degree of the collateral line;
   (3) *Public propriety* in the second degree;
   (4) Spiritual relationship.
   (5) Crime resulting from adultery with a promise OR attempt at marriage, even by a merely civil act.

3. Impediments of a major grade are all the others.

This distinction is made to indicate that those of minor grade are more easily dispensed. Note: Although all these are minor degree, they are diriment impediments.

MARRIAGE IN DANGER OF DEATH

Canon 1043: In the danger of death, the local ordinaries *for the peace of conscience,* and, if the case warrants it, for the *legitimation of offspring,* both to *the form observed in the celebration of marriage* and as to all *ecclesiastical impediments,* public or occult even multiple, *except impediments* arising from the *sacred order of priesthood* and from *affinity in the direct line of a consummated marriage* can dispense their own subjects wherever they may be, and all persons actually staying in their territory, provided that scandal be removed, and, if a dispensation of disparity of cult or mixed religion is granted, the usual prescribed promises must be given.

Canon 1044: In the same circumstances as mentioned in Canon 1043 and only for cases in which the local ordinary cannot be reached, the pastor as well as the priest who assists at the marriage, according to Canon 1098: 2, and the confessor for the internal forum and in the act of confession only, have the same faculties of dispensing.

1. To clarify these canons, it is best to study all the elements involved separately. We all know that the Church grants extraordinary faculties on extraordinary occasions. From the common law, Canon 882, in danger of death, grants to any priest all the faculties necessary to absolve the dying person from all censures, sins, even though the priest has no faculties in that particular territory. This (C. 1043-44) is a complicated canon, but it can be made clear if each part is studied separately. The Church gives these very extensive powers of dispensation to the local ordinary and also to the priest mentioned there, when there is danger that a party may die before the priest can in the ordinary mode of communication get a dispensation from the Holy See. By ordinary communication we mean a personal interview, letter, cablegram, etc.

What about telephone or telegraph? It is not absolutely impossible to contact the Holy See in our day and age. However, the committee for the authentic interpretation of the code, Nov. 12, 1922, condemned the use of the telephone or the telegraph in such cases, because these are extraordinary means; and, moreover, are not safe. Furthermore, in 1891, the Papal Secretary of State, had declared that "the Supreme Pontiff *orders* that all applications or favors made to the Roman Curia by telephone or telegraph shall be ignored, and that he wants the bishops to do the same."

2. Ordinaries of places are those mentioned in Canon 198, viz, bishops, (residential) not merely a titular bishop or an auxiliary, unless he is also a vicar general; an abbot nullius; vicar general; apostolic administrator, papal apostolic; prefect apostolic; or temporary administrator during a vacancy.

3. The circumstances requisite for the use of the powers here granted are: (a) *danger of death;* (b) *for the sake of relieving a person's conscience;* (c) for the *legitimation of children;* (d) *dispense from the form of marriage;* (e) *dispense from all*

and each ecclesiastical impediments, public, occult or multiple; (f) *that all scandal be removed;* (g) *that the cautiones or guarantees be given if the dispensation from disparity of cult or mixed religion be given at the time.*

4. Canon 1040 explicitly states that "no one except the Holy Father has the power to dispense from prohibitive or diriment impediments, unless it has been granted him by common law or by special apostolic indult. *The primary factor of this canon is the salvation of souls.* Therefore, the law is set up for this particular purpose. *Due to certain circumstances, the distance of the Holy See, the urgent necessity, as well as the danger of death,* Canon 1043 provides a means whereby the Ordinary of the Place and others do not have to have permission from the Holy Father or the Holy See, neither does he need a special indult to grant certain important dispensations. Why? Because the common law gives the Ordinary these faculties, these same faculties are given to the pastor and other priests mentioned in that Canon.

5. *Danger of death is one of the requisites to use these faculties;* this *does not mean immediate* or *extreme danger* (articulo mortis) but any *ordinary danger* which arises from (1) *internal cause* and (2) *external cause.* An *internal intrinsic cause* such as an accident, where injury is sustained; disease, illness, or a serious operation, such as surgery. *Extrinsic* or *external* might be special or unusual circumstances that place persons in danger of death. These may come from two sources; (1) *natural causes* and (2) *social causes.*

Natural causes, such as catastrophes, i.e., earthquakes, epidemics, mine disasters, innundations.

Social causes, i.e., a serious disturbance of peace and public order from bloody revolutions, insurrections, invasion by enemies, mobilization, civilians who reside in war zones carrying on battle, civilians exposed to air attacks, dangerous missions, prisoners awaiting capital punishment.[1]

6. *Must we be certain of death?* Certainty is not required but the law of probability is sufficient to use these faculties. *If no actual danger of death is present objectively,* but prudently determined probable, the faculties are valid and can be used.

1. Dowdell, *Celebration of Marriage in Danger of Death,* Vatican Press, Rome, 1944, p. 529.

Other requisites for the valid use of these faculties are either *peace of conscience* or *legitimation of children* or both together. Peace of conscience is sufficient in itself. The ordinary, pastor, etc., who uses these faculties should keep in mind that *it is unnecessary that both parties seek peace of mind.* If only one of them seeks this, this party does not have to be the one who is in danger of death, nor the one who has the impediment to the marriage.[2] The reason for peace of mind need not be the need for sacramental absolution.[3]

It is not necessary that the confession be *Sacramentally Valid.* Nor is it necessary that absolution be given (by the confessor) from an impediment in the Internal Forum. It may be, for example, to remove the proximate occasion of sin, or some grave cause of contention, such as a legal controversy over property, reparation of injury or loss of reputation. An example of *peace of mind: Mrs. Smith, a Catholic, calls you about her husband, an unbaptized, who is dying.* They are not married validly. Mr. Smith does wish to become baptized, and he is willing to do anything to give peace of mind to Mrs. Smith. Mrs. Smith does not want to go to confession. The pastor can't get in touch with the ordinary. Mrs. Smith was in a convent before and was never dispensed from vows. She is also related to Mr. Smith as a second cousin. The dispensation can be granted and the marriage validated.

Legitimation of Children:[4] 1. When peace of mind is not sought, but merely the legitimation of children, there is a rare case. Authors do not agree on this. 2. Suppose the children were spurious, i.e., *adulterine* (born while one of the parties was in vows or sacred orders), in virtue of Canon 1051 the children could not be legitimated. Canon 1051 "a dispensation from a diriment impediment...." "There is granted also *ipso facto* the

---

2. Clays Bowaaert-Simenon, *Manuale Juris Canonis,* Gandae et Leodin, No. 250.

3. Bouscaren-Ellis, *Comm. on Code of Canon Law,* Bruce, 1956, p. 487.

4. *The Jurist,* "The Philosophy of Legitimacy," Jan., 1943, pp. 64-116.

legitimation of children in case any have already been born *or* were conceived by the parties who are being dispensed, *with the exception, however, of adulterine and sacrilegious children.*" Now, this canon deals with normal cases and not cases in danger of death.

2. Nor could the children already born, by subsequent marriage of the parties, be legitimized according to *Canons 1114* and *1116,* when the only reason for granting the dispensation is the legitimation of offspring. *Canon 1114:* "Children who are conceived or born, of a valid or putative marriage, are considered legitimated *unless,* at the time of conception the *marriage contracted was forbidden to the parents* because of *solemn religious profession* or *the reception of sacred orders.*" *Canon 1116* "by a subsequent marriage of the parents whether a true marriage or a putative marriage (one in good faith), whether newly contracted or validated, even though not consummated, the children are legitimated provided that the parents were free to marry." Wernz-Vidal, Gasparri, Ojetti, De Smet and others. It must be noted that in case of sacrilegious offspring, that a dispensation from the diriment impediment of solemn vows or sacred orders at the hour of death, secures the legitimation of the children *not yet born.*

For adulterine and sacrilegious children already born: Some authors claim that the faculties of Canons 1043 and 1044 can be used even in the case of adulterine and sacrilegious children *already born,* because it could facilitate (after the marriage is contracted) in obtaining an indult of legitimation from the Holy See. The phrase *"ad consulendum legitimationi prolis"* is the reason for using the 1043 and 1044 Canons which contain the faculty to dispense from such marriage impediments. Moreover, there are other authors who hold the *probable opinion* that adulterine or sacrilegious children already born is included in this extraordinary faculty of 1043 and 1044. It is safe to follow this opinion until the Holy See declares otherwise. According to this viewpoint then such *children already born or to be born* are legitimized immediately even though one of the parties should die before the marriage contract is made, or, for some other reason, the marriage does not take place.

7. *Dispensation from Impediments:* (1) This canon is dealing with ecclesiastical law, therefore, any impediment of divine or natural law cannot be dispensed, e.g., a previous bond of marriage, consanguinity, etc. (2) The power to dispense includes all impediments prohibitive and diriment, public and occult of ecclesiastical law except the priesthood and affinity in the direct line arising from a consummated marriage (affinity in the direct line would mean the wife's mother, grandmother, daughter, and vice-versa). The Church sometimes (rarely) does dispense from affinity in the direct line for a man and his mother-in-law, a stepfather and a daughter of his wife by another man (refer Lydon, Canon Law, page 178). A dispensation would be needed in the collateral line, second degree inclusive. The dispensation is needed for affinity in the collateral line, second degree inclusive, e.g., Jack and Mary, catholics, are married, Mary dies, Jack needs a dispensation to marry her sister, which is the first degree, her first cousin, her aunt, her niece. He would need no dispensation for a second cousin marriage. This canon gives faculties for dispensations which are rarely given by the Holy See under normal circumstances, e.g., sacred orders or third degree of crime.

In danger of death: to be sure that no consummation took place and proof cannot be had for this, the sworn testimony or statement by the parties that they have been baptized and are under no impediment would suffice.

8. *Avoid Scandal:* If the scandal results, this alone would not invalidate the dispensation. If the impediment is public, the dispensation should be public, e.g., the parties lived in public concubinage. In an occult case, when people consider their marriage as valid, it seems that no scandal could result. Scandal could result if the person would be in sacred orders or vows and lived in this condition in the territory in which he is known.

9. *Disparity of Cult or Mixed Religion:* Here the cautiones or guarantee is required for validity of the dispensation. The Holy See did require this promise explicitly, but since 1941 it is sufficient that the promise be given at least implicitly. (AAB 33-294). In the case of *children already born* the controversy existed until 1941, are these included in the guarantees made by the non-Catholic party? The Holy Office in 1941 says that it did not pertain to *children already born.* The guarantees are made

for children *TO BE BORN*. However, the parents should try to bring up all children already born into the Church. Canon 1061 requires that all the guarantees be made in writing. Since this prescription is for *liceity only*, the marriage would be valid. In case of grave necessity, there is not time to discuss the promises to the parties, the dispensation would be valid, all things being equal. In case of necessity when one must hurry, one may use the dispensation from the diaconate, etc. Notification of this dispensation should be sent to the chancery if given in the external forum, or sent to the Sacred Penitentiary or the chancery for the secret archives as the case warrants, if given in the internal non-sacramental forum.

FACULTIES GRANTED BY THESE CANONS

Canons 1043 - 1044 - 1045 - 1098:

1. *ORDINARY OF THE PLACE*
   has ordinary power

2. *PASTOR*
   has ordinary power

3. *ASSISTANT PASTOR*
   has delegated power from the Ordinary through letter
   has delegated power through statutes
   has delegated power from the pastor

4. *STRANGE PRIEST*
   acts as assisting priest simply according to 1098 because even without him a marriage before two witnesses is valid.
   acts as confessor - has jurisdiction from Canon 882. No ordinary jurisdiction here because a confessor does not have an office as such.
   acts as pastor - power given him *a jure* by Canon 1044. Since he does not have an office, does not have ordinary jurisdiction.

5. *CONFESSOR*

has power from diocesan facilities
a jure - Canon 882

The above list includes all the clerics mentioned in Canons
1043-45 and 1098 who are *qualified to act in danger of death.*

ORIENTAL LAW

It is of particular interest to note that in Canon 34 which
is the parallel to our Canon 1044, but differs in substance insofar
as *curates or assistant priests* in a parish are explicitly mentioned
to have the same power as the pastors. "... eadem dispensandi
facultate pollet tum parochus, *tum vicarius cooperator...*" of
whom no mention is made in the Latin Code, Canon 1044. Hence,
it is that many canonists have a good opinion that a curate that
has general delegation to assist at marriages, though not explicitly
mentioned in Canon 1044, would possess the same power as that
given to the pastor and the non-delegated priest of Canon 1098.
To argue otherwise is to create an anomaly in law of a non-
delegated priest who would actually have more power than
a legitimately delegated priest.

Another interesting fact is that the Oriental Code, Canon
34: 2, includes the substance of the response of the Code Commission given in 1922, that it is to be considered impossible to
reach the ordinary in the circumstances of this canon and Canon
35, (Canon 1045) CIC, if the only means of contacting the ordinary is by telephone or telegraph.

Again in Canon 36 (1046) CIC the curate (vicarius cooperator) is explicitly mentioned among those who granting a dispensation in the external forum in virtue of the preceding canons
and are exhorted to inform the ordinary immediately and that
a record be made in the matrimonial register. It is only logical
that he (curate) be explicitly mentioned here.

CASE: SICK CALL

You are an assistant at St. Mary's Church. The telephone
rings at 2:00 a.m. Mrs. White tells you that her husband, Mr.
White, is at the point of death and would like to have a priest

come to him as soon as possible. Mr. White is a Catholic. You hear his confession. Through the confession you learn the following:

1. Mr. and Mrs. White were married in the Baptist Church and the marriage was never validated.

2. There are three children (6 - 8 - 10) and one child on the way. The three children attend the Catholic school.

3. Mrs. White, non-baptized, is Mr. White's second cousin.

4. After this, Mr. White mentions that he was also in the seminary and received the subdeaconate, but due to an argument with his bishop, he left the seminary without getting a dispensation and later entered into this marriage. Mrs. White does not know of this fact; moreover, Mr. White wished to conceal this fact from her.

Now, Mr. White is very sorry for what he did and wishes to die in peace. He begs you to straighten out this marriage, and he also tells you that Mrs. White will cooperate but is ashamed of witnesses being present. How should this case be handled?

MARRIAGES IN URGENT NECESSITY

Canon 1045:   1. Ordinaries of Places can, under the conditions laid down at the end of 1043, grant a dispensation from all the impediments mentioned in the said Canon 1043, whenever an impediment is discovered; *when everything is already prepared for the marriage,* and the marriage cannot, *without probable danger of great harm,* be deferred until a dispensation is obtained from the Holy See.

2. *This faculty* can be used also *for the validation of a marriage* already contracted, if there is the same danger in the delay and there is not sufficient time for recourse to the Holy See.

3. *In the same circumstances* all the persons mentioned in Canon 1044, have the same faculty,

but only for occult cases in which not even the local ordinary can be reached or in which he could not be reached without great danger of violating a secret.

---

1. *The Ordinary:* Whenever all things are prepared for the wedding and one discovers an impediment which is diriment, the ordinary may dispense from all ecclesiastical impediments, except those two mentioned in Canon 1043, whenever there is not enough time to approach the Holy See; scandal must be avoided; and whenever it is a mixed marriage, requiring a dispensation of mixed religion or disparity of cult, the necessary promises must be made. According to the probable opinion, they can dispense from the juridical form of marriage (priest and two witnesses).

2. *The same privilege is given to others besides the Ordinary*: Pastors, the strange priest of Canon 1098, and confessors have the same faculty, in the same circumstances whenever the ordinary cannot be reached, OR, whenever he can be reached but would involve the danger of disclosing the secret.

3. Impediments discovered only before the wedding—*not yet dispensed*: In this case it need not be the day of the wedding when they have already arrived at the church, or a few days before the wedding which would cause grave injury through postponement. If the wedding must be celebrated within a shorter time for some reason, this canon may be used. If the ring is not engraved or the invitations have not been sent out as yet, we can still use the privilege if other preparations are made. Even if the parties withheld the fact of the diriment impediment until the day of the wedding, a dispensation could be given according to Canon 1045.

Lack of Time

If the lack of time to make the recourse is present, then this canon could be used. Of course it must be kept in mind that any extraordinary means, as telephone or telegraph, are not to be used.

Probable Danger of Great Harm

Absolute certainty is not required; the probable danger of great harm is sufficient. The probability depends on a reasonable estimation of the matter which may result in serious consequence, as e.g., scandal, family feuds, loss of finances, danger of breaking the sixth commandment, loss of reputation. If there is a doubt whether the reasons are grave enough, this doubt is sufficient to grant the dispensation. This dispensation is for their own subjects, taking all the precautionary measures that no scandal will result; and the guarantees must be given if the marriage deals with a mixed marriage or disparity of cult. It must be noticed that the pastor's faculties are limited by "occult cases" whenever the ordinary cannot be reached, or if he can be reached it would be violating a secret, e.g., (a) natural secret; (b) professional secret; (c) sacramental secret (Jone, Oesterle).

According to some authors, if the pastor approaches the ordinary for a dispensation and the ordinary failed to respond, the pastor may go ahead according to Canon 1045: 3, whenever a grave and urgent cause is present. In such a case, he should notify the ordinary at once of the dispensation and circumstances of the case. This also includes impediments *public* in nature and *occult* in fact, which we call an *occult case,* as e.g., the pastor forgets to get the dispensation and realizes this only on the day of the wedding, he may go ahead.

JURISDICTION

A *FORUM* is a place for the transaction of official business—
judicial or *administrative*.

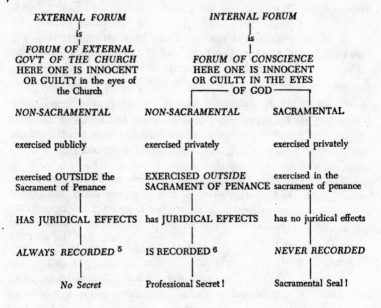

EXTERNAL FORUM	INTERNAL FORUM	
is	is	
FORUM OF EXTERNAL GOV'T OF THE CHURCH HERE ONE IS INNOCENT OR GUILTY in the eyes of the Church	FORUM OF CONSCIENCE HERE ONE IS INNOCENT OR GUILTY IN THE EYES ——— OF GOD ———	
NON-SACRAMENTAL	NON-SACRAMENTAL	SACRAMENTAL
exercised publicly	exercised privately	exercised privately
exercised OUTSIDE the Sacrament of Penance	EXERCISED *OUTSIDE* SACRAMENT OF PENANCE	exercised in the sacrament of penance
HAS JURIDICAL EFFECTS	has JURIDICAL EFFECTS	has no juridical effects
ALWAYS RECORDED [5]	IS RECORDED [6]	NEVER RECORDED
No Secret	Professional Secret !	Sacramental Seal !

5. Always recorded in the Parochial records and the Diocesan Chancery.
6. Recorded in the Secret Archives: Diocesan or Sacred Penitentiary, Rome.

MODE OF RECORDING DISPENSATIONS

Canon 1046:   The pastor or the priest mentioned in Canon 1044, shall notify the ordinary of the place as soon as possible regarding the dispensation granted for the external forum; and the dispensation must be recorded in the marriage register.

Whether it is a new marriage, or a validation, it must be recorded. This marriage must also be recorded in the baptismal book, if the party or parties were baptized in that parish; otherwise it must be recorded in the parish of baptism.

Canon 1047:   Unless the rescript of the Sacred Penitentiary provides otherwise, a dispensation from an occult impediment, granted for the internal non-sacramental forum must be registered in a book to be carefully kept in the Secret Archives of the diocese referred to in Canon 379; nor is any other dispensation necessary for the external forum, even if the occult impediment afterwards becomes public; but one is needed if the dispensation has been granted only in the internal sacramental forum.

This canon is clear when the dispensation from the impediment is given by the Sacred Penitentiary. However, when this dispensation is given in connection with the sacramental forum, another dispensation is needed. This is so, not because the dispensation in the internal forum is invalid but because there is no way in proving this in the external forum. If a dispensation was given outside of confession in the internal non-sacramental forum, a record of this should be made in the secret archives of the chancery, and if this cannot be done for some reason, then it should be sent to the secret archives of the Sacred Penitentiary.

Canon 1048:   If a petition for the dispensation has been sent to the Holy See, ordinaries of places must not use their faculties, if they have any, except as provided in Canon 204: 2.

If the ordinary has power and perhaps through forgetfulness wrote for a dispensation, and later realizes that he has such power, he should wait until he hears from the Holy See. But if an urgent or grave cause arises requiring action, he may go ahead and grant the dispensation. He need not wait. If no grave cause arose and the ordinary did grant the dispensation, it would be valid, but *illicit*. In this case he should notify the Holy See afterwards that he dispensed according to Canon 204: 2.

Canon 1049: 1. When there is a question of marriages already contracted or *to be contracted*, one who has a general indult to dispense from some particular impediment, unless the indult itself expressly provides otherwise, can dispense from it even if the same impediment is multiple.

2. One who has a general indult to dispense from several impediments of different kinds, diriment or impeding, can dispense from the same even though they are public, when they occur in one and the same case.

This may arise when a dispensation is needed for the impediment of consanguinity which is multiplied, or the impediment of affinity and one of mixed religion. This would not be so if the faculties were given for a particular case.

Canon 1050: If it happens that together with a public impediment or public impediments from which a person can dispense in virtue of an indult there concurs another impediment from which he cannot dispense, he must apply to the Holy See for all of them; if, however, the impediment or impediments from which he can dispense are discovered after the Holy See has granted the dispensation, he may use his faculties.

Canon 1051: By a dispensation from a diriment impediment granted either in virtue of ordinary power in virtue of Canon 1043-44, or power delegated through a general indult, not however by a rescript in particular cases, legitimation of children also is granted in case any have been already born or conceived by the parties who are being dispensed, with the exception of adulterine and sacrilegious offspring.

Legitimation takes place automatically regarding children already conceived or born when a dispensation is given from a diriment impediment by ordinary power or in virtue of a general indult, but not by rescript in a particular case. In other words, by the act of dispensing a diriment impediment, legitimation takes place ipso facto which is implicitly contained in the dispensation. Before the Code (1918) a declaration had to be explicit regarding legitimation. This is not necessary now. Whenever a dispensation is given in view of marriage, if the marriage does not take place, and it is not the fault of the parties, (e.g., one of the parties dies suddenly) legitimation takes place. Some authors claim that if the marriage does not take place because of the *fault of the parties* legitimation takes place just the same. (Payen, 291; Cappello, 358, Bous, 496). It must be noted here that children born at the time parents are incapable of marrying, e.g., prior marriage, solemn vows, sacred orders, these children are not legitimized. One must write to the Holy See for such legitimization.

IMPLICIT DISPENSATIONS

Canon 1052: A dispensation from an impediment of consanguinity or affinity, granted for a certain degree of the impediment, is valid, even though in the petition or grant there be an error about the degree, provided the degree really existing is inferior, or even though another impediment of the same kind, in an equal or inferior degree, has been concealed in the petition.

If, for example, the petitioner asked for a dispensation of consanguinity in the third degree (second cousins) and mentioned that they were first cousins (second degree in the collateral line) it is considered as valid because the greater includes the lesser; but if the dispensation was asked in the reverse order, it would not be valid. Sometimes we have a case of double consanguinity or affinity, in the same degree or in an inferior degree, if this is not mentioned the dispensation will be valid. Jack and Jill may be second cousins in two ways, when they have two common ancestors, first cousins in one way and second cousins in another. The dispensation would be valid in this case even though they did not mention it in the petition. It is good to remember that when the relationship is mixed in some way as third degree touching the second, the *longer line determines the degree* (Canon 96: 3), in this case it is satisfactory to say that they are related in the third degree. It is another question when we deal with relationship of second degree touching the first (uncle and niece); it would not be satisfactory to say that it is second degree of consanguinity alone according to the interpretation of the Sacred Congregation; the ordinary himself must apply for such a dispensation and say that they are related 2° touching the 1° and indicate that it is an *uncle - niece case,* in order to be sure of the validity of the dispensation.

Canon 1053:   A dispensation granted by the Holy See from a marriage RATUM NON - CONSUMMATUM, or PERMISSION GRANTED TO CONTRACT ANOTHER MARRIAGE ON ACCOUNT OF THE PRESUMED DEATH OF THE OTHER PARTY, ALWAYS IMPLIES a dispensation from the impediment arising from *adultery with the promise,* or *attempt at marriage,* if the case warrants it, but by no means from the impediments mentioned in Canon 1075; 2 and 3.

Just in case this particular impediment existed in any of these two cases, which is common to these cases, this canon implicitly grants the dispensation.

ORIENTAL LAW

Canon 1053   (43)

It is interesting to note that both disciplines grant the implicit dispensation from the *impediment of crime which arises from adultery with a promise, or attempt of marriage in* two cases, namely, (1) when the Holy See grants a dispensation from a non-consummated marriage, and (2) whenever permission to remarry has been granted on the presumed death of a spouse. However, the Oriental case contains the words: "... etiam ab iis qui potestatem habent infra Sedem Apostolicam, licentia ..." which are not found in Canon 1053 (CIC). However, after the promulgation of the Oriental Code in 1949, the Code Commission explained that the implicit dispensation of Canon 1053 is valid and effective also when the permission to remarry on the presumed death of a spouse is given by the ordinary of the place. *In other words, the implicit dispensation, from the impediment of crime in the presumption of death case handled by the ordinary of the place, was not included in the permission to remarry until this was included in the Oriental Code in 1949 and later for the Latin ordinaries when the Code Commission gave this interpretation.*

OBREPTIO ET SUBREPTIO

Canon 1054:   A dispensation granted from a minor impediment is not invalidated by any defect, whether of misstatement (obreptio) or omission (subreptio) even though the only final cause stated the petition is false.

---

1. This canon deals with Minor Impediments exclusively (cf. C. 1042: 2).

2. *Obreptio* is a misstatement, or statement of a falsehood; while *subreptio* is an omission or concealing a fact in the petition.

3. According to Canon 40, truth is an essential condition for the validity of every rescript; however, this canon makes an ex-

ception for the minor impediments, which is an extraordinary concession.

4. The dispensation must be asked for a specific impediment, otherwise the dispensation is not granted and would be invalid, e.g., if one asks for a dispensation of public propriety and it was actually one of affinity, the impediment would still remain undispensed, and sometimes when a dispensation is valid, when they conceal a truth or state a falsehood, but the petitioner may be punished for so doing.

Canon 1055: Dispensations from public impediments committed to the ordinary of the petitioners are to be executed by the ordinary who gave the testimonial letter or who forwarded the petition to the Holy See, even though the parties, at the time when the dispensation is to be executed, have left their domicile or quasi-domicile in his diocese and have departed to another diocese, never to return, notification should be sent to the ordinary of the place in which the parties intend to contract marriage.

Today when people move around frequently, it is possible that a rescript may come to the ordinary of the petitioners. Since these dispensations are granted usually for the external forum *in forma commissoria* it is to be executed by the same ordinary who asked for it. This same ordinary may, even though the parties moved to another diocese, execute this rescript and send notification of it to the ordinary where the marriage is to take place. There are no restrictions on the rescript (Bouscaren, 499). For a dispensation in the internal forum, an approved confessor would handle this.

Canon 1056: With the exception of some small offering to defray the expenses of the chancery in dispensations for persons who are not poor, ordinaries of places and their officials are forbidden, and any contrary custom is reprobated, to demand any payment on the occasion of granting a dispensation, unless the faculty to do so has been expressly given them by the Holy See; and if they do exact anything, they are bound to restitution.

Canon 1057: Those who grant a dispensation in virtue of the power delegated to them by the Apostolic See must expressly mention the pontifical indult in the dispensation.

This is also done when a dispensation is granted in virtue of the quinquennial faculties.

CHAPTER IV

PROHIBITIVE IMPEDIMENTS

IMPEDIENT IMPEDIMENTS

Canon 1058: 1. A marriage is rendered illicit by the following simple vows:
    (1) of Virginity;
    (2) of Perfect Chastity;
    (3) not to marry;
    (4) to receive Sacred Orders;
    (5) to embrace the religious state.

2. No simple vow renders a marriage invalid unless this has been decreed for certain persons by special provision of the Holy See.

Vows: Impediment to Marriage

I. Definition: A vow is a free deliberate promise made to God to do something which is possible. It is an act of religion, differing from a simple resolution insofar as it binds under pain of sin (Lev 27; Eccles 5:3). A vow is *public* when it is accepted by a competent ecclesiastical authority, otherwise it is private. Vows are either simple or solemn. A vow is solemn when it is recognized by the Church as such and when taken in a religious order approved by the Holy See. As to their effects, solemn vows render certain acts invalid, e.g., one in solemn vows who marries contracts marriage invalidly, whereas one in simple vows marries illicitly.

II. Simple Vows: *Prohibitive Impediments to Marriage:*

(1) *Vow of Virginity:* The object of this vow is to keep one's virginity intact; the state of virginity is lost irrevocably by a consummated solitary sin or by the first deliberate act of sexual intercourse. This vow is usually taken along with the vow of chastity and the vow not to marry.

(2) *Vow of Perfect Chastity:* is one whereby a promise is made to refrain either perpetually or temporarily from every sexual pleasure, complete or incomplete, of mind and body. If one should contract marriage while he is bound by this vow, such marriage is illicit until dispensed; moreover the right to the conjugal act is forfeited unless the other party demands his debt in which case the one in vows must render it.

(3) *Vow not to Marry:* This vow has celibacy for its object. If one contracts marriage, he sins against this vow, but not in exercising his marital rights. If the marriage bond is dissolved, the vow still remains.

(4) *Vow to receive Sacred Orders:* This vow has for its object the reception of Sacred Orders which are the subdiaconate, diaconate, and priesthood. If one with such vows marries, he indirectly violates the vow because it would make the fulfillment of the vow impossible.

(5) *Vow to enter Religious Life:* This impediment arises when one makes a vow to enter a religious order or congregation of solemn vows. However, if one did all in his power to become a religious, but failed to meet with the requirements necessary for the religious life or for some other reason after making an honest effort, the vow would not be binding.

No simple vow invalidates marriage unless it has been declared as such by special precept of the Holy See, (CIC C. 1058: 2). The Society of Jesus has such a precept and thereby becomes a diriment impediment.[1]

III. Oriental Law: The legislation is similar to the Latin Code; however, the vow of receiving the subdiaconate (which is a minor order) or major orders is an impediment only when a particular rite demands the observance of celibacy for these orders. This is the case for the reception of the subdiaconate among the Armenians, Italo-Albanians and Malabar rites; for

1. Gasparri-Seredi, *Fontes*, N. 153, Vol. 1, p. 269.

the reception of orders (Major) among the Syrian and Coptic rites.

IV. Dispensation: Vows can be dispensed by the Church. Due to their character, vows are established by the Church as impediments and as such only the Church can dispense from these vows (CIC C. 1307-15). Among the private vows, *only two* are reserved to the Holy See: (a) Vow of perfect chastity and (b) vow to enter a religious order. Vows taken in a religious order of Solemn Vows cannot be dispensed except by the Holy See. Vows (simple) taken in a diocesan congregation must be dispensed by the local ordinary. Although, when the congregation is of Pontifical right, not the ordinary but the Holy See dispenses. IN DANGER OF DEATH, the ordinary, pastor and others may dispense. Cardinal Spellman of New York announced at the National Convention of the Canon Law Society of America in September, 1963, that the bishops of USA are proposing to abolish the impeding impediments, except in mixed religion, when the Code is revised.

LEGAL ADOPTION

Canon 1059:   In those regions where a legal relationship arising from adoption renders marriage illicit according to civil law, the marriage is also illicit by canon law.
(Cf. 1080)

For Christian marriage, the Code gives canonical force to the civil law in each state or country. Whatever the law of the state determines regarding this impediment is usually accepted by the Church. If the state or country enacts a law making legal adoption a diriment impediment, the Church recognizes it also as a diriment impediment. Some countries as Italy, Spain, Poland consider it as a diriment impediment. France, Germany, Hungary, Switzerland and Belgium consider it a prohibitive impediment. Puerto Rico retains it as a diriment impediment.[2]

2. Ayrinhac-Lydon, SS., *Marriage Legislation,* 2nd ed., Benziger Brothers, N.Y., 1952, p. 98.

Oriental Law

This law includes legal guardianship (which the Latin Code omits) if this is an impediment in civil law.

Mixed Religion — Law of 1918 to March 31, 1970

Canon 1060: The Church everywhere most strictly forbids the contracting of marriage between two baptized persons of whom one is a Catholic and the other is a member of a heretical or schismatic sect; and if there is danger of perversion for the Catholic party and the children, the marriage is forbidden also by Divine Law.

COMMENT: Although the principles of mixed marriage remain the same, nevertheless some elements of this canon have been mitigated; for example, we could say: "The Church everywhere permits the contracting of marriage between two baptized persons—one Catholic and the other Protestant."

1. Mixed religion in general could mean (a) a marriage between a Catholic and a baptized non-Catholic person, or (b) a marriage between a Catholic and a non-baptized person. However, canonically speaking, *mixed religion* is restricted to a marriage between a *Catholic and a baptized non-Catholic*.

2. Whenever the baptism of the non-Catholic is doubtful, we have here an impediment either of mixed religion or disparity of cult. What it actually is we do not know. *After* a marriage, the burden of proof rests upon the presumption in favor of the validity of the baptism and of the marriage until it is proven otherwise. *Before* marriage, when applying for a dispensation it is granted for *mixed religion and disparity of cult ad cautelam.*

3. In this precautionary method, all the possibilities are covered in such a doubtful case. If in the eyes of God the person is baptized validly in the Protestant sect, the *mixed religion* dispensation would apply and takes effect, the other would not.

And if in the eyes of God, the person is not actually baptized, the *disparity of cult* dispensation would take effect, the former would not. The precautionary phrase *ad cautelam* then prevents any further difficulties.

4. Communism or Atheism: If any person belongs to any atheistic sect, (Communism is in this category), those persons are considered as belonging to an atheistic sect. The dispensation of *mixed religion* or *disparity of cult* is needed according to whether the person is baptized or not.

5. Danger of Perversion: Whenever there is danger of perversion of the Catholic party or the children of a mixed marriage, the divine law gravely prohibits such a marriage. As long as such danger exists, the Church cannot grant a dispensation. The necessary conditions must be fulfilled before a dispensation is granted.

CONDITIONS FOR DISPENSATIONS

Canon 1061: This canon listed the necessary conditions for obtaining a dispensation for mixed religion. (No longer applicable)

Canon 1062: This canon advised the Catholic party of the obligation of converting the non-Catholic party. (No longer applicable)

Canon 1063: This canon was a prohibition forbidding the Catholic party from going to a non-Catholic minister. (No longer applicable)

The Motu Proprio, *Matrimonia Mixta* of Pope Paul VI, promulgated March 31, 1970, which went into effect Oct. 1, 1970, is the new mandate governing mixed marriages. The Episcopal Conferences of each country proposed guidelines suitable to their territories.

The Former Law

A person is excommunicated who contracts marriage before a non-Catholic minister with the religious rites (*communicatio in sacris*) [3] with heretics, which implies approval of heresy (C. 2319). Regarding the doubt of two Catholics who would go through such a ceremony (the Code was silent about this), Pope Pius XII in his Motu Proprio, Dec. 25, 1953 (AAS, 46-88; Digest, Vol. IV, C. 2319) expunged from Canon 2319: 1, #1, the qualifying clause, *contra praescriptum canonis 1063*: #1. As a result, this penalty is now incurred *by any marriage contracted or attempted by Catholics* before a non-Catholic minister as such, e.g., if both parties were Catholics, OR if one was unbaptized, OR if no Catholic marriage took place beforehand. (The excommunication of the Third Council of Baltimore, n. 127, is no longer in effect.)

DECREE ON MIXED MARRIAGE — March 18, 1966

Due to the fact that this decree has been abrogated in part, since the promulgation of *Matrimonia Mixta*, of March 31, 1970, we find it worthwhile to reiterate number seven of this decree.

"The excommunication provided for by Canon 2319, 1, 1, for those who celebrate a marriage before a non-Catholic minister is abrogated. The effects of this abrogation are retroactive."

The Code has no penal law for those marrying before a civil officer, judge, magistrate or Justice of the Peace. However, we must check the synodal law of each diocese. Some have enacted a penal law for excommunication of those who attempt marriage before a civil magistrate; these laws are enacted because of the frequent abuse in particular territories.

---

3. Orientals, Cf. New Legislation under C. 1094.

NORMS FOR MIXED MARRIAGES (March 31, 1970)

The history of mixed marriages is rather peculiar because many different policies have developed on this type of marriage over the years. In some instances, certain bishops were wont to grant a limited number of dispensations over a certain period of time; norms were given for the performance of such marriages in the rectory or sacristy of the church; later developments found such marriages performed in the church but outside the altar rail, and in some dioceses without flowers on the altar, without music, without lighted candles; as time went on permissions were granted for the wedding to take place inside the altar rail, with music but no singing and with flowers on the altar; finally we have new norms which permitted the Mass in which the Catholic party alone received Communion during the service.

Today, with the Norms of March 18, 1966 abrogated or, rather supplanted by the Motu Proprio, *Matrimonia Mixta*, the Apostolic Letter of Pope Paul VI, March 31, 1970, we find very broad privileges regarding mixed marriages. Due to the changing times and conditions in our modern pluralistic society, the results of Vatican II and the rise in mixed marriages in general, Pope Paul deemed it necessary to promulgate these norms March 31, 1970, which became effective August 1, 1970 in Canada and became effective on October 1, 1970 in the United States. These changes came about because the former legislation on this matter did not lead to Christian unity. Although the Pope continues to discourage mixed marriages, he felt that these norms were necessary to promote Christian unity.

Laws should be clearly known and understood by all concerned. In this case not only the Catholic priest and Catholics in general, but also the non-Catholic minister as well as the non-Catholic layman and civil officials should be acquainted with these new norms. It is essential then to know what these norms are: the changes in the law, how they are applied to each individual, and all the circumstances surrounding each case.

Since mixed marriages are increasing, Pope Paul VI has

shown his pastoral concern for them by issuing these norms, trying to safeguard, however, the existing principles of divine law, and the inherent natural right of men and women to contract marriage and beget children.

These norms do prescribe a twofold obligation upon the Catholic party to a mixed marriage according to the circumstances instituted by divine law for the salvation of souls. The Catholic has the duty "of preserving his or her own faith; nor is it ever permitted to expose oneself to a proximate danger of losing it." "Furthermore, the Catholic partner in a mixed marriage is obliged . . . as far as possible, to see to it that the children be baptized and brought up in that same faith and receive all these aids to eternal salvation which the Catholic Church provides for her sons and daughters." These are not merely ecclesiastical mandates but divine commands.

The only dilemma in such a mixed marriage is that of the children's upbringing and education. Both parties have equal responsibility in this matter, and, as such, could lead into difficulty between two believing Christians, namely, the one Catholic, the other non-Catholic. Because of this, Pope Paul VI points out that there cannot be a uniform canonical discipline on mixed marriages as in the past. By issuing this Apostolic Letter on mixed marriages, Pope Paul VI wished to bring this new legislation up to the proper perspective with the teaching of Vatican II as expressed especially in the *Decree on Ecumenism* and the *Declaration on Religious Freedom.*

The Norms on Mixed Marriages
(Motu Proprio — March 31, 1970)

1. A marriage between a Catholic and a baptized non-Catholic (Protestant or Orthodox) requires a dispensation for lawfulness. This norm is the same as it has always been. Without this dispensation a Catholic may not marry *lawfully* with a non-Catholic Christian. If a Catholic does marry before a

priest, without this dispensation, the marriage would be valid but illicit or unlawful. To rectify this situation, the marriage must be convalidated in the Church; the parties then would be considered in good standing in the Church.

2. A marriage between a *Catholic* and a *non-baptized non-Catholic* (for example, a Moslem, Jew, Hindu or any non-Christian) requires a dispensation for the *validity* of the marriage. Without this dispensation the marriage is invalid.

3. A *just cause* based on "the nature and circumstances of times, places, and persons" is needed for the dispensations mentioned in norms 1 and 2. The canonical reasons listed in canon 1061, 1, 1, are no longer required . . . such as advanced age, pregnancy, etc.; a *just cause* would be the spiritual well-being, or peace of their personal and family relationships. Pastoral rather than canonical reasons would suffice.

4. To obtain the dispensations mentioned in norms 1 and 2, the Catholic party:
   1) "shall *declare* that he is ready to remove dangers of falling away from the faith."
   2) must "make a sincere *promise* to do all in his power to have all the children baptized and brought up in the Catholic Church."

COMMENTARY: The impediment of mixed religion or disparity of cult comes from the divine law to safeguard the danger of perversion of the Catholic party or their offspring. Both of these impediments are prohibitive by the divine law; but in view of ecclesiastical law, mixed religion is merely a prohibitive impediment, while disparity of cult is a diriment impediment, and as such, would render a marriage invalid if this dispensation would be lacking.

In issuing this norm 4, Pope Paul is attempting to preserve the divine law obligation of Catholics while at the same time he is keeping in mind the principles of ecumenism and of religious freedom. Hence, for every Catholic this is a grave obligation: to live his faith and to pass it on to his offspring.

It must be remembered that this obligation is imposed upon the Catholic only in the degree to which this is concretely possible. This obligation is qualified according to the norm; it (the obligation) "is imposed according to the various situations." The Catholic baptism and the education of the children is to be undertaken "as far as possible." In other words, the Catholic promises "to do all in his power" because no one is bound to do the impossible. This is a departure from the law of 1918 which stated that no dispensation could be given unless a *guarantee* was given. These norms do not require a guarantee.

A Catholic is asked to respect the sincere conscience of his non-Catholic partner, just as he wants his own conscience to be respected. Harmony must be sought in the family, especially when it comes to the education of the children. Here there must be the *give* and *take* idea. A Catholic is asked only to do *what is possible,* and no more in a given situation.

Therefore, dispensations may be granted even when it is uncertain that the children will actually be raised as Catholics. The norm seems to imply more the sincerity, the attitude and intention of the Catholic rather than the actual raising of children. The success in raising the children as Catholics may vary according to the attitude of the non-Catholic party. Sometimes it will be possible and in other situations it might be impossible, in which case the Catholic is not obliged to do the impossible.

The norm "to do all in his power" does not mean that the Catholic must exert pressure or undue strain on the non-Catholic party which would destroy the harmony of the marriage, or contribute to the breaking up of the marriage. Is the promise also a guarantee? These norms do not insist on a guarantee that children will be *baptized and brought up Catholics.* It is merely a promise. It merely indicates that the Catholic should be aware of his obligation and be ready to fulfill his duty to the best of his ability in the situation. More than this is not demanded. Not even moral certitude is needed that the children will be brought up in the Catholic faith. This drastic change has taken place in respect to the sincere conscience of the non-Catholic party.

Vatican II declared: "All men are to be immune from coercion on the part of individuals or of social groups and of any human power, in such wise that no one is to be forced to act in a manner contrary to his own beliefs, whether privately or publicly, whether alone or in association with others, within due limits ... parents, moreover, have the right to determine, in accordance with their own religious beliefs, the kind of religious education that their children are to receive" (Declarations on Religious Freedom, 2-5), and, insofar as other Christians are concerned the Second Vatican Council decreed that "Catholics must gladly acknowledge and esteem the truly Christian endowments from our common heritage which are to be found among our separated brethren . . . nor should we forget that anything wrought by the Holy Spirit in the hearts of our separated brethren can be a help to our own edification. Whatever is truly Christian is never contrary to what genuinely belongs to the faith; indeed it can always bring a deeper realization of the mystery of Christ and the Church" (Decree on Ecumenism, n. 4).

5. "The non-Catholic party must be clearly informed of these promises which the Catholic party has to make." This is a major change in the law. No promises in writing or declarations of any kind are required by the non-Catholic party. Everyone has the right to live according to his convictions and to use legitimate means to share them with others. This right is a sacred duty which must be carried out with prudence, tact, and the respect for the conscience of others. In short, all that is required of the non-Catholic party is that he be aware of the promise and obligation made in conscience by the Catholic party.

6. "Both parties are to be clearly instructed on the end and essential properties of marriage, (which) are not to be excluded by either party." In other words, marriage instructions must be given. This is an essential pastoral obligation. Both parties must be informed of the essential ends of marriage: (1) unity, that is, marriage between one man and one woman and (2) permanence, that is, with no divorce in mind for the future.

7. Within its own territorial competence, it is for the Bishops' Conference to determine the way in which these declarations and promises, which are always required, shall be made: whether by word of mouth alone, in writing, or before witnesses; and also to determine what proof of them there should be in the external forum, and how they are to be brought to the knowledge of the non-Catholic party, as well as to

lay down whatever other requirements may be opportune.

8. The canonical form is to be used for contracting mixed mar-

riages, and is required for validity, without prejudice, however, to the provisions of the Decree *Crescens Matrimoniorum* published by the Sacred Congregation for the Eastern Churches on 22nd February, 1967.[4]

9. If serious difficulties stand in the way of observing the canonical form, local Ordinaries have the right to dispense from the canonical form in any mixed marriage; but the Bishops' Conference is to determine norms according to which the said dispensation may be granted licitly and uniformly within the region or territory of the Conference, with the provision that there should always be some public form of ceremony.

10. Arrangements must be made that all validly contracted marriages be diligently entered in the books prescribed by canon law. Priests responsible should make sure that non-Catholic ministers also assist in recording in their own books the fact of a marriage with a Catholic.

     Episcopal Conferences are to issue regulations determining, for their region or territory, a uniform method by which a marriage that has been publicly contracted after a dispensation from the canonical form was obtained, is registered in the books prescribed by canon law.

11. With regard to the liturgical form of the celebration of a mixed marriage, if it is to be taken from the Roman Ritual, use must be made of the ceremonies in the *Rite of Celebration of Marriage* promulgated by our authority, whether it is a question of a marriage between a Catholic and a baptized non-Catholic (39-54) or of a marriage between a Catholic and an unbaptized person (55-66). If, however, the

4. Cf. AAS 59, 1967, p. 166.

circumstances justify it, a marriage between a Catholic and a baptized non-Catholic can be celebrated, subject to the local Ordinary's consent, according to the rites for the celebration of marriage within Mass (19-38), while respecting the prescription of general law with regard to Eucharistic Communion.

12. The Episcopal Conferences shall inform the Apostolic See of all decisions which, within their competence, they make concerning mixed marriages.

13. The celebration of marriage before a Catholic priest or deacon and a non-Catholic minister, performing their respective rites together, is forbidden; nor is it permitted to have another religious marriage ceremony before or after the Catholic ceremony, for the purpose of giving or renewing matrimonial consent.

14. Local Ordinaries and parish priests shall see to it that the Catholic husband or wife and the children born of a mixed marriage do not lack spiritual assistance in fulfilling their duties of conscience. They shall encourage the Catholic husband or wife to keep ever in mind the divine gift of the Catholic faith and to bear witness to it with gentleness and reverence, and with a clear conscience. They are to aid the married couple to foster the unity of their conjugal and family life, a unity which, in the case of Christians, is based on their baptism too. To these ends it is to be desired that those pastors should establish relationships of sincere openness and enlightened confidence with ministers of other religious communities.

15. The penalties decreed by canon 2319 of the Code of Canon Law are all abrogated. For those who have already incurred them the effects of those penalties cease, without prejudice to the obligations mentioned in number 4 of these norms.

16. The local Ordinary is able to give a *sanatio in radice* of a mixed marriage, when the conditions spoken of in numbers 4 and 5 of these norms have been fulfilled, and provided that the conditions of law are observed.

17. In the case of a particular difficulty or doubt with regard to the application of these norms, recourse is to be made to the Holy See.

DUTIES OF THE ORDINARY AND PASTORS

Canon 1064: Ordinaries and other pastors of souls:

1. must deter the faithful from mixed marriages in so far as it is possible;

2. if they cannot impede them, they shall strive by all means lest they contract in violation to the laws of God and the Church;

3. after mixed marriages have been celebrated either in their own territory or outside of it, they shall carefully see to it that the parties faithfully discharge the promises they have made;

4. in assisting at such marriages, they must observe the prescriptions of Canon 1102.

Canon 1065: 1. The faithful must also be deterred from contracting marriage with those who have either notoriously abandoned the Catholic faith even without joining a non-Catholic sect, or with those who have become members of societies condemned by the Church.

2. The pastor must not assist at above-mentioned marriages unless he consulted the ordinary, who after considering all the factors, may permit him to assist at the marriage, provided there be a grave reason and the ordinary in his prudent discretion judges that adequate measures have been taken to insure the Catholic education of all the children and the removal of danger of perversion from the other party.

An unworthy party to marriage does not necessarily mean that this is an impediment. Whenever a non-Catholic becomes a convert and is a member of the Masons, permission can be obtained from the Apostolic Delegate for him to retain *passive membership*.

PUBLIC SIN AND CENSURE

Canon 1066: If a public sinner or one who is notoriously under censure refuses to go to sacramental confession, or to be reconciled with the Church beforehand; the pastor must not assist at his marriage, unless there be a grave reason, concerning which, if it is possible, he should consult the ordinary.

All these precautionary measures are taken to prevent the individual from committing a sacrilege. If the matter is known only through the confessional, and he will not become reconciled, nothing can be done because of the seal of confession.

BURIAL FOR CATHOLICS INVALIDLY MARRIED

The common problem of burial in a mixed marriage case is the request to have permission to bury the non-Catholic party in a Catholic cemetery in order that both parties and their offspring could share a common plot. According to a survey made in the United States, it was discovered that some dioceses permit the non-Catholic to be buried in consecrated ground.

Catholics, invalidly married, who died without the sacraments or without any sign of repentance, but who brought up their children in the faith, and who themselves attended Mass regularly, cannot be buried with a Christian burial ceremony according to Canon 1240: 1. These are usually ligamen cases that could not be validated. The survey found that some dioceses permit prayers at the funeral parlor or at the grave, with burial in consecrated ground. Others were more strict, by permitting non-liturgical prayers at the funeral parlor, or at the grave, but denying burial in consecrated ground. Since Vatican II, each diocese has a different policy. Some are more lenient than others. One would have to consult the guidelines of his own diocese.

CHAPTER V

DIRIMENT IMPEDIMENTS

INTRODUCTION

1. A diriment impediment is some definite fact of circumstance which renders a person incapable of making a valid marriage contract.

2. There are 13 diriment impediments:
   1 Want of Age - Canon 1067
   2 Impotence - Canon 1068
   3 Previous and Existing Marriage - Canon 1069
   4 Disparity of Cult - Canon 1069
   5 Sacred Orders - Canon 1072
   6 Solemn Vows - Canon 1073
   7 Abduction - Canon 1074
   8 Crime - Canon 1075
   9 Consanguinity - Canon 1076
   10 Affinity - Canon 1077
   11 Public Propriety - Canon 1078
   12 Spiritual Relationship - Canon 1079
   13 Legal Relationship - Canon 1080

3. The impediments that chanceries meet most often are in this order: (1) disparity of cult; (2) consanguinity; (3) affinity; (4) crime arising from adultery.

DIRIMENT IMPEDIMENTS

Want of Age - Canon 1067

1. A man before completing his sixteenth year, and a woman before completing her fourteenth year cannot contract a valid marriage.

2. Although a marriage contracted after the aforesaid age is valid, yet pastors of souls should try to deter young people from marrying before the age at which, according to the received customs of the country, marriage is usually contracted.

A man before the completion of his sixteenth year and a woman before the completion of her fourteenth year cannot contract a valid marriage. Although the marriage is a valid contract after the aforesaid age, nevertheless, pastors of souls should deter young people from making such a contract before an earlier age than is commonly the custom in their respective country.

(1) The impediment of age arises from physical capacity. The restriction is one of ecclesiastical law because by the natural law children who have sufficient discretion and have a general knowledge of what marriage means and are willing to enter the contract may marry validly. The natural law has no direct age requirement. The theory is that actual power to generate is not necessary since it is consent of the parties, not carnal relation, that makes the marriage contract. Mental capacity is required for making a valid matrimonial contract.

(2) The canonical impediment of age binds only the baptized, whereby, it recognizes a marriage valid only when the parties have completed the canonical age - 16 for a male, 14 for females. The age must be determined by Canon 34, Section 3, whereby a boy who was born on September 1, 1940, has canonically completed his sixteenth year only after midnight of the sixteenth birthday, namely, September 2, 1956. He could not get married on the day itself of the sixteenth birthday. It would be invalid. It must be after his sixteenth birthday. What could be

said of the girl? She cannot contract a valid marriage, only the day after her fourteenth birthday.

(3) Dispensation. If parties marry under the established age, the impediment ceases with the lapse of time; however, the marriage remains invalid; a validation is necessary according to the form of marriage.

The fact that the law permits parties to marry at 16 and 14, it is of utmost importance that parents discourage these early teen-age marriages, as mentioned in Canon 1034.

Impotency

Canon 1068:   1. Impotence, antecedent and perpetual, whether on the part of the man or the woman, whether known to the other party or not, whether absolute or relative, invalidates marriage by the law of nature itself.

2. If the impediment of impotence is doubtful either in law or in fact, the marriage is not to be hindered.

3. Sterility neither invalidates marriage nor renders it illicit.

---

(1) What is impotency? The codifiers did not define it. Canonists do not agree as to its real definition. All agree, however, that when there is an incapacity or inability to have natural sexual intercourse, this case would constitute impotency and would invalidate marriage. The inability to perform a natural sexual act (Human Act - copula) namely, penetration of the vagina by the male organ and the emission of true semen in it, is called impotency. For example, on the part of the man: When the man is deprived of both testicles; when he cannot have an erection; or if the sex organs are out of proportion. On the part of the woman: the absence of a vagina, the vagina is out of proportion or prevents penetration.

(2) *Sterility*. All agree that sterility is the case when natural sexual intercourse can take place, while at the same time both

parties possess all the organs necessary for generation, but are not capable of generating offspring. For example, the parties are too old; women who have reached the age when ovulation ceases; women who have no ovaries; no uterus.

Generation is a twofold process: First, the *human act* called *copula;* and second, the *physiological process,* that is, the natural process of generation which takes place in a man or woman for the generation of children. The *physiological* includes the development of the ova in the ovaries of the female and the sperm in the testicles of the male. When copula takes place, during a fertile period, the sperm goes from the vagina to the uterus and on to the fallopian tubes of the female. At the same time the ovum or female germ cell released from ovary of the female meets the sperm somewhere enroute. When the sperm penetrates it, they are united. *This union we call fecundation.* Here we have a human being in its embryonic stages. This embryo descends from the tube and enters the uterus. Here it attaches itself to the wall of the uterus, develops to maturity, after approximately nine months, a child is born.

(4) From what has been said, we have first, the human act of generation, controlled by the will, that is copula; the penetration of the vagina by the male organ and the emission of true semen into the vagina; the natural process of generation, which cannot be controlled directly by the will. *Whatever hinders the human act of generation,* that is, *normal copula, is considered* impotency. Whatever hinders the *physiological process is considered sterility.* (In the medical profession, this distinction is not accepted. At times our definition of sterility is considered impotency by the medical profession.)

(5) Impotence is commonly defined as the incapacity to perform the marital act, that is, when the parties are incapable of "having copula which is in itself suitable for generation."

How do we determine *when* copula is in itself suitable for generation? This is not clear. If a woman lacks ovaries or has a hysterectomy, her acts are not suitable for generation. In other words, the controversy concerns the case when intercourse is possible, but the organs are lacking which are essential to beget offspring. The decisions of the Holy See must be our guide. As long as a married couple are capable of having normal conjugal relations, they are not impotent. What is considered here is that the conjugal act depends on the human will, not on the physiological process which follows the act. If the parties are able to have the conjugal act, that is sufficient; the fact that they are incapable of having children is a defect of nature.

TYPES OF IMPOTENCY:

(1) *Antecedent* is that which existed before the marriage.

(2) *Subsequent* if it arose after the marriage.

(3) *Perpetual* if it cannot be cured by licit means and is not dangerous to life through an operation.

(4) *Temporary* if it disappears naturally or can be cured by licit means and not dangerous to life through an operation.

(5) *Absolute* whereby the marital act cannot be had with any person whomsoever, for example: sexual organs are too large.

(6) *Relative* is an impediment only in regard to certain persons.

(6) *Doubtful Impotency:* a.) If the impotency is doubtful by either doubt of law or doubt of fact, marriage can take place even though this impediment is of natural law. The reason for this is because it is difficult to solve such doubts, the Church maintains that it is a probable and prudent doubt; the Natural Law to marry prevails.

b.) If there is a doubt regarding the impediment of impotency *before the marriage,* an investigation must take place. After the investigation, if the doubt persists, marriage could take place.

c.) If *after the marriage,* a doubt of the impediment of impotency arises, after the parties have tried marital relations, an investigation as to whether the impotency was antecedent and perpetual must be made. If it is certain that antecedent and perpetual impotency is present, action should be taken to begin process for declaration of nullity.[1]

1. Bouscaren, I. Lincoln, S.J., *Canon Law Digest,* Vols. II, III, IV.

VENEREAL DISEASE AND MARRIAGE

Nothing is mentioned in Canon Law on venereal disease as an impediment to marriage since this is primarily a moral problem. However, if this disease is the cause of impotence, it could render the marriage invalid since impotence is a diriment impediment. According to the natural law a person who has such a disease (e.g., syphilis, this is a contagious disease) is forbidden to marry unless he or she informs the other party of this condition because of the grave danger to the other spouse in the use of marriage. (*The diseased party is prohibited to marry by virtue of the natural law and by the law of charity.*) These people should be exhorted not to marry because of the possibility of giving birth to defective children. The state may enact reasonable health laws regulating or forbidding marriage to such people, but this regulation should be limited insofar as the prohibition should be temporary and only as long as the individual is not restricted by his natural right to marry.

Although the Encyclical, *Casti Connubii,* condemns the various means the state might use upon people who are naturally fit for the married state, and upon the suspicion that they would bring forth defective offspring; nevertheless, it also conveys the teaching that even these people are to be instructed on the harm they can inflict upon society and should be dissuaded from entering marriage for their own good as well.

Each year syphilis kills over 5000 Americans. A survey conducted by the American Social Health Association in cooperation with the American Medical Association revealed that almost 90% of syphilis cases go unreported. Expert opinion suggests that possibly one and a half million people are now afflicted with untreated syphilis. Because of the danger and threat to society, further details are given here for pastoral counseling.

What is VD? The two most common venereal diseases are syphilis and gonorrhea. They are infections caused by different germs. Syphilis is caused by one of the *spirochete* group of organisms ("T. pallidum"), and the *gonococcus germ* ("N. Gonor-rhoeae") causes gonorrhea. Gonorrhea frequently is called clap, dose, strain, morning dew, drip, running range, or gleet.

What are the signs? 1) This disease has three stages which are the same in both men and women. The first is a painless sore, usually on or around the sex organs which appears about 10 or 90 days after infection. This will go away by itself but the disease remains.

2) From one to six months after the appearance of the sore, called a "chancre," other signs may appear. These are skin rashes, spotty but temporary baldness, headaches, fever, sore throat and small, flat sores in moist areas of the body. Syphilis is most contagious during the second stage when it is more apt to be acquired by intimate contact without sexual intercourse. Kissing may be a method of infection if a person has the sores in the mouth.

3) When the early signs of syphilis have disappeared many persons believe themselves cured, but this very seldom happens. The syphilis is only "latent" or quiet. The germs are still in the body and may localize in the brain, causing mental illness; in the eyes to cause blindness; or in the body causing crippling or heart disease. Sometimes this happens years later.

What is gonorrhea? Gonorrhea is had when there is a pus discharge from the sex organs, sometimes accompanied by pain-ful, burning feelings during urination. These symptoms persist awhile and then may get better by themselves in a few weeks. But—the infection remains and does its work for years, fre-quently causing permanent sterility in women (the inability to have children) by a condition which blocks the passages where the sperm and ovum meet in the process of fertilization. The germs of gonorrhea may be transmitted from the mother to the eyes of children during birth, causing blindness.

Congenital Syphilis: A woman with syphilis can give the

disease to her unborn child. The disease in the child is called congenital syphilis (congenital does not mean inherited, but acquired during pregnancy). With treatment, however, the mother can protect her expected baby from the disease. If she is not treated, the child may be born dead, or prematurely. Symptoms of syphilis in a baby are open sores, rashes, a weakened condition or sniffles. Occasionally there are no symptoms and if the child is not treated eventually, blindness, deafness, paralysis, insanity or even death may occur.

Because the disease is so widespread throughout the USA today, everyone is warned by the medical association to protect themselves with high standards of conduct. One should not hide the facts but get medical care early. The physician's knowledge of this problem is kept confidential.

Prior Bond of Marriage

Canon 1069: 1. One who is bound by a previous marriage bond, even though it was not consummated, invalidly attempts marriage, without prejudice however to the Privilege of the Faith.

2. Even though the prior marriage be invalid or dissolved for any reason, it is not lawful to contract another until the nullity or dissolution of the former shall have been established according to law and with certainty.

1. This impediment is of the divine law and binds all men both Christian and pagan. There is no exception. One who was married before is forbidden to marry again, unless the first marriage is declared null or has been dissolved. The Privilege of the Faith is the only exception to this rule insofar as the first marriage is dissolved, not before, but at the very moment the second is contracted.

2. A prior marriage is dissolved by the death of one of the

parties, whereby the surviving party is free to marry. *This freedom must be verified by*:

(1) Authentic documents: death certificate, ecclesiastical or civil; where the ordinary does not require a *nihil obstat,* the pastor may allow the new marriage to take place.

(2) Gathering proof from witnesses when authentic documents are not available; this, of course, is submitted to the ordinary for the *nihil obstat.*

(3) Having recourse to presumptions mentioned in an Instruction of the S.C. of the Holy Office, May 13, 1868.[2] Strict proof is impossible in some cases and in such circumstances, the proper authorities can decide with moral *certainty* on the basis of the presumption that the party is dead.[3]

(4) *Cases decided by the Sacred Congregation of the Sacraments*: AAS III-26 (1911); AAS VII-40, 235:476 (1915); AAS VIII-151 (1916); AAS IX-120, (1917); AAS XIV-96 (1922); Instruction AAS III-102 (1911); Instruction AAS XIII-348 (1921).

It must be noted that in PRESUMPTION OF DEATH cases, the validity of the second marriage depends upon the fact whether the *former spouse is actually dead.* PERMISSION IS BY NO MEANS A DISPENSATION. If it happens that the spouse is still living, THE SECOND MARRIAGE IS INVALID. Permission is given only under these circumstances. "What God has joined together let no man put asunder."

INSTRUCTION OF THE HOLY SEE ON PRESUMPTION OF DEATH CASES

1. Prolonged Absence or Civil Declaration is Insufficient: The

2. Instruction of the Holy See: AAS 2-199.

3. "Presumption of Death Case," *The Jurist,* July 1959, Vol. XIX; also *Canon Law Digest,* Vol. I, p. 508. Cf. Appendix in this volume.

mere lapse of time, prolonged absence, e.g., the five or seven year period established by civil authorities or other presumptions of death considered by civil law, is insufficient.

2. Official Documents: Interested parties should obtain, if possible, official documents proving the death of the party concerned, e.g., the church, hospital, army or other institutional records. The Department of Vital Statistics which operates in each State sometimes provides important information of this kind. This department is usually located in the State's capital city.

3. Two Witnesses: When official documents cannot be obtained, the testimony of two trustworthy witnesses should be obtained, provided these witnesses:
   (1) knew the deceased;
   (2) know the fact of his death;
   (3) agree on the circumstances, e.g., the time and cause of the death.
   (4) state whether they were related to each other, or were friends or associates of the deceased.

4. First Class Witness: One first class witness of the deceased may suffice if this witness can provide adequate circumstantial evidence.

5. Hearsay Evidence: [4] Sometimes hearsay evidence may suffice (*tempore non suspecto*) and it coincided with information already available.

6. Conjectures: Presumptions based on:
   (1) age;
   (2) moral character;
   (3) physical or mental status;

4. Fraenkel, F., *Missing Persons,* N.Y. 1950.

(4) affection for his or her family;

(5) correspondence (letters);

(6) any circumstances which would give reasons to presume he or she would be heard from if they were alive at the time.

7. Rumor: One should resort to rumor if there is any foundation here.

8. Newspapers, Radio, T.V., Government Agencies, F.B.I.: The results of investigations through these media could be used if sufficient grounds are present for the presumption.

9. Holy See: Whenever any other doubts that are serious are present, the matter must be referred to the Holy See (H.O. 2, July 1898, AAS XXXI, 252).

10. References to Other Cases: (1) *Earthquake in Messina 1908*: The Sacred Congregation of the Sacraments demanded that each case be investigated separately according to the decree of 1898.

(2) *Russian-Japanese War*: A decree of 1910 gave the same instructions. Incidentally, lapse of time in this case was only three years. The decision gives a good review of circumstances in wars, floods, earthquakes, etc.

SOURCES OF INFORMATION

Cases of Servicemen or Former Servicemen:

Whenever a tribunal is handling a case of this kind, it may be necessary to conduct a special investigation in order to obtain information or additional information on a case already started about the party in question. The following addresses may be helpful:

The address of the Military Ordinariate:
> Military Ordinariate
> 30 East 51st Street
> New York, New York 10022

For the Army:
> Casualty Branch
> Adjutant General's Dept.
> War Department
> Washington, D.C. 20025

For the Navy and Marine Corps:
> Bureau of Medicine and Surgery
> Navy Department
> Washington, D.C. 20025

For the Coast Guard & Merchant Marine:
> Military Morale Section
> U.S. Coast Guard Headquarters
> Washington, D.C. 20025

To find out whether a person has died in a certain locality, write to:
> Bureau of Records and Vital Statistics
> State Dept. of Public Health
> (The major city or state capital)
>> e.g., For California:
>> Bureau of Records & Statistics
>> State Dept. of Public Health
>> 631 Jay Street
>> Sacramento, California 95814

DECLARATION OF NULLITY

   I. Lack of Form
  II. Diriment Impediment
 III. Nullity Arising from Other Causes

I. Lack of Form:

A prior attempted marriage is proclaimed invalid by the *declaration of nullity* because of the *defect of form* (C. 1097). No formal process is used here. The ordinary after close examination is the competent authority to declare the nullity.

The following documents are sent to the ordinary for this *Declaration of Nullity*:

(1) Certificate of Baptism;
(2) Certificate of Confirmation and First Holy Communion;
(3) Record of the Civil Marriage;
(4) Record of the divorce (photostat from the clerk of the Circuit Court);
(5) Sworn statement that the marriage was never validated in the Church, that is, celebrated in the form prescribed by the Church.

II. Diriment Impediment:

The ordinary may grant a nullity on a prior marriage by simple summary judicial process (C. 1990) which is based on the following diriment impediments:

(1) Disparity of cult;
(2) Holy Orders;
(3) Solemn Vows;
(4) Ligamen;
(5) Consanguinity;
(6) Affinity;
(7) Spiritual Relationship.

When these impediments (or impediment) can be proved by authentic documents and one is certain that no dispensation had been obtained (C. 1990).

Another impediment could arise from *Crime*: A marriage could be declared invalid, if a person bound by a previous marriage *commits adultery* and *promised*, or *attempted marriage* with this same person.

III. Nullity of Marriage Arising from Other Causes:

To grant a nullity on a previous marriage arising from other causes, would be *defective consent,* impotence, force and fear; in these cases a formal *judicial trial must take place and two concordant sentences rendered.* Cf. Instr. of S. C. Sacr. August 15, 1936, Art. 220.

N.B.: The question of a presumed death is considered not directly under the impediment of ligamen (a previous and existing marriage) but it is a corollary because many of these cases are introduced for processing without any direct reference to this impediment (ligamen).

Another corollary to this impediment would be Common Law Marriages:

COMMON LAW MARRIAGE

A *Common Law Marriage* is one that omits the canonical form (C. 1094), as well as the civil form of marriage and the parties live together as husband and wife. This is a marriage without any ceremony whatsoever, that is, it is one without either minister or witnesses assisting; the man and woman live together as husband and wife and act as such before society.

Whenever a *Common Law Marriage* is permitted, the civil law requires (when there are no impediments) that (1) the *parties exchange their consent mutually.* (The manner and form is not determined by civil law and hence considered immaterial); (2) *they must have the intention* to contract a marriage here and now (*de presenti*); (3) the parties must cohabit with each other. This third condition required by civil law seems to be a contradiction. It is difficult to see how this condition can be a constituent of a Common Law Marriage. Objectively speaking and also from the canonical point of view, the *mutual consent* and the *proper intention* are sufficient. *Cohabitation* is merely a proof of such a marriage. To retain it as a condition to constitute marriage is a contradiction.[5]

The statutes of the following states do not prohibit common law marriages: Colorado, Georgia, Maine, Michigan, Mississippi, Montana, New Hampshire, Ohio, South Carolina, Vermont and Wyoming. It is interesting to note that although Arkansas, Vermont and Wyoming do not prohibit common law marriages by statute, the courts of these states will not recognize common law unions as valid marriages. This, of course, would be detrimental to the civil effects, property rights, inheritance, etc.[6]

On the other hand, some states *prohibit* common law marriages by statute, but the civil courts of these same states continue to recognize these unions as valid marriages. These states are: Alabama, California, Florida, Idaho, Indiana, Iowa, Kansas, Oklahoma, Pennsylvania and Rhode Island. The following states prohibit common law marriages *by statute*: Arizona, Arkansas, California, Delaware, Illinois, Kentucky, Louisiana, Maryland, Massachusetts, New Hampshire, New Mexico, North Carolina, North Dakota, Oregon, Utah, Vermont, Virginia, West Virginia, Wisconsin, Wyoming, Hawaii, Puerto Rico.[7]

Principles:

1. The fact that a man and woman may live together for many years cannot be construed that this relationship automatically becomes a valid common law marriage with the lapse of time. The first two conditions mentioned above: *mutual consent and intention* must take place, otherwise this relationship amounts to *mere concubinage,* even though people publicly consider them married.

5. Long, Jos., *A Treatise on the Law of Domestic Relations,* 3rd ed., Indianapolis, 1948, p. 91.

6. Koegel, Otto E., *Common Law Marriage,* Catholic Univ., Washington, 1922.

7. Mackay-Mandell, *Law of Marriage and Divorce,* N.Y., p. 8.

2. It is also erroneously believed by clergy and laymen alike, that relationships of this kind *are not valid* common law marriages, when they actually are. These cases should be carefully checked. After a divorce, individuals easily change their minds then choose (*post factum*) the type of opinion that suits their needs here and now; they may change their story.

3. Catholics cannot contract a valid common law marriage.

4. *Unbaptized parties must observe the prescribed form of the civil law.* If common law marriages are recognized by the state, then the unbaptized contract a *valid* common law marriage in that state. If it is forbidden by the state, then the common law marriage would be invalid. The state regulates the form of marriage for them.

A common law marriage is recognized as *valid* by the Church between *two baptized non-Catholics* as well as between an *unbaptized person* and a *baptized non-Catholic,* irrespective of the civil law of a particular state, because these people are subject to the laws of the Church. Therefore, these cases must be carefully scrutinized by pastors and especially by the chancery to ascertain whether such common law marriages constitute an impediment of a prior bond, in which case it would invalidate a subsequent marriage. We should keep in mind that the solution of such cases is *not* determined by the fact that the civil law recognizes such marriages as valid, but rather by the very fact that mutual consent and proper intention in virtue of the natural law *was* or *was not given.* It must be kept in mind that for such people no legislation exists requiring a specific formality for the celebration of their marriage.[8]

5. When the parties to a common law marriage wish to become Catholics, (in those states that prohibit a common law marriage) they must obtain a license and renew their consent in order to fulfill the requirements of civil law. It is also advisable that the same procedure be followed even in those states that recognize common law marriages despite the fact that they do not require it.

8. Cloran, Owen, M., *Previews and Practical Cases on Marriage,* Vol. I, Bruce, 1960, pp. 231-235.

6. Regarding convalidation of a marriage in civil law, this is done by reason of the theory of *consent persevering* and this applies only to the marriage of the unbaptized.

7. The unbaptized persons who contract a common law marriage are bound by the diriment impediments of civil law.

8. If one or both of the parties to the common law marriage is a *baptized* non-Catholic, they are not bound by the impediments of the civil law, but are bound by the diriment impediments of the ecclesiastical law.

Proving a Common Law Marriage

1. According to Canons 1081 and 1014, a common law marriage of a baptized non-Catholic enjoys the presumption that it is valid. When such a marriage lacks proof, registration of witnesses to same, the testimony given with an oath of the parties themselves can be accepted as proof of their marriage, provided no other marriage is prejudicial to this testimony.

2. *Cohabitation*: Cohabitation and the public knowledge of the marital status establishes a presumption of such a marriage contract. This presumption is corroborated by various concomitant circumstances:

(1) whether both parties registered as husband and wife at hotels when traveling;

(2) whether the man introduced the woman in social circles as his wife;

(3) whether they acted as husband and wife in legal matters, for example:

(a) having a joint bank account;

(b) filing their income tax together;

(c) registering together when voting;

(d) making out their last will and testament in such a way that he legally considered her his wife;

(e) taking out insurance policies declaring one of the parties as beneficiary;

(f) whether the income tax report of the man had any

reference to the woman as his wife;

(g) whether they referred to themselves as **Mr.** and **Mrs.** in public;

(h) whether they were registered in the post office or in the telephone directory as husband and wife;

(i) whether they intended to live this way until death.[9]

FORM TO DETERMINE COMMON LAW UNIONS

1. Do you believe in the sanctity of an oath? ....
2. Do you realize the gravity of perjury and its serious consequences? ....
3. Do you solemnly swear to tell the whole truth and nothing but the truth in answering all the following questions? (Touching the Holy Gospels) ....
4. Name? ....
   Address? ....
   Place of Birth? .... Age? .... Occupation? ....
5. Father's name? .... Mother's maiden name? ....
6. Were you ever baptized, sprinkled, or christened in any religion? ....
   When? .... Where? ....
   What denomination? ....
7. Have you ever lived with anyone in a common law union? ....
   With whom? ....
   Was this party married before he (she) lived with you? ....
   When? .... Where? ....
   With whom? ....
   Was the former spouse living at the time you cohabited? ....
8. What is the present name and address of the person with whom you lived in common law? ....
9. Was this party ever baptized, christened or sprinkled in any religion? ....
   When? .... Where? ....
   What denomination? ....
10. How long did you live together? ....
11. When did you begin living together? ....
12. Where did you spend this time together? ....
13. Why was there no marriage ceremony? ....

9. Doheny, *Canonical Procedure in Matrimonial Cases*, Vol. I, Bruce, 1937.

14. Did you look upon yourselves as husband and wife? ....
    What was the opinion among your relatives, friends, neighbors, trades folk, etc.? ....
    Give names and addresses: ....
15. Did you call yourselves Mr. and Mrs? ....
    Did you ever register at work or for income tax purposes, charge accounts, insurance, mail box, and telephone directory, as Married?
    ....
16. Did others consider you as married to each other? ....
    Who? ....
    What is their present name and address? ....
    ....
    Why did they consider you married? ....
17. Did you consider that you had a right to him (her)?............................
    Why? ....
18. Did you ever tell him (her) that this was no marriage? ....
    Did you ever tell anyone else? ....
    Who? .... Address? ....
    Why did you do this? ....
19. Did you ever mention that you really should get married? ....
    To whom? ....
    What is their present name and address? ....
    ....
    Why did you mention this? ....
    What was the answer to this? ....
20. Did you intend to live this way until death? ....
    Did either of you make a will? ....
    How did you provide for the other party? ....
21. Did you own property together? ....
    In what name is it listed? ....
22. Did you have any children? ....
    Were they registered as children of Mr. and Mrs? ....
23. Did you think it was a sin to live thus? ....
24. Did the other party consider it a sin to live thus? ....
25. Did you ever go through any kind of a marriage form together, i.e., in which marriage consent was expressed, even privately? ....
26. ADDITIONAL QUESTIONS: ....
    ....
27. Do you swear to the truth of the above statements? ....

DATE: ....
                                                                    SIGNATURE
PLACE: ....
                                                             SIGNATURE OF PRIEST
SEAL:

Disparity of Cult

Canon 1070: 1. A marriage contracted by a non-baptized person with a person who was baptized in the
Catholic Church or who has been converted
to it from heresy or schism, is null.

2. If a party at the time of the marriage was commonly regarded as baptized, or if his or her
baptism was doubtful, the marriage must be
regarded as valid according to Canon 1014,
until it is certainly established that one of the
parties was baptized and that the other was
not.

A marriage is considered null when contracted between a
non-baptized person and a person who was baptized in the Catholic Church, or who has been received into the Church from
heresy or schism.

If the party at the time of the marriage was commonly held
to have been baptized, or if his or her baptism was doubtful,
the marriage must be considered doubtful (Canon 1014) until
it is proved with certainty that one party was baptized and one
was not.

This canon deals with three items: (1) persons born in the
Catholic Church; (2) persons received into the Catholic Church
from heresy and schism; and (3) a doubtful baptism.

INTRODUCTION

Historical Aspect

1. The natural and divine laws govern the impediments of *mixed religion* and *disparity of cult* because of the consequent danger to the faith and morals of the Catholic party.

2. In the Old Testament we have a positive law which forbids marriage between a Jew and a Gentile (Ex 34:16 and Dt 7:3).

3. Marriages between Jews and Christians, in the early Church, were considered legitimate by Christian emperors and they then influenced many of the Church councils.

4. From the 12th century to the new Code of Canon Law in 1918, all marriages were considered invalid which were contracted between a baptized person and a non-baptized person, unless a dispensation was obtained. This included baptized Protestants. Because of this legislation, many marriages were null.

5. This impediment is from divine law if there is a danger of perversion either to the Catholic party or their offspring, and a dispensation cannot be given until the danger is removed. However, this is considered a prohibitive impediment of the divine law only, because we have no positive proof that such a marriage is invalid by divine law.

Ecclesiastical Law: According to ecclesiastical law, it is a diriment impediment regardless of whether there is a danger or not.

For example, from the facts and circumstances that children are being raised Catholics and the wife practices her Catholic religion without any interference from her unbaptized husband is not sufficient in itself of the guarantee. Canon 21 must be followed: "A law passed to guard against some danger remains binding even for individual cases in which the danger does not exist." The danger of perversion is a serious matter. The removal of the danger is a condition for the dispensation from the ecclesiastical law.

In summary, before 1918 and the New Code, the diriment impediment existed in all marriages of one probably baptized or for heretics and schismatics, and the non-baptized. After 1918, the impediment exists only in marriages where one party is not baptized and the other is baptized in the Catholic Church, or converted to it from heresy or schism.

THE ORIENTAL CODE

It may be well to point out here the differences between the Latin Code and the Oriental Code of Law. Canon 60, 61 states: "A marriage contracted by a non-baptized person with a baptized person is null." This implies that baptized non-Catholics validly cannot marry a non-baptized person; this includes Oriental schismatics. Hence, the Oriental Code, dealing with the impediment of disparity of cult, is more restrictive than the Latin Code. In other words, the Oriental Code is similar to the Latin legislation before 1918. This impediment is retained according to the particular discipline. It also includes Oriental schismatics and retains the impediment of disparity of cult.

In ecclesiastical circles there are discussions about returning to this legislation as it was before 1918, because of the high divorce rate which results among the great number of non-Catholics who enter into such a marriage, or wish to enter a marriage with Catholics. They must resort to the complicated and involved process of the Privilege of the Faith. If we had the pre-Code legislation, our chanceries would not be tied down to all the necessary paper work and routine which is involved now. It would all be solved simply by the declaration of nullity, as it is done in the Oriental Church.

Conversion to the Catholic Church

The second item considered in this canon is conversion to the Catholic Faith from heresy, schism, or any other religion.

The manner in which conversion takes place into the Catholic Church (after which the member is called a convert): the so-called A.B.C. formula is used: (A) Adjuration of heresy and profession of faith, (B) Baptism which is given conditionally, and (C) Confession sacramentally with conditional absolution. If the individual was baptized validly in a heretical sect, A and C are used. If one was never baptized, he is baptized absolutely.

The third element in this canon — *The Non-Baptized Party. There is a basic disparity or inequality regarding religion between a Catholic and a non-baptized person.* After questioning the party concerned, relatives, friends and acquaintances should be questioned, and records of churches where the non-baptized party lived for more than 6 months should be investigated.

One should investigate: if other members of the family were baptized, and if the parents were baptized and whether they were religiously inclined. If there is a doubt then there is a strong presumption that the party may have been baptized; if the parents were religious, we can presume they were baptized. Baptism is not usually presumed if the parents of the non-Catholic party frowned on baptism, did not have any children baptized, or had no records in the church.

Cases of Orientals and Non-baptized Persons

Case No. 1: Canon 1070: *Mary, a Byzantine (Ruthenian) Catholic* was raised from childhood in the Roman Catholic Church. She attended Mass and received her Holy Communion there. Later when she planned her marriage with a non-baptized person, the pastor of the Latin Church obtained a dispensation from the disparity of cult. The Latin pastor performed the ceremony. Some time later the marriage ended in separation and divorce. Mary then married another non-baptized person outside the Church, but now this person wishes to take instructions and come into the Catholic Church. Mary wishes to have her second marriage validated. *This marriage can be validated* due to the fact that the Latin rite ordinary invalidly granted the dispensation from the disparity of cult which resulted in an invalid marriage because the Latin ordinary has no subject and therefore no jurisdiction in the case, even though Mary attended the Latin Church during her lifetime.

Case No. 2: The ordinary of the Military Ordinariate in the USA enjoys faculties for Catholics of both the Eastern and Latin Rite subjects in the service. Chaplains may obtain the necessary dispensations from the Military Ordinariate, for example, for a Byzantine Catholic and a non-baptized person.

Susan, a Byzantine Catholic in the U. S. Army, plans to marry a non-baptized person in the city where they are sojourning. The chaplain promised to marry them during this sojourn. The chaplain went to the local ordinary of the place, who lived close by and obtained the dispensation from disparity of cult. The chaplain performed the marriage in the parish church. Some years later Susan separated and got a divorce. Her marriage was declared invalid on the score that the Latin ordinary did not have jurisdiction for either of these two parties. If the chaplain would have obtained the dispensation from the Military Ordinariate, the marriage would have been *valid*.

Canon 1071: The prescriptions of Canons 1060-1065 pertaining to mixed marriages must also be applied to marriages in which an impediment of disparity of cult exists.

Who Are the Persons Born in the Catholic Church?

(1) All adults who are validly baptized in the Catholic Church.
(2) All children of Catholic parents; also those of a mixed marriage, who have been baptized with the intention of belonging to the Catholic Church.
(3) All persons in danger of death who have been baptized by a Catholic. This may be baptism conferred by a layman or a priest, even though the party was uncon-

scious.

(4) Children born of non-Catholics or were born of an invalid marriage are validly baptized in the Catholic Church when their parents' consent is given and a promise that the child will be brought up as a Catholic.

Manner of Baptism

The baptism takes place with the remote matter: water, and the proximate matter: the washing or ablution by infusion, immersion or aspersion. When any of these are used, the one baptizing must use the form simultaneously; "I baptize you, in the name of the Father . . . ." The moral unity must exist between the ablution and the form. *Re: Protestant ministers*: They must have the *proper intention*, regardless of what their opinion might be. As long as the minister has the general intention: *to do what Christ instituted*, or he follows the Scripture as *all the Christians do in conferring Baptism*. When the proper ritual of Baptism is used, we can presume the proper intention. This brings up the question: *Are non-Catholic baptisms valid?* This question is frequently asked. We must distinguish. For a general principle, we could use this: If the minister used the proper matter and form and does what *Christ intended*, the baptism is valid. Hence, we cannot say, as some erroneously believe, that all non-Catholic baptisms are invalid. Ordinarily doubtful baptisms are considered valid. According to the response of the *Holy Office* to certain ordinaries in the U.S.:

Whether baptism conferred by the Disciples of Christ, Presbyterians, Congregationalists, Baptists, Methodists, is to be presumed invalid, when the necessary matter and form were used, because the minister did not have the intention to do what the Church does, or what Christ instituted, or whether such baptism is to be considered valid, unless the contrary is proved in a particular case. REPLY: In the negative to the first part; in the affirmative to the second part.[10] In other words, *in practice*,

10. S. C. Holy Office, Dec. 28, 1949, AAS 41-650.

baptism in these particular sects is considered valid until the contrary is proved, which means that each baptism could be subjected to a careful investigation of a particular locality at the time of the baptism, as well as the method and practice of the individual minister in the administration of the sacrament. These investigations are not easy but, when done, are rewarding.

Cases exemplifying deceptive records and circumstances of Baptism

Case No. 1: Father A was sufficiently satisfied with a beautifully embossed baptismal certificate stating from a certain non-Catholic church that the person concerned was baptized. Father B doubted the baptism of the church. An investigation took place. The rector of the church of the baptism directed the investigators to his curate who took care of such matters. When asked what form he used, he was confused. "Do you have a baptismal font?" he was asked. He replied he did not use one. "Do you issue certificates?" His answer was: "All the members of our church are baptized in this church when they sign our golden book of baptism. We then issue the certificate of baptism. This was the case regarding your party."

Case No. 2: One non-Catholic minister stated that he baptized more solemnly than Catholics do. He exclaimed that while he poured the rose water on the person to be baptized, his wife sang with the accompaniment of the organ from the choir loft. He issued a certificate of baptism. We must be very careful in accepting baptismal certificates from non-Catholic churches.

Case No. 3: This case is very interesting. Mary had been married and divorced and now, after taking instructions, wished to marry a Catholic, if her Privilege of the Faith was granted in Rome. In the process it was discovered that her minister issued a baptismal certificate, thus making her first marriage a *ratum* marriage, since the other party was also baptized. Mary protested that she was never baptized. Investigation was made in the parish where she was baptized. Fortunately, the minister was courteous in permitting the examination of the baptismal record. The records showed that the former minister entered the baptism several times at different times. Mary's baptism was recorded only partially and not like the others. The records showed that Mary was baptized a day after the wedding when she was on her honeymoon. Moreover, the date, October 12 (which was in the record), the date of marriage, was made into a 13, i.e., October 13, whereby baptism was to have been conferred on October 13. He was asked if the former minister was forgetful. He said he was 80 and very forgetful, the reason for his retirement. "How did you know?" said the minister. He replied: "Well, the records indicate forgetfulness." What really happened was that the minister began entering the marriage record into the baptismal book and realized that it was the wrong book. He left it go and did not finish entering the names, etc. Someone later changed the date, which was written in blue ink, and made a 3 out of 2 with black ink. The fact that the entry was incomplete, the minister forgetful, the date changed, the time of baptism listed when the party was away, and additional evidence was given by relatives. Therefore, from this internal evidence, we concluded that she was never baptized, thus substantiating her statement and the Privilege of the Faith case was carried through.

The Impediment of Mixed Religion of the Synod of Trullo (691)

Due to the controversy of the impediment of disparity of cult (mixed religion [11]) enacted by the Council of Trullo (A.D. 691), which went on for several years, it is necessary to clarify some of these issues. In the Latin Church the impediment of mixed religion has not been an invalidating prohibition of mar-

11. *Canon Law Digest*, V, 13-14.

riage since about the thirteenth century. In the Eastern Churches, the severity of the prohibition was once sharpened by conflicts regarding christological heresies, but here, too, the impediment has not been considered diriment for hundreds of years. However, a gradual development in Catholic and Orthodox teaching over the many years of separation parallels this fact. Since Vatican II it coincides in a shared acceptance of the sacramentality of marriages of baptized persons and the intimate relationship existing between Christian marriage and the eucharistic community of the Church.

Since there is a common bond of belief today in the sacramental hierarchical dimensions of marriage, it is difficult to understand the contradiction between the publicized jurisprudence of the Roman Rota and the pastoral practice of the Orthodox Church regarding the impediment of "mixed religion." The discordance exists between an interpretation of the binding force of Eastern law derived from the Canon 72 of the Council of Trullo (691) and some Canonists. (In summary, Canon 72 stated that marriage between the Orthodox and heretics are forbidden, under the penalty of excommunication, and must be dissolved.) On the basis of a canonical theory of jurisdiction followed in recent years, the Orthodox faithful are considered still bound to the impediment enacted by this council.

The earliest use of the impediment of the Council of Trullo as a possible ground of nullity is found in a private reply given to the Bishop of Worcester by the Sacred Congregation of the Oriental Church on December 1959.[12] Since that we have public record of the fact that this impediment has been upheld by the Oriental Congregation, and used to invalidate many marriages by the Congregation of the Doctrine of the Faith, and more recently by the Roman Rota. Two cases ("documentum libertatis") were granted by the Holy Office, Feb. 10, 1960.

Five such cases were reported in the Roman Replies for

12. The terminology "Mixed Religion" was never used in the time of Trullo. This term was unknown; instead, "disparity of Cult" was used, which has a different meaning today.

1965. The Canon Law Digest Supplement, through 1965, records three cases. In each of these cases one party was a validly baptized member of the Orthodox Church and the other party was validly baptized as a Protestant. All these marriages occurred before motu proprio *Crebrae Allatae*, May 2, 1949. It was Cardinal Coussa's contention that after this motu proprio Canon 72 of Trullo was abrogated for the Orthodox. He was wrong.

Therefore, it can be stated that motu proprio *Crebrae Allatae* was not intended for the Orthodox and as such, Canon 72 of Trullo still holds. Moreover, a rescript dated May 22, 1969 declared invalid a marriage of an Orthodox with a validly baptized Protestant *contracted in 1956: Constare de invaliditate matrimonii in casu ex canone 72 Concilii Trullani quod adhuc suam vim tenet.*[13] This now clearly contradicts the former theory and sustains the opinion that the motu proprio did not affect the matrimonial law of the Orthodox Churches.[14] To understand the controversy better, one should read *The Impediment of Mixed Religion.*[15]

At first, decisions regarding Canon 72 of Trullo were handled administratively and reserved explicitly to the competency of the Holy Office; subsequently in particular cases local ordinaries (Latin and Oriental) were instructed to decide the cases. By virtue of the apostolic constitution *Regimini Ecclesiae Universae* of August 15, 1967 and the decree *Integrae servandae* of December 7, 1965, these cases should now be handled judicially, with appeal to normal tribunals of second instance and then, if necessary, to the Roman Rota.[16]

"The Roman Church, whose primacy among its sisters we accept ... separated itself (from us).... When therefore, because of these circumstances, the Church assembles a council with its Western bishops, without our knowledge of what is happening, it is right that its bishops should accept its decrees and observe them .... But although we are in accord with the Roman Church concerning the Catholic faith, how could we,

13. Pro. No. 2911/59m.
14. *The Jurist,* XXIX, 1969, p. 387.
15. Bassett, *The Jurist,* Vol. XXIX, Oct. 1969, pp. 383-415.

because we do not keep assemblies at the same time she does, accept decisions which have been taken without our advice, and of which we even do not know anything." [17]

Sacred Orders

Canon 1072: Clerics in Sacred Orders who attempt marriage do so invalidly.

1. Sacred Orders are the Subdeaconate, Deaconate, Priesthood, Bishopric.

2. This is an ecclesiastical impediment which became established for the Latin Church at the Council of Trent, stemming from the Lateran Council of 1139.

3. Celibacy had been encouraged in the Church for centuries, since the fifth century.

4. Since it is only an ecclesiastical impediment, it could be dispensed by the Holy See, but this is seldom done for the priesthood. The *Deaconate and Subdeaconate*: in danger of death, Canons 1043 and 1044 provide for such dispensation out of the Subdeaconate and Deaconate.

5. Clerics who are constituted in Major Orders when they attempt marriage even by a civil ceremony, incur an *ipso facto* excommunication which is reserved simply to the Holy See. Canon 2388: By common law such clerics lose their ecclesiastical office which they may hold (Cf. C. 188: 5). In addition, they become irregular *ex delicto* (C. 985: 3).

6. On May 4, 1937, the Sacred Penitentiary added a more severe penalty for an attempted marriage by a priest; it is now a *specialissimo modo* censure reserved to the Holy See.

Solemn Vows:

Canon 1073: Likewise marriage is invalidly attempted by reli-

16. Cf. *Ephemerides Juris Canonici*, XXIII, 1967, p. 334.

17. Bishop Nicetos of Nicomedia in an address to Anselm (1136) **during** their discussion of the Roman Primacy.

gious who have pronounced either solemn vows or vows which by special provision of the Holy See are endowed with the power of invalidating marriage.

1. Anyone who attempts marriage in solemn vows: this marriage is rendered invalid by this canon. Here we exclude Sacred Orders.

2. Vows taken in a religious institute are public and are either simple or solemn. The distinction between these is the fact that a simple vow renders an attempted marriage illicit or unlawful, while solemn vows render an attempted marriage invalid (Cf. C. 529). This is one of the ecclesiastical prohibitions.

3. By special provision of the Holy See, the Jesuits have a simple vow whereby an attempted marriage is rendered invalid.

4. *Penalty*: A person in solemn vows who attempts marriage incurs an excommunication simply reserved to the Holy See. The guilty partner incurs the excommunication also (C. 2388: 1). Solemn vows are so-called because they are recognized by the Church as such. The solemnity is considered not so much in the external ceremony but in their object or effects; *whereby solemn vows render certain actions invalid whereas simple vows render them illicit*. Ecclesiastical law gives this invalidating effect.

5. *Dispensation*: A person in solemn vows can obtain a dispensation from the Holy See. The obligation of solemn vows arises from the divine law and as such cannot be dispensed while the vow is in effect. But by exercise of jurisdiction, which the Holy Father has, he can relax this vow, and in so doing relaxes the obligation.

Abduction

Canon 1074: 1. Between the abductor and the woman abducted with the intention of marriage, there can be no marriage as long as she remains in the power of the abductor.

2. If the woman, after having been separated from the abductor and put in a free and safe place, consents to have him as her husband, the impediment ceases.

3. As regards the nullity of marriage, the violent detention of a woman is held equivalent to abduction; that is, when the man, for the purpose of marriage, violently detains a woman in the place where she is staying or to which she has freely come.

1. This is an ecclesiastical impediment: the factors herein considered came under force and fear before the Council of Trent; this invalidated the marriage. In other words, the Council of Trent considered the factor of abduction along with force and fear. The Code includes not only abduction but also the violent detention of a woman.

2. The second paragraph also indicates that if she freely consents in the place of detention, the marriage is still null because she must be brought to a safe place to make the consent freely.

3. A distinction should be made here. Suppose a man abducts a person for reason of sexual relations and not for marriage. The woman afterwards consents to marry him. In this case, there is no impediment; but if she is abducted for sexual relations and afterward is detained for the purpose of marrying, the impediment would be there. Since this is an ecclesiastical impediment, it would not affect the unbaptized.

Crime

Canon 1075: The following persons cannot validly contract marriage:

1. Persons who, during the existence of the same lawful marriage, have consummated adultery together and have mutually promised each other to marry, or have attempted marriage even by a mere civil act;

2. Those who, likewise during the existence of the same lawful marriage, have consummated adultery together, and one of whom has killed the lawful spouse;

3. Those who, even without committing adultery, have by mutual cooperation, physical or moral, killed the lawful spouse.

A valid marriage cannot be contracted in the following cases of crime:

I. *First Degree of Crime*: (1) *Adultery* - Adultery must be taken in the true sense, namely, one party at least is bound by a valid marriage.

(2) *Adultery must be consummated* - That is, the penetration of the vagina and the depositing of the seed therein. The use of contraceptive devices during intercourse would eliminate this impediment. Of course, the parties would have to prove this.

(3) *Formal Adultery* - This means that at least one of the parties is a married person. Affected ignorance, that is, when something is done, but not enough to find out if the other party is married, on the part of one of the parties, if the other party is married, would excuse.

Crass or supine Ignorance (i.e., indifference), when one realizes the gravity of the obligation and should find out, but does not, probably excuses in this case because of the doubt of law and fact.

Condition - The promise must be absolute and sincere; it must be serious and mutual, exteriorly manifested and accepted during the existing marriage. The promise of marriage must be upon the fact of the dissolution of the present marriage by the death of the party espoused, not by divorce (Cipos, par. 123).

Today, divorced persons who marry again during the lifetime of the other party, and consummate the attempted marriage, fall under this degree of the impediment of crime. If one is validating such a marriage later, a dispensation from this impediment is needed and one should apply for it in the chancery.

II. *Second Degree of Crime*: The second degree of crime is when adultery is committed and one of the adulterers kills the lawful spouse. Two factors make up this impediment: First: true adultery, and second, one adulterer kills either his own spouse or the spouse of the other party or both spouses. The adultery must precede the killing of the spouse. There must be murder with the intention of marrying. We say it must precede the murder because after the murder one cannot call it adultery because the party is already dead. To kill one's spouse for the purpose of collecting insurance or to inherit property is no impediment (Cipos, par. 123).

III. *Third Degree of Crime*: The third degree of crime is when no adultery takes place but the cooperation to murder the lawful spouse takes place. First, both must be accomplices, physical and moral, to the murder. The intention to marry must be present. This is presumed unless the contrary is proved. If adultery took place, this would be an additional impediment. In practice, give the entire case to the chancery so they would understand the situation.

Dispensation: Ordinaries can give a dispensation which they have from the quinquennial faculties for the first degree of crime. The Apostolic Delegate grants a dispensation for the second degree of crime. The ordinary can grant it in the second degree only in occult crime cases. For the third degree of crime, dispensation must be obtained from the Apostolic Delegate. Whenever murder is public, the Church does not dispense. Ordinaries and pastors and all those listed in Canons 1043 and 1044 may dispense from all three in danger of death.

Consanguinity

Canon 1076: 1. In the direct line of consanguinity, marriage is invalid between all the ancestors and descendants *whether legitimate or natural.*

2. In the collateral line, marriage is invalid up to the third degree inclusively, but the understanding is that the matrimonial impediment is multiplied only as often as the common ancestor is multiplied.

3. Marriage must never be permitted if there exists a doubt that the parties may be related by consanguinity in any degree of the direct line or in the first degree of the collateral line.

Consanguinity is the relationship between persons, based on carnal relationship, or carnal generation. Consanguinity does not arise from blood transfusions. Consanguinity exists in the *direct line,* if one of the persons is the *direct ancestor* of the other, that is, persons who descend from each other. For example, *Father, Daughter, Granddaughter, Great-granddaughter,* etc.

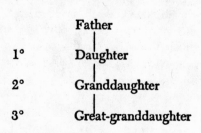

Consanguinity in the Indirect Line

This indirect line is also called *oblique line, transverse line* but usually it is called the *collateral line,* if neither person is the direct ancestor of the other, but both are descended from a common ancestor, as for example, brother and sister, first cousins, etc.

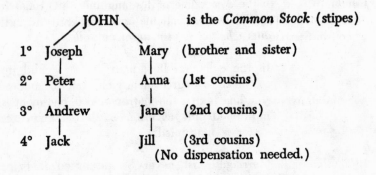

In the preceding diagram: *Joseph and Mary are brother and sister* and 1° removed from the common stock (Peter); *Peter and Anna are first cousins* and 2°; *Joseph and Anna* are in the 2° 1°, second degree touching the first (*in secundo gradu tangente primum*) OR Uncle and Niece: *Andrew and Anna* are in the third degree collateral mixed with the second degree 3° 2°, that is (*second cousins-first mixed*); *Andrew and Jane* are in the 2° degree, or a second cousin degree. Since 1918, there is *no dispensation needed for third cousins 4° collateral of consanguinity.* Marriage between *Brother and Sister* is *Probably Null* in the natural law itself. The Church never grants a dispensation in such a case or even when it is probable that the parties are related in this manner. If non-baptized people are related in this way and already married, the Holy Office does not forbid a priest to baptize them.

Uncle - Niece Marriages

We have a special instruction of the Sacred Congregation of the Sacraments, August 1, 1931, regarding such marriages. No dispensation will be granted without very special reasons. The ordinary himself must write the petition to Rome for such a dispensation, *or*, at least, sign the petition, *and* give his views on the reasons for asking such a dispensation (AAS XXIII, 1931, p. 413). These marriages should be discouraged, as well as cousin marriages.

Diagraming

It must be kept in mind that there is no impediment of consanguinity unless one of the parents, of one party wishing to get married, was at least a first cousin of one of the parents of the other party.

When determining the degrees of relationship, use the following:

(1) To make two persons *Brother and Sister,* give them a common ancestor.

(2) To make two persons *First Cousins,* give them a common Grandparent.

(3) To make two persons *second cousins,* give them a common Great-grandparent.

(4) To make brothers *Full Brothers,*

```
A _____ B
        |
Leo ____|____ John
```

(5) To make brothers *Half-Brothers,*

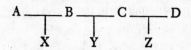

MANNER OF COMPUTING THE DEGREES

The degrees are computed in this way:

Direct Line: Compute it according to the *number of generations*, or, according to the *number of persons* in the line, *without counting the ancestor* (Stipes).

Collateral Line: Compute it according to the *number of generations* in one branch, *if the branches are equal;* if the two branches are *unequal, count the longer branch* (C. 96).

CONSANGUINITY CASES

Case No. 1: Jack and Mary come to your rectory to arrange for their marriage. Jack tells you that he is the first cousin to Mary's mother; he is also a nephew to Mary's father. Do you need a dispensation?

Case No. 2: While Peter and Eva are going over their marriage plans with the pastor, they mention that they are related; their fathers were first cousins, and Peter's mother was a second cousin to Eva's father. Is a dispensation needed?

Case No. 3: Father John of St. Joseph's encounters this dilemma. Susie and James wish to marry, but their fathers were half brothers, and their grandmothers were half sisters.

Case No. 4: Joseph and Rosemary wish to marry but they present the pastor with this consanguinity problem: Joseph's father is Rosemary's uncle on the father's side and Rosemary's mother is Joseph's aunt on the mother's side.

Case No. 5: Donald and Teresa signed an engagement contract a year ago. Now they are preparing for their wedding. In the investigation the pastor discovers that their *grandfathers* are brothers and their fathers are brothers and their mothers are sisters.

Case No. 6: Owen plans to marry Lea, but they are related: Their mothers are first cousins and their fathers are brothers.

Case No. 7: After filling out the preliminary investigation papers, Ted and Zia left the rectory, but returned later to find out how he was related to Zia (which he forgot to mention). Their common father married two first cousins successively.

Case No. 8: Peter and Julia are engaged. Father Thomas discovers that they cannot marry unless a dispensation is obtained. Julia's father, Christian, is Peter's brother, and Julia's mother is first cousin to both Peter and Christian.

Case No. 9: In a discussion before marriage, the parents of the couple reveal to Matilda that it might be impossible to marry Blane because she is related to him. Matilda's grandfather was a brother to Blane's grandfather and Matilda's grandmother was a sister to Blane's grandmother.

Case No. 10: Father Charles encountered some difficulty with the couple, Pat and Lulu, when they came to arrange for their wedding. Lulu's father was a brother to Pat's grandfather on his mother's side; Lulu's mother was a sister to Pat's grandmother on her mother's side and Lulu's father was a brother to Pat's grandfather on his mother's side. In this case, three sisters - G, H and D, of the Denby family marry three brothers, F, E and C, of the Smith family. Peter, the son of the first pair F and G Smith, marries Joanne, the daughter of the second pair, E and H. Peter and Joanne have a son, Patrick, who plans to marry Lulu, the daughter of the third pair C and D.

Case No. 11: Clement and Jenny have been dating for several years. They now plan to marry. In their conversation with their pastor, he is dubious whether it is possible but told them he would work out a solution. Checking the family tree, he finds the following. Clem's grandfather, Tom Fulton, and Joe Fulton are brothers. Rose, Jean and Fay Jones are sisters; Tom marries Fay and they have a child, Rita. Joe marries Jean and they have a child, Nicholas. Rita and Nick marry and have a daughter Jenny. Fay dies (i.e., Tom Fulton's wife). Tom now marries Rose, the other Jones sister. The grandson Clement now wishes to marry Jenny. Give the schema.

Case No. 12: Dora and Bob plan on getting married, but they are related. Their fathers are brothers, and Bob's mother is the first cousin to Dora's father.

Case No. 13: Fay and George are in doubt whether they can get married because they are related. Fay's father is the grandfather of George by a former marriage; he is also an uncle to Fay's mother.

Case No. 14: Sam and Rose decided to get married. They have a problem. Sam's father was the grandfather of Rose by a former marriage, and Sam's mother was the grandmother of Rose by a former marriage.

Case No. 15: Steve, a widower, and his son Junior get married to Kate and her daughter, Jane, respectively. The daughter of Steve and Kate now wishes to marry Leo, the son of Junior and Jane.

Case No. 16: John of the Melchite rite wishes to marry Helen of the Byzantine rite. Helen is John's second cousin, once removed. Can they marry without a dispensation? Would the case be the same if John and Mary were of the Latin rite?

CONSANGUINITY

Case No. 1: Jack and *Mary* come to your rectory to arrange for their marriage. Jack tells you that he is the *first cousin* to Mary's mother; he is also a *nephew* to Mary's father. Do you need a dispensation?

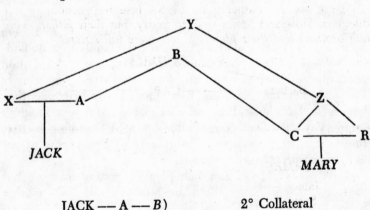

JACK — A — B)	2° Collateral
MARY — C — B)	
JACK — X — Y	2°)
MARY — R — Z — Y — 3°)	3° 2° Collateral

(Dispensation needed.)

Case No. 2: While *Peter* and *Eva* are going over their marriage plans with the pastor, they mention that they are related; their *fathers* were *first cousins*, and *Peter's mother* was a *second cousin* to *Eva's father.*

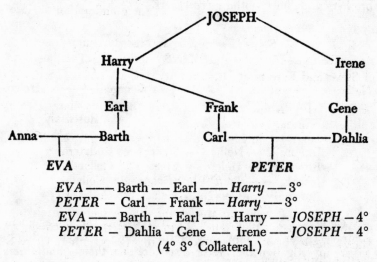

EVA —— Barth —— Earl —— *Harry* — 3°
PETER — Carl —— Frank —— *Harry* — 3°
EVA —— Barth —— Earl —— Harry —— JOSEPH — 4°
PETER — Dahlia — Gene —— Irene —— JOSEPH — 4°
(4° 3° Collateral.)

Case no. 3: Father John of St. Joseph's encounters this dilemma. *Susie* and *James* wish to marry, but their *fathers* were *half-brothers* and their *grandmothers* were *full sisters*.

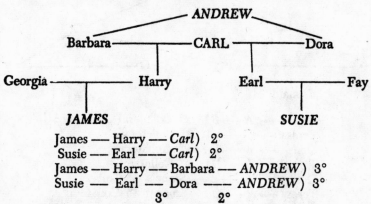

James —— Harry —— *Carl*) 2°
Susie —— Earl —— *Carl*) 2°
James —— Harry —— Barbara —— *ANDREW*) 3°
Susie —— Earl —— Dora —— *ANDREW*) 3°
3°   2°

Case No. 4: *Joseph* and *Rosemary* wish to marry but they present the pastor with this consanguinity problem. Joseph's father is Rosemary's *uncle* on the *father's* side and Rosemary's mother is Joseph's *aunt* on the *mother's* side. (Their fathers are brothers and their mothers are sisters.)

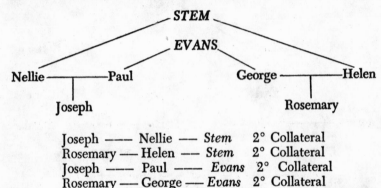

Joseph	—— Nellie ——	*Stem*	2° Collateral
Rosemary	—— Helen ——	*Stem*	2° Collateral
Joseph	—— Paul ——	*Evans*	2° Collateral
Rosemary	—— George ——	*Evans*	2° Collateral

Case No. 5: *Donald* and *Teresa* signed the engagement contract a year ago; now they are preparing for their wedding. In the investigation the pastor discovers that their *grandfathers* are *brothers*, their *fathers* are *brothers*, and their *mothers* are *sisters*.

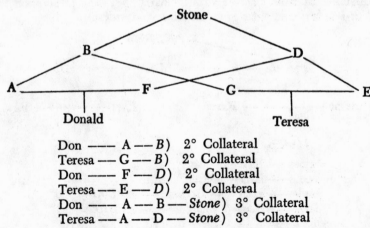

Don	—— A —— B)	2°	Collateral
Teresa	—— G —— B)	2°	Collateral
Don	—— F —— D)	2°	Collateral
Teresa	—— E —— D)	2°	Collateral
Don	—— A —— B —— Stone)	3°	Collateral
Teresa	—— A —— D —— Stone)	3°	Collateral

Case No. 6: *Owen* plans to marry *Lea*, but they are related. Their mothers are *first cousins* and their fathers were *brothers.*

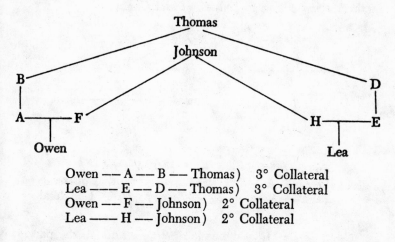

Owen —— A —— B —— Thomas) 3° Collateral
Lea ——— E —— D —— Thomas) 3° Collateral
Owen —— F —— Johnson) 2° Collateral
Lea ——— H —— Johnson) 2° Collateral

Case No. 7: After filling out the preliminary investigation papers, *Ted* and *Zia* left the rectory, but returned later to find out how he was related to Zia (which he forgot to mention). Their father married two *first cousins* successively.

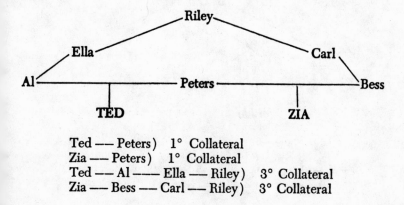

Ted —— Peters) 1° Collateral
Zia —— Peters) 1° Collateral
Ted —— Al ——— Ella —— Riley) 3° Collateral
Zia —— Bess —— Carl —— Riley) 3° Collateral

Case No. 8: *Peter* and *Julia* are engaged. Father Thomas discovers that they cannot marry unless a dispensation is obtained. Julia's father, Christian, is Peter's *brother*, and Julia's mother is *first cousin* to both Peter and Christian.

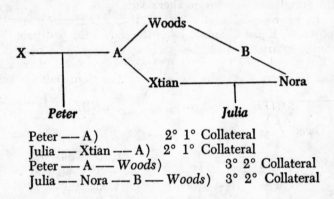

Peter —— A)   2° 1° Collateral
Julia —— Xtian —— A)   2° 1° Collateral
Peter —— A —— *Woods*)   3° 2° Collateral
Julia —— Nora —— B —— *Woods*) 3° 2° Collateral

Case No. 9: In a discussion before marriage, the parents of the couple reveal to *Matilda* that it might be impossible to marry *Blane* because she is related to him. Matilda's grandfather was a *brother* to Blane's grandfather and Matilda's grandmother was a *sister* to Blane's grandmother.

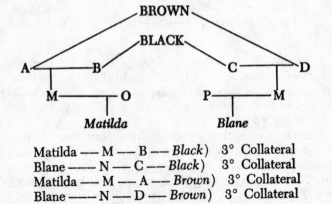

Matilda —— M —— B —— *Black*)   3° Collateral
Blane —— N —— C —— *Black*)   3° Collateral
Matilda —— M —— A —— *Brown*)   3° Collateral
Blane —— N —— D —— *Brown*)   3° Collateral

Case No. 10: Father Charles encountered some difficulty with the couple *Pat* and *Lulu* when they came to arrange for their wedding. Lulu's father was a *brother* to Pat's grandfather on his father's side; Lulu's mother was a *sister* to Pat's grandmother on her mother's side and Lulu's father was a *brother* to Pat's grandfather on his mother's side.

In other words, three sisters, G, H and D Denby marry three brothers F, E and C Smith. Peter the son of the first pair F and G Smith marries Joanne, the daughter of the second pair, E and H; this couple PETER AND JOANNE have a son, Patrick who plans to marry Lulu, the daughter of the third pair C and D.

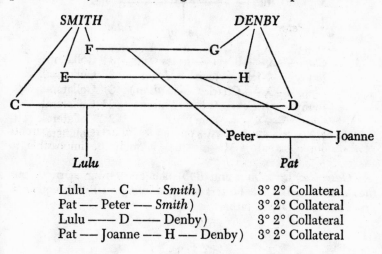

Lulu —— C —— *Smith*)	3° 2° Collateral
Pat —— Peter —— *Smith*)	3° 2° Collateral
Lulu —— D —— Denby)	3° 2° Collateral
Pat —— Joanne —— H —— Denby)	3° 2° Collateral

Case No. 11: *Clement* and *Jenny* have been dating for several years. They now plan to marry. In their conversation with their pastor, he is dubious whether it is possible but told them he would work out a solution. Checking the family tree he finds the following.

Clem's grandfather, Tom Fulton, and Joe Fulton are *brothers*. Rose, Jean and Fay Jones are *sisters*. Tom marries Fay and they have a child Rita. Joe marries Jean and they have a child, Nicholas. Rita and Nick marry and have a daughter, Jenny. Fay dies (Tom Fulton's wife). Tom now marries Rose, the other Jones sister. The grandson, *Clement*, now wishes to marry *Jenny*. Give the schema.

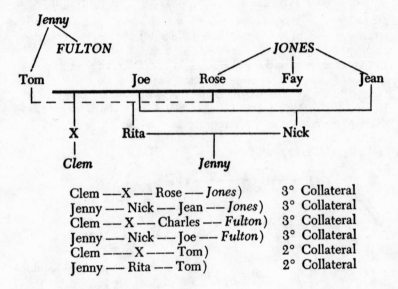

Clem ——X —— Rose —— *Jones*)   3° Collateral
Jenny —— Nick —— Jean —— *Jones*)   3° Collateral
Clem —— X —— Charles —— *Fulton*)   3° Collateral
Jenny —— Nick —— Joe —— *Fulton*)   3° Collateral
Clem ——— X ——— Tom)   2° Collateral
Jenny —— Rita —— Tom)   2° Collateral

Case No. 12: *Dora* and *Bob* plan on getting married, but they are related. Their fathers are *brothers*, and Bob's mother is *first cousin* to Dora's father.

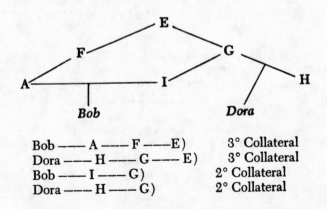

Bob —— A —— F ——E)   3° Collateral
Dora —— H —— G —— E)   3° Collateral
Bob —— I —— G)   2° Collateral
Dora —— H —— G)   2° Collateral

Case No. 13: Fay and George are in doubt whether they can get married because they are related. Fay's father is the *grandfather* of George by a former marriage, he is also an *uncle* of Fay's mother.

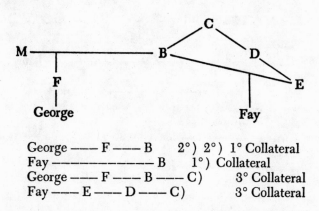

```
George ——— F ——— B      2°) 2°) 1° Collateral
Fay ———————————— B      1°) Collateral
George ——— F ——— B ——— C)      3° Collateral
Fay ——— E ——— D ——— C)      3° Collateral
```

Case No. 14: Sam and Rose decided to get married. They have a problem. Sam's father was the *grandfather* of Rose by a former marriage, and Sam's mother was the *grandmother* of Rose by a previous marriage.

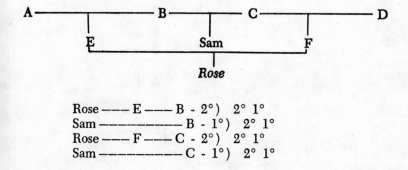

```
Rose ——— E ——— B - 2°)   2° 1°
Sam ———————————— B - 1°)   2° 1°
Rose ——— F ——— C - 2°)   2° 1°
Sam ———————————— C - 1°)   2° 1°
```

Case No. 15: *Steve*, a widower, and his son *Junior* get married to *Kate* and her daughter, *Jane*, respectively. The daughter of Steve and Kate now wants to marry Leo, the son of Junior and Jane.

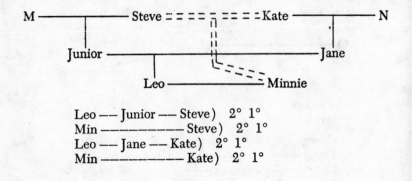

Leo —— Junior —— Steve) 2° 1°
Min ———————— Steve) 2° 1°
Leo —— Jane —— Kate) 2° 1°
Min ———————— Kate) 2° 1°

ORIENTAL COMPUTATION

Canon 66: 2. Marriage is invalid in the collateral line to the 6°: Examples:

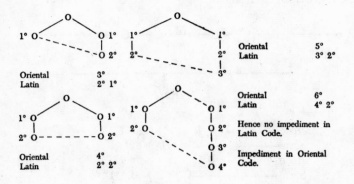

ORIENTAL LAW

The diriment impediment of consanguinity and affinity differ as to the manner of computation and applicability. Canon 66 of the Oriental Law provides that marriage between blood relatives in all degrees of the direct line are null and void; furthermore, blood relations in the collateral line nullifies marriage up to the sixth degree inclusive; in case of a doubt concerning relationship in any degree of the direct line or up to the second degree of the collateral line inclusive, marriages are never permitted. Canon 66 has a fourth provision not to be found in its Latin counterpart, Canon 1076. This provision gives the Oriental version of the Canon 96 CIC, namely, the manner in which the degrees of consanguinity are to be computed.

The Oriental code computes the degree of consanguinity by taking into consideration *all generations on both sides* of the collateral line, whereas the Latin Code takes into consideration only the one, *the longer line*. At first sight the casual observer might be inclined to think that this computation is the same as the third degree in the Latin Code, but this would be true only if there would be an unequal number of generations on both sides of the line. However, if one side of the line should have four or five generations and the other one or two, the Latin Code would permit marriage in the fourth and fifth generations whereas the Eastern Code would prohibit the same. Interritual marriages frequently take place and hence a situation might take place where a Latin would plan to marry an Oriental to whom he might be related in the fourth or fifth degree of consanguinity often in the collateral line. According to his own law, the Latin may contract marriage validly whereas the Oriental could be disqualified from contracting a valid marriage without a dispensation. Which law prevails? Cappello proposes the principle of communication of freedom from the Latin subject to the Oriental party; moreover, if there still remains doubt regarding this (doubt of law), Canon 15 CIC could be applied, namely, that the law does not oblige here.[18] E. Herman disagrees with this interpretation.[19] Since this conflict of laws creates a doubt, we are free to follow this (Canon 15 CIC) until the Holy See declares other-

18. Cappello, F., *De Matrimonio*, VI, 1947, pp. 487-488.

19. Herman, Emil, "Adnotationes," *Periodica de Re Morali Canonica Liturgica*, Rome, 1949.

wise. We might add that some authors suggest that the safest would be to obtain a dispensation from the proper Eastern Hierarch (Ordinary) who can dispense the Oriental party.

Affinity

There are also some differences regarding the affinity (unlike the Latin Code). The Oriental Code recognizes as a diriment impediment affinity between blood relations of the spouses and the so-called affinity (ex trigeneia) which arises from two valid marriages (even if not consummated) when the spouses contract marriage successively with the same third party or with two different persons related to each other by blood. For example; John marries a widow, Margaret, who had a son Joseph by her first marriage. Some time after Margaret dies and John marries another person, Susan. John subsequently dies. *Later Susan wishes to marry Joseph.* In this case, we find that there exists the impediment of affinity arising from trigeneia: *the degree of affinity of Susan's late husband John to Joseph. The degree of John's affinity to Joseph then depends upon the degree of consanguinity of John's first wife to Joseph.* Since Margaret was Joseph's mother (1°), between John and Joseph we have simple affinity in the first degree and we find then that Susan is related in the same degree of affinity to Joseph arising from *trigeneia*, or a successive marriage with the same third party, namely, two different persons related to each other by blood.

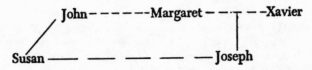

In the direct line affinity nullifies marriage in all ascending and descending degrees similar to the Latin Code but, unlike the Latin Code, marriage contracted in the fourth degree inclusive in the collateral line is considered null.

Affinity (ex digeneia) which exists between the blood relatives of the two parties nullifies marriage up to the fourth degree inclusive.

Affinity

Canon 1077: 1. Affinity in the direct line in any degree invalidates marriage; in the collateral line it invalidates it up to the 2° degree inclusive.

2. The impediment of affinity is multiplied:
1° as often as the impediment of consanguinity from which it arises is multiplied;
2° whenever marriage is repeated successively with a blood relative of a deceased spouse.

Canon 97: 1. Affinity arises from a valid marriage, either ratified or ratified and consummated.

2. It exists only between the woman and the blood relatives of the man.

3. It is computed in such a way that the same persons who are blood relatives of the man are related by affinity in the same line and degree to the woman and vice versa.

---

1. Affinity comes from a valid marriage. It extends to all degrees in the direct line. A man could not, e.g., marry his wife's mother, grandmother, daughter, or granddaughter, and vice versa.

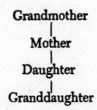

Grandmother
|
Mother
|
Daughter
|
Granddaughter

2. The brothers of the husband are not related by affinity to the sisters of the wife.

3. The Church rarely dispenses from affinity in the direct line.

4. *Henry VIII of England:* Henry VIII got a dispensation to marry Catherine, his sister-in-law, who was his brother's wife; Arthur never consummated the marriage, is the alleged opinion. When Henry VIII decided to marry again, he claimed that the affinity dispensation was invalid, even when given by the Pope of Rome, because it was an impediment of the Divine Law.

5. Canon 1043-44 grants the faculty to dispense with all ecclesiastical impediments but affinity in the direct line of a consummated marriage is restricted here.

6. In 1957 the disputed question among authors was presented to the Holy See: whether affinity contracted in infidelity became an impediment for marriage which was entered into after baptism even of only one of the parties. The answer was Affirmative (AAS 49-77).

Affinity: Twenty-six states in the United States do not have affinity as an impediment. The following have degrees of affinity that annul marriages: Alabama, Georgia, Iowa, Kentucky, Maine, Maryland, Massachusetts, Connecticut, Delaware, Michigan, Mississippi, New Hampshire, Oklahoma, Pennsylvania, Rhode Island, South Carolina, Tennessee, Texas, Vermont, Virginia, Washington, West Virginia and District of Columbia. Every state varies regarding this impediment. Alabama, e.g., forbids the son to marry his stepmother or the widow of his uncle. The father may not marry the widow of his son. The father may not marry the daughter of his wife, or the daughter of his son. It is best to check the laws and statutes of each state.

CASES OF AFFINITY

Case No. 1: Joseph marries Mary who dies within a year. Joseph then wants to marry Mary's sister, Ann.

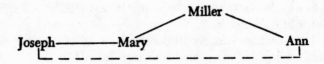

Case No. 2: Susie and Lea are sisters. Helen and Rose are sisters. Susie and Lea are first cousins to Helen and Rose. John marries Lea. How is he related to the other three in virtue of the impediment of affinity?

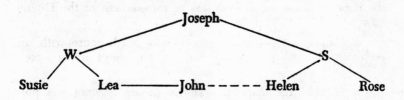

1. Lea and John marriage
    John to Susie ——— 1°
    John to Helen ——— 2°
    John to Rose ——— 2°

2. John and Helen marriage
    John to Rose ——— 1°

Public Propriety

Canon 1078: *Public Propriety*

> The impediment of public propriety arises from an invalid marriage, whether consummated or not, and from public or notorious concubinage; it annuls marriage in the first and second degree of the direct line between the man and the blood relations of the women and vice versa.

1. It must be noted that this impediment arises from an invalid marriage, consummated or not consummated, and it must be from concubinage which is public or notorious. Thereby, any attempt at marriage in the first and second degree of the direct line between the man and the blood relations of the woman would render this attempted marriage invalid.

2. What kind of invalid marriage are we considering here? The code does not distinguish; neither shall we.

3. In 1929 the Code Commission did give a definition regarding public propriety insofar as it settled the question that this impediment does not arise from the mere fact of a civil marriage when there is no cohabitation (Chap. AAS. 21-170).

4. An invalid marriage is one that has the appearance of marriage but is invalid because of some diriment impediment or force or fear or lack of consent, etc.

5. What is concubinage? When two people live as husband and wife with the intention of having sexual relations and this union does not even have the appearance of marriage. If this is publicly known, the impediment arises; if it is not publicly known, there is no impediment. For example: John and Mary live in concubinage in a hotel. They are thought to be man and wife; therefore, there is no impediment - the crime is not public.

6. *The Unbaptized*: The unbaptized are not bound by this ecclesiastical impediment. If one is baptized, it binds directly the baptized and indirectly the unbaptized party. However, the unbaptized are not bound by the impediment if they give up their concubinage at the time of conversion; if they continue after the baptism, they incur this impediment.

7. *Dispensation*: This is not like affinity insofar as it extends to the direct line only and not to the collateral line. Hence, this would be concubinage, provided it is public or notorious.

INVALID MARRIAGES AND CONCUBINAGE

An invalid marriage is different technically from concubinage. They are both similar insofar as both are *immoral* because these people have *no right* to the conjugal act. They are different insofar as an *invalid marriage* has some juridic act involved (the ceremony which accompanied it), whereas in *concubinage* no such act took place. A marriage is considered *invalid* only when the prescribed form is used and a diriment impediment is present. It must be remembered that we can obtain a *sanation for an invalid marriage,* but we cannot sanate a case of *concubinage.* In the former (invalid marriage) some form of juridic act took place, whereas in concubinage people are living together as married people, preceded by no celebration of marriage or, in other words, lacking this juridic act. No consent was given to marriage in concubinage. When a sanation is given, the consent to marriage must be persevering at the time it is granted. In applying for a *sanatio in radice,* every priest should keep this in mind, namely, the difference between concubinage and an invalid marriage. A dispensation for a *sanatio* for a concubinage case would be invalid.[20]

Spiritual Relationship

Canon 1079: The only spiritual relationship which invalidates marriage is that mentioned in Canon 768.

1. That spiritual relationship annuls marriage only which is mentioned in Canon 768: "The minister of baptism and the sponsor contract spiritual relationship from baptism with the person baptized only." In other words, because of baptism, the minister and the sponsor or sponsors contract spiritual relationship whereby the impediment to marriage arises with the baptized person.

2. The Code does not distinguish whether this pertains to solemn or private baptisms. Therefore, we do not consider this question. There is, however, no impediment between the parents and the minister, or parents and sponsors.

3. On one baptismal certificate, we found the minister of baptism was also the sponsor. Is this possible? According to the Sacred Congregation of Rites, 1873, if the bishop wants to be sponsor in confirmation, he can appoint a proxy to act as sponsor. One author (Wernz [21]) states there is a double relationship; the

20. Monitor Eccles. 1962, pp. 541-555.
21. Wernz, Jus. Decretal., IV, n. 492, ftn. 67.

proxy sponsor does not contract any spiritual relationship whereby it would become an impediment. Does one incur the spiritual relationship if he acts as sponsor at a conditional baptism? No, he would incur spiritual relationship with the person if the same individual were present for the first baptism, as well as the conditional baptism. If a non-baptized person acted as sponsor, did he become related spiritually to the baptized if he was baptized in the Church? No, because it is an impediment of ecclesiastical law and he was not held by the law at the time he acted as sponsor.

4. Dispensation: The ordinary can dispense from this impediment by his quinquennial faculties.[22]

Legal Relationship

Canon 1080: *Legal Relationship*

Persons who according to the civil law are regarded as incapable of marrying each other because of a legal relationship arising from adoption, cannot validly contract marriage together according to canon law.

All persons who by civil law are disqualified in marrying certain persons because of legal adoption are likewise disqualified in contracting a valid marriage according to canon law. Such invalidating laws are found in Puerto Rico; also in Massachusetts, Rhode Island and Connecticut (Cf. Alford, *US MAT. Comparatum* No. 163, N58, ch. 15).

Dispensation: A dispensation from this impediment must be obtained from the Apostolic Delegate.

---

22. Oriental Law: In the new code for the Orientals, the sponsor contracts relationships with the person baptized and with this person's parents. However, spiritual relationship does not arise between the minister and the person baptized. This is an important point when dealing with Orientals.

CHAPTER VI

MATRIMONIAL CONSENT

QUALITIES

Canon 1081: 1. Matrimony is effected by the consent of the parties legitimately expressed between persons capable according to law; which consent no human power can supply.

2. Matrimonial *consent is an act of the will* by which *each party gives and accepts a perpetual and exclusive right over the body,* for acts which are of themselves suitable for the generation of children.

---

1. *Contract of the parties:* Every contract made by individuals comes under the law of reason whereby it implies a transfer of rights and obligations; as such, there can never be a marriage without real consent of both parties.

2. In order that this contract produce effects, the parties must be juridically qualified. *The marriage consent is an act of the will with a definite object. The act of the will must really exist, (actually or virtually).* Act of the intellect, the disposition of one's mind, various opinions, errors of judgment are considered

only insofar as these affect the will. *The consent must be mutual.*
The object of this consent is the perpetual and exclusive right
over each others body for the exercise of actions that by their
very nature pertain to the procreation of children. This right is
the essential object of the true marriage contract by virtue of
the natural law and the divine positive law. Custom, circumstances of the times, state or ecclesiastical laws can never change
this.

3. The consent must be lawfully expressed as determined
by Canon 1094. However, there are also state laws which must
be considered. The capacity of the persons is determined by
natural law; for the baptized by canon law; for the unbaptized
by the state law.

4. True consent is very important so much so that the contract would be invalid if certain obstacles were present, such as:

(1)	Insanity	C. 1081
(2)	Ignorance	C. 1082
(3)	Error	C. 1083
(4)	Simulation	C. 1086
(5)	Force and Fear	C. 1087

5. When all the conditions mentioned above are fulfilled
in the external forum, we consider the marriage contract valid
because every act: (the giving and accepting, the holding of
hands, the words expressed) was in perfect order externally.
However, if we examine the act itself - the essential factor or
marriage, namely, the mutual consent to marry according to the
established standards (unity, indissolubility, procreation of children, etc.) we find that sometimes the *interior* dispositions of
the contractants do not correspond exactly to those of the exte-
rior acts. In order to have a valid marriage, the interior dispositions must conform to the external, otherwise it is possible that
the contract would be invalid.

6. Before a marriage, the pastor seldom meets with such
a problem. These conditions are withheld and usually arise when,
after a separation or divorce, one of the parties claims nullity
on the grounds that the consent was not mutual or for some other
condition made at the time of the contract, and asks permission
to enter into a new marriage.

REQUISITE KNOWLEDGE

Canon 1082: 1. In order that matrimonial consent be given properly, it is necessary that the contracting parties fully understand that marriage is a permanent union between a man and a woman for the procreation of children.

2. This ignorance is not presumed after puberty.

1. Lack of knowledge may be due to:
(1) ignorance, (2) error, or (3) fraud.

Ignorance is the lack of knowledge. In reference to marriage, if one of the parties did not know that marriage is a permanent union of a man and woman for the purpose of begetting offspring, such a marriage would be invalid. Ignorance, of course, would have to be proven without a doubt.[1] The contract of marriage requires consent in the transfer of rights. In this serious transaction there cannot be a true and valid marriage without the real consent of both parties. The consent, freely given, *alone* constitutes marriage. Such was the teaching of the Roman law, Church Fathers (regarding the Blessed Mother and St. Joseph), the teaching of St. Thomas and the Council of Trent. *Consent is an act of the will regarding a definite, specific object.* Therefore, regarding a definite, specific person in the contract of marriage.

ERROR OF FACT

Canon 1083: 1. Error regarding a person renders marriage invalid.

2. Error regarding the quality of the person, even if it is the cause of the contract, invalidates marriage *only*:
(a) if the error regarding the *quality amounts to an error of person;*

1. AAS XIII, 1921, p. 56; Cappello, n. 582.

(b) if a free person contracts marriage with
a person whom he or she considers free,
but who is on the contrary in a condition
of slavery in the proper sense.

1. Here we have two types of error of fact:
    (1) Error of Person, and
    (2) Error of the Quality of the Person.
The first invalidates marriage; the second invalidates marriage only under certain conditions.

2. If the error concerned the identity of the other party as, e.g., Joseph marries Mary thinking she is Rose. Today, this is hardly possible; but if he does the marriage would be invalid.

3. If the error concerned some quality or characteristic of the other party, provided that this certain quality or characteristic expected is such that it amounted to *error concerning the person*, e.g., marrying a slave girl thinking she was free.

4. *The Essence of the Marriage Contract Is the Consent. The Essential Object of the Consent Is the Person; it is not the qualities of the person. Qualities are something accidental to marriage; these qualities, even though insignificant in themselves are sometimes very important to the other party.* It is true that the injured party *hoped, wished, thought, believed* that his spouse possessed this or that quality, but the *"die is cast," the consent was given—the contract was made—the marriage is valid.* This is an *error* or *false judgment made by the injured party* regarding the personal qualifications of the other spouse. The Church could make such an error a nullifying factor but it does not because this factor would only cause greater confusion. Human beings are not perfect, as we all know; therefore, it is self-evident that there would be no end to such problems. In practice, it is almost impossible to prove that an error in quality amounts to error of the person. This is possible *only* when the injured party can give full proof that the quality of the party amounted to a *conditio sine qua non*.

5. John marries Jane *under the condition* (in writing or before qualified witnesses) that Jane is a wealthy woman, or that Jane is of noble birth which she claimed; or that Jane was never in a mental institution. *After the marriage,* John learns that Jane is not a wealthy woman, nor is she of noble birth, etc. This marriage would be considered invalid.

Fraud: Fraud or deception in which a person is misled into error could happen through misrepresentation through one's conduct, by deceptive speech or even silence. In *civil courts,* fraud, *if proven,* invalidates marriage. But in *ecclesiastical courts,* fraud does not invalidate a marriage no matter what grave injustice or injury was incurred by the other party *because a valid marriage is indissoluble.* What measures could one take against a fraudulent marriage? A prolonged courtship is one way. A lifetime project should always be carefully planned and evaluated. The sexual aspect of marriage is only one phase of the married life, and young people lose sight of all the other important aspects. Too often young people marry each other without knowing too much about one another. During the war years this was a common occurrence. Soldiers away from home were lonely, had a casual meeting and married immediately and were sorry later. Prolonged courtship is one way to offset fraud. If a *party fears* that he is being deceived by the party he intends to marry, he should *put this condition into writing or before witnesses;* make this statement on what he expects of the other, or what he does not expect of the other party. Only in such a case would fraud invalidate the marriage. It is a quality of the person which is considered in this error.

ERROR OF LAW

Canon 1084: Simple error regarding the unity, or indissolubility, or sacramental dignity of marriage, even though it is the cause of the contract, does not vitiate matrimonial consent.

Whenever a person makes a civil contract, he is bound by all the obligations contained therein and he cannot be excused

from these because these obligations are much different than what he thought them to be. So too, all the principles and characteristics which constitute marriage *as instituted by God* remain intact and stable regardless what a married person thinks, wishes, or believes them to be. His way of thinking does not change these principles. Errors, mistakes, judgments or private opinions of persons regarding the principles of marriage cannot be given any consideration in judging marriage cases. While ignorance is a lack of knowledge, error is mistaken knowledge or the making of a false judgment.

1. *Concomitant Error*: An error when there is *no real influence on the consent,* that is, the consent would have been given even though the error existed at the time.

2. *Antecedent Error*: An error which has such influence that if the truth had been known, the consent would not have been given. If a person was in such a frame of mind that he would refuse to give consent if the condition had been known, this is called an *interpretative will*. Since it actually did not take place the marriage is valid. The case is such that we consider *not what would have been done, but what actually did take place.*

3. *Simple Error*: Error is simple when it remains in the mind (intellect) without passing over into the will. We have *simple error in the mind* when it exists *there* in a *speculative way* without actually becoming incorporated in the choice made by the will. For example, a person may have a *simple error in the mind* regarding indissolubility, unity, the sacramental character of a marriage; nevertheless, the will wishes to contract a marriage that is valid according to the law of nature. (The speculative factor in the intellect did not pass over into the category of the will). *The actual fact is that the will selected marriage without any conditions or reservations.*

A non-Catholic, wishing to come into the Church as a convert and in order to marry a Catholic, asks for a declaration of nullity on his first marriage because he always *thought* (as all Protestants do) that he could divorce his wife anytime. This is *simply* an *erroneous idea* about the indissolubility of marriage (remaining speculatively in the intellect); this simple error always carries with it the *presumption that one wishes to get married according to God's plan.* Therefore, if this non-Catholic *merely thought* he could get a divorce,[2] or *believed* he could get a divorce, or *wished* he could get a divorce, or *hoped* he could get a divorce, *this simple speculative error remains in the intellect and never passed over into the will.* This marriage is valid. As long as the error remains in the mind (intellect), *no positive act of the will is placed* regarding it. This is also called *theoretical error. A positive act is a fact which must be proved.* It is never presumed!

A Qualified Error: A qualified error is opposed to simple error. When the simple error passes over from the *intellect to the will* and becomes an *intention,* this error is called *qualified error.* Since this *process is invisible,* the party entertaining this *process must make it visible.* This is done by bringing it into the external forum. This is possible and can be done when this same party has the final product—this Qualified Intention *in writing* or *can prove it with the help of witnesses.* If the above mentioned convert can prove[3] that he married with the agreement that the marriage could be dissolved by a civil divorce at the will of either party, the marriage would be considered *invalid.* Here the general notion of divorce which Protestants hold passes from the *intellect* into the *will* to form this *intention.* Strictly speaking, it is not so much the error that causes the invalidity of the mar-

---

2. The same is true if a woman marries a man whom she *believed* or *hoped* to be temperate and after the marriage turns out to be a confirmed alcoholic.

A man marries a woman *thinking* or *believing* she is a virgin, but after the marriage, learns that she is one of loose morals or a prostitute.

3. Proof: In writing or before qualified witness.

riage as the *presence of two conflicting intentions*: *one to contract a real marriage,* the other *to contract a dissoluble marriage* (with the intention of a divorce).

Canon 1085: The knowledge or opinion of the nullity of marriage does not necessarily exclude matrimonial consent.

Here again is a repetition of the former laws stressing the principle that an error concerning one's opinion or belief does not invalidate a marriage contract. This prevails over one's private opinion. For example, John contracts marriage with Anna on June 10, 1950, knowing that he left a wife in Europe; he knows that a diriment impediment exists and this marriage to Anna will be invalid; at the same time he does everything to contract marriage, thus giving matrimonial consent. John learns later that his wife died in Europe on May 30, 1950. Is his marriage to Anna valid despite the fact that he thought he had a diriment impediment? John and Anna are married validly despite the fact of what he *thought*. In any case, the validity or invalidity of the marriage does not depend upon what the parties *believe* or *think* at the time of the marriage, but rather what actually and objectively takes place according to the principles of law.

The intention to contract a real marriage is always presumed unless the contrary is proved. When a Catholic contracts a mixed marriage before a civil magistrate, he generally knows that it is invalid. However, when a *sanatio in radice* is granted, it presupposes that a natural valid consent was given at the time of this marriage, and that this valid consent is still persevering; therefore, there is no need for a renewal of consent. If a mere mock marriage took place, the valid consent would be absent.

INTERNAL CONSENT

Canon 1086: 1. The internal consent of the mind is always presumed to be in agreement to the words or signs used in the celebration of marriage.

2. But if one or other of the parties by a positive

will exclude marriage itself, or all the rights
to the conjugal act, or any essential property
of marriage, *the contract is invalid.*

1. This canon expresses the presumption of law regarding
the existence of the internal consent, when the words expressed
and the signs shown externally, in the celebration of marriage,
take place. This internal consent must exist in the parties at the
same time. If the positive act of the will regarding consent was
excluded, this fact must be proved in the external forum. We
exclude here the simple error of the mind, or an interpretative
will.

2. A positive act of the will which opposes the very nature
of the matrimonial contract, or opposes the essential properties
of marriage, makes the marriage null and void. If the parties
cannot prove this fact in the external forum, the law presumes
this marriage a *valid contract.* In the forum of conscience, it
is not a valid marriage, in which case an ecclesiastical court
could grant a separation. If the case exists whereby they must
live together for some reason, they have an obligation to validate
this marriage by giving their consent. If the lack of consent was
merely *internal* it suffices that the party who did not give the
consent, give this consent *now* by an internal act. If the lack
of consent was shown publicly or outwardly, the consent should
be given in the same way: publicly or outwardly as the case
may be (C. 1136).

3. We may have total simulation (or a fictitious marriage)
if the positive act of the will (the intention) is not to contract
marriage at all. The acts are merely done without giving internal
consent. This could happen if one marries merely to inherit a
property or to gain a high social position, etc.

4. We may have *partial simulation* when one excludes some
of the essential obligations of marriage, for example, one does
not wish to have the conjugal act which is *per se* suitable for
generation of offspring; or excludes the essential properties of
unity and indissolubility. In this case, partial simulation makes

the marriage invalid.

5. Simulation is difficult to prove. The testimony of the interested party taken under oath is not accepted as sufficient proof; neither is the testimony of the two parties accepted as sufficient proof. Conjectures arising from the circumstances may throw some weight on the case itself. If, for example, a man ran off immediately after the marriage ceremony and made a declaration that he never gave his consent to this marriage, we would have a very good and a strong presumption that his consent was simulated. When there is a doubt, the presumption of law is in favor of the validity of the marriage (C. 1014).

6. We may have a matrimonial dilemma. We might have a case in which the parties are *certain* and the confessor is *certain* that this particular marriage is null for lack of consent. But it is impossible to prove it satisfactorily in an ecclesiasatical court. A second marriage is not permitted. Cohabitation might be obligatory, but conjugal relations would be unlawful. Hence, we have a conflict between the internal and external forum.

7. Such a conflict is even worse if a person who simulated consent, later, being free of the first wife, contracts a valid marriage with another party. In the external forum, wife #1 would be his legitimate wife, he would be bound to live with her but could not have marital relations with her. Wife #2, which is his second wife would be his real wife (in the forum of conscience) in the eyes of God, with whom he could have marital relations, and there is no possibility of revalidating the first marriage.

8. Much research has been done on this conflict between the *internal* and the *external* forum. It is a dilemma recognized by canonists and theologians alike. The result of this research will be found in the section on *Second Marriages* entitled "The Good Faith Solution."

SEXUAL ANOMALIES AND MARRIAGE

The history of Canon Law reveals to us that from time to

time we must reflect upon the law and the times in which we live. The recent Ecumenical Council has awakened in us the need of such an examination and reflection. The program of Scripture, Liturgy and Dogma has been accelerated, but Canon Law has not yet been considered in its true perspective. It is a challenge which we must face sooner or later.

One of the items for real study is the problem of sexual anomalies which come to our attention in tribunals and seem to be increasing in number. Canon Law does not consider these personality problems; and the jurisprudence of the Roman Rota, which is usually the guiding factor for canonists and tribunals, has thrown very little light on the subject; in fact, it gives little attention to such problems.

Today we find all kinds of moral delinquents, sexual perverts, psychotics, neurotics, sociopaths, etc. *It is the belief of many psychiatrists and canonists that those individuals afflicted with sexual anomalies should not enter into marriage.* The unfortunte part about these people is that the problem really begins after marriage when the partner is unable or unwilling to accept the responsibility of an indissoluble union. The result is separation and divorce. What is the solution of so many problems today?

Ordinarily these problems are handled under the headings of impotency, insanity, or *ratum non-consummatum* marriages. Most of our difficulties stem from the fact that it is difficult to define adequately the sexual pervert, psychopath, the moral degenerate, the compulsive sexual offender, etc., or to obtain valid evidence. The problem could be approached (1) from the personal incapacity of the person to enter a true marriage with the aid of the psychologist and psychiatrists; (2) and upon the defects of the intellect and will which prevent a person from giving the true consent.

One Catholic psychiatrist [4] gives a clear description of sex-

4. Cavanagh, John, R., M. D., "Sexual Anomalies and the Law"; also *The Catholic Lawyer*, IX, 1963, 4-31.

ual perversions which he considers sexual anomalies: namely voyeurism, exhibitionism, transvestism, fetishism, sadism, masochism, necrophilia, incest, rape, troilism, prostitution, sodomy, bestiality, pedophilia, nymphomania and homosexuality.

It is possible and conceivable that a person with a sexual anomaly which has reached the state of an obsessive, irresistible, compulsive urge would have a personal incapacity whereby he would not be able to elicit a free and deliberate act which is required in matrimonial consent. There is a possibility for a man to have a right understanding of marriage, but because of some defect to be incapable of right action of the will to elicit the act of marriage.[5] In two cases,[6] the Roman Rota has treated of the personal incapacity of the parties to marriage.

Can a marriage be declared null on the basis of homosexuality?

It is interesting to note the opinion of Oesterle [7] who divides homosexuality into *primary* and *secondary* homosexuality: *Primary* is always based on the character of the person, possibly innate, of indigenous cases; *secondary* is considered when the person acquires the anomaly during life, often by seduction. He divides it further into *facultative* and *obligatory* homosexuality: *facultative* refers to bisexual attraction; *obligatory* is such that in relation to persons of the opposite sex the person is absolutely impotent. If the definition of Oesterle is followed regarding the obligatory homosexual, and if proof is given that the party never had any inclination toward the other sex, the nullity of the mar-

---

5. St. Thomas, Summa Theol., I-IIae, q. 77, 2.

6. S. R. R. Dec. XXXIII, Dec. XV, 1941, p. 144.

S. R. R. Dec. XXXIII, Dec. XLIV, 1941, p. 488.

7. Oesterle: Animadver. in Sent. S. R. R. Feb. 23, 1951; *Il Diritto Eccles.*, LXII, 1951, pp. 730-750; "De Relatione Homosexualitatis ad Matrim.," *Revista Espanola de Dir. Canonica*, X, 1955, p. 28. "Voluntas se obligandi et voluntas non adimplendi . . . in ordine ad prolis generationem," *Perfice Munus* XXXIV, 1960, p. 45, "Von der psychischen auf die Ehen," *Oesterreiches Archiv. for Kirchenrechf*, XII, 1961, pp. 305-337.

riage because of impotence might be relatively easy to establish. On the other hand, *facultative homosexuality* could be more easily consummated rendering the marriage indissoluble. In this case the solution of the problem could be had only by separation *a mensa et toro.*

The question whether a marriage can be declared null on account of homosexuality can be answered only as far as we can determine whether the case is one of *obligatory* or *facultative* homosexuality. When the homosexuality is so fixed and ingrained that it becomes obligatory, or if it has become so since childhood, and this can be established by proof, then we would have a practical case of impotence *absoluta et insanabilis.* On February 16, 1940, the Roman Rota gave some practical direc-tives for examining cases of functional impotence when it considered an interesting case regarding a man who had the sexual anomaly of practicing sodomy.[8] Some of the questions suggested by the Roman Rota are: whether a person in question suffered a sickness or a pathological condition, either congenital or acquired; at which age did the vice begin; and from what cause, e.g., from morbid dispositions, from defect of discipline of parents, from a seducer, or from excesses in adolescence? Oesterle wrote extensively on homosexuality and the invalidity of marriage. His works should be consulted for further information on these problems.

Oesterle is of the opinion that the marriage with a homosexual can be annulled on three grounds: (1) *exclusio matrimonii ipsius*: lack of an intention to enter a true marriage; (2) *exclusio fidelitatis;* (3) *exclusio iuris ad coniugalem actum.* He attempts to prove the nullity of a marriage on homosexual grounds by emphasizing that homosexuality is in its essence incompatible with marriage; due to the lack of will power to break away from such a habit, which as a result, good faith is lacking at the time of marriage.

8. S. R. R. Dec. XXXII, 1940, Dec. XV, pp. 141-154.

Arguments that Homosexuality is Incompatible with Marriage

1. When considering Canons 1081 and 1086, the homosexual could not have the proper intention and the will to enter a true marriage due to the fact that under the outward appearance of marriage he retains the desire to continue his homosexual relations.

2. In considering the same Canons (1081-1086), the homosexual proposes to commit sins against matrimonial fidelity, and these propositions can be substantiated by the gathering of evidence *before and after* the said marriage.

3. Moreover, in virtue of Canon 1081, the true matrimonial consent is not given in the sense that the man and woman reciprocally hand over and receive the perpetual and exclusive right to each other (*ius in corpus*).

According to Canon 1086, any person who externally manifests consent but inwardly does not invoke the corresponding act of the will would simulate consent, since the contract of marriage requires four elements: (1) the intention to make a true contract, (2) the intention to bind oneself to the matrimonial contract, (3) the physical and moral capacity to bind oneself, and (4) to fulfill the obligations that are undertaken. *How then could a homosexual physically and morally be able to make a contract binding him to the object of the contract?* We are certain that a person cannot enter into a valid contract who cannot dispose freely of the object of the same contract. Moreover this must be an object which is both physically and morally possible. Since we know that no one is obliged to the impossible, nor is he able to oblige himself to it; therefore, we can state that for these reasons the marriage of a homosexual is invalid: (1) the homosexual is incapable of restraining himself from homosexual relationships; (2) the homosexual does not permit the exclusive right to marital intercourse, and often excludes it entirely. Thus, we can conclude that homosexuality is incompatible with marriage.[9]

9. *The Jurist*, Vol. XXIII, Oct. 1963, pp. 394-422.

Neither the Code nor the Roman Rota has given us any solution to this present day problem. To cope with this situation, it will be necessary for us to (1) consider the present day study and systems of modern psychology and psychiatry; (2) to get an adequate definition of the homosexual, sadist, etc.; (3) to study the concept of error and fraud which are related to such sexual anomalies and marriage; (4) to define the concept of the constitutionally immoral, the sexual psychopathic, etc., and their inability to fulfill the obligations of marriage; (5) to establish that heterosexuality is a condition of a valid marriage; and (6) to establish homosexuality and other sexual anomalies as diriment impediments of marriage. It is the hope of the canonists that the revision of the Code of Canon Law, now under consideration, will give serious thought to such problems.

In 1964, a Canadian Tribunal submitted a marriage case on homosexuality (Lesbianism) which set a precedent. In this particular case, consent was given according to the prescriptions of the Code and as such, this marriage would be considered valid, but, two psychiatrists out of three offered their expert opinion, not on canonical principles but solely on psychological grounds and the Roman Rota granted a nullity in this case.

Traditional jurisprudence of the S. R. Rota has always (until recently) sought the source of nullity in the contractant's mental inability to elicit sufficient consent during the wedding ceremony. This is not the case here; the woman did elicit sufficient consent but did not have what they called the *facultas discretiva* or discretionary power. This discretionary power is not whether one is able to know (*cognoscere*) the obligations, but, *whether one has the necessary power or aptitude to undertake (suscipere) these obligations.* Hence, this woman was fully aware of the obligations and did give the proper consent according to the Code but she did not have the power or aptitude to undertake the obligations of a true married life. Therefore the marriage was declared null.

FORCE AND FEAR

Canon 1087: 1. Likewise is invalid a marriage entered into through FORCE or grave FEAR which was unjustly exercised by an external agent such that in order to escape from it a party was compelled to choose marriage.

2. No other fear, even though it be the cause of the contract, entails the nullity of marriage.

1. Force and fear are correlative terms. *Force* is the physical impulse from an external agent which cannot be overcome, as for example, when an unjust moral force with blows or threats is used. *Fear* is the trepidation of the mind because of an impending evil.

2. *Absolutely grave fear* is such that will overcome the mind and will of a normal firm and steadfast person because of a grave injury or loss he or she would suffer. For example, the loss of life or limb, fortune, liberty or reputation from an external agent. (*Internal fear* - such as one's own imagination, would be ruled out in this case).

3. *Relative grave fear* is such that will overcome the mind and will of certain individuals according to their capacity. *Reverential fear* would be one of these. For example, the fear of being ejected from the parental home; the fear of offending one's parents or one's superiors; for certain over-sensitive people, this could amount to grave fear.

4. *Fear must be unjustly inflicted from an external agent.* Natural causes are excluded. We have this fear when human justice is violated in forcing a certain marriage. If, for example, a young man is threatened with his life or with bodily harm, and he has no way of escaping except through marriage, his marriage would be considered null. Threat of a seducer with imprisonment or marriage could not be considered as unjustly inflicted. This is a *just penalty*, but a better alternative would be

to impose a fine or demand support of the child. *A principle one should use in evaluating force and fear cases is to judge whether there was any other alternative than marriage.*

5. It is questionable whether force and fear is an impediment of the natural or of ecclesiastical law. We have various opinions in this matter.[10]

Canon 1088: 1. In order that marriage be contracted validly it is necessary that the contracting parties be present either in person or by proxy.

2. The parties must express matrimonial consent in words, and they may not use equivalent signs if they are able to speak.

This canon applies to both Catholics as well as non-Catholics who are baptized. Before the Council of Trent, it was possible to contract marriage by means of a letter. After the Council of Trent, authors disputed whether this was possible for a valid marriage. We have proof of this even as late as 1910, in which the Roman Rota upheld the validity of such a marriage. The man gave his consent to marriage by letter which he sent to the girl. The girl went to her pastor with a witness and expressed her consent there. The marriage took place in 1900.[11] The Code ruled out this form of marriage; although it states explicitly that marriage can be contracted through a proxy.

PROXY MARRIAGE

Canon 1089: 1. Without prejudice to the statutes of the diocese, which may be imposed in addition hereto, in order that marriage may be contracted by proxy, a special mandate is required to contract it with a certain person, which man-

10. Woywood, Commentary, p. 750.
11. AAS II, pp. 297-309.

date must be signed by the principal and by either the ordinary of the place, the pastor where the mandate is given, or by a priest delegated by either of these, or by at least two witnesses.

2. If the principal cannot write, this fact must be indicated in the mandate itself and another witness must be added who shall himself also sign the document; otherwise, this mandate is invalid.

3. If the principal who gave the mandate should have revoked it, or he became insane before the proxy contracted the marriage in the principal's name, this marriage would be invalid, even though the proxy or the party to the marriage knew nothing about this revocation.

4. In order that the marriage be valid, the proxy must fulfill this office in person.[12]

According to Clark,[13] proxy marriages are not recognized in the United States. However, we have an unusual case in which Federal Judge Lowell of Boston, Mass., upheld the validity of a marriage contracted in this way. This case happened in 1924 in

12. Proxy Marriage:
    (1) Most authors agree that the principal party of proxy marriage cannot authorize a proxy to substitute another proxy for himself.
    (2) One must make out a special mandate for a proxy marriage; it is not proper to give a general mandate to place all the legal acts of the proxy marriage.
    (3) The mandate must indicate the specific person that will marry by proxy. It would be unlawful to give the proxy a mandate to choose a partner and marry her for him (by proxy).
    (4) The date and name of the place should be indicated where the proxy marriage is to take place.
13. Clark, *Contracts*, p. 381.

which a United States citizen went to the Portuguese Consulate in Philadelphia and obtained a certificate whereby he contracted marriage by proxy to a person in Portugal.

Canon 1090: Marriage can also be contracted through an interpreter. [All things being equal, if the pastor is satisfied with all the other preliminaries, he may go ahead with the marriage; but if there is time he should consult the ordinary.]

Canon 1091: The pastor must not assist at a marriage which is to be contracted by proxy or through an interpreter, unless there is a just cause and there is no doubt regarding the authenticity of the mandate and the veracity of the interpreter, and if there is time, he must have the permission of the ordinary.

CONDITIONAL MARRIAGE CONSENT

Canon 1092: When a condition is attached to the marriage contract and not withdrawn before the marriage, the following rules govern the case: A condition once placed and not revoked:

(1) If it is a condition concerning a *future* event which is *necessary,* or *impossible,* or *immoral,* but not contrary to the substance of marriage, it is to be considered as not having been made.

(2) If it concerns the *future* and *is contrary to the substance of marriage,* it renders the marriage invalid.

(3) If it concerns the *future and is licit,* it suspends the validity of the marriage.

(4) If it concerns the past or the present, the

marriage will be valid or not, according as
the matter concerning which the condition
is made, exists or not.

1. We usually do not meet marriages based on conditions.[14]
In most cases, conditional marriages remain a secret, because
it is unlawful to have a condition. If it was made before the marriage *in writing or before two witnesses* whereby it can be proven
in the external forum, the marriage would remain valid until the
contrary proof is obtained by the ecclesiastical authorities.

2. If the pastor discovers that a condition was placed, he
must warn the parties not to cohabit. The pastor should investigate the case and act prudently in the matter in order to avoid
any scandal. Sometimes the Church permits a marriage to be
contracted conditionally for grave reasons.

3. A condition is some circumstance which is attached to
the consent and upon which the contract of marriage depends.
We must distinguish between a *cause* and a *condition* of marriage. A woman marries a man because she *believes or thinks*
that he is a millionaire. Here we have no condition; it is a *cause*.
This is merely an error and the contract would be valid despite
the fact that she *would not have married* had she known the
true facts that he was not a millionaire (*error dans causam con-
tractui*).

I. Illustrations of Future Conditions

1. Those not contrary to the substance of marriage:
     (1) *Necessary Future Conditions*: "I marry you now on
          condition that the sun rises tomorrow." If this is a
          serious statement, the marriage is valid only on that
          condition. If the sun did not rise, it would be invalid.
          People usually do not make such conditions seriously.
     (2) *Impossible Future Conditions*: "I marry you on con-

14. In the year 1930, the Roman Rota received **thirteen such cases;**
it accepted one and rejected the rest. AAS XXIII, 1931.

dition that you learn the Russian language within a week."

(3) *Immoral Future Conditions*: "I marry you on condition that you have an abortion; or on condition that you kill your father." The marriage would be valid only when this condition is fulfilled.

(4) *Licit Future Conditions*: "I marry you only on condition that you pass your Ph.D. examination." The marriage is valid when this condition is fulfilled.

2. Those contrary to the substance of marriage:

(1) "I marry you now on condition that you agree like all non-Catholics, that I can divorce you any time during the marriage." "I marry you now on condition that I could live with other women."
Note: *If the parties agree to practice birth control, this may be gravely sinful, but it does not invalidate the marriage.*

II. Illustrations of Past Conditions:

(1) "I marry you now on condition that you have had a hysterectomy or vasectomy." If this is not true, the marriage would be invalid.

III. Illustration of a Present Condition:

(1) "I marry you on condition that you are wealthy." If the party is not, the marriage is invalid.

All these cases are true on condition that these statements are made seriously. Furthermore, to prove that such conditions were made, proof must be given of this in *writing* (*tempore non suspecto*), or *before two witnesses;* otherwise, such conditions would be valid only in the internal forum (forum of conscience).

Canon 1093: Even though a marriage had been contracted in-

validly because of an impediment, the consent
which has been given is presumed to persevere
until its revocation shall have been proved.

It is argued among authors whether marriage consent could
be present if only one of the parties knew of a diriment impediment, and thus knew that a valid marriage could not be contracted. They here declare that the marriage consent is here
presumed to exist in such a case.

INSANITY

Insanity cases seem to be increasing more and more in our
generation as shown statistically in our marriage tribunals. Why
this is so, is difficult to say. It is generally known that there are
more people in mental institutions than there are students in all
our colleges and universities in the United States. The study of
mental illness among the insane belongs to the field of medicine,
but it also becomes an object of study for ecclesiastical and civil
lawyers because of the great influence it has upon *the ability of
persons in this state in placing legal acts.* Mental illness is such
that it can diminish or even totally destroy a person's capacity
for legal acts, and as such, it can disqualify him for marriage.[15]

Insanity is an obstacle to making a valid contract of marriage because the mental defect deprives one of the *use of reason*
and therefore, renders one incapable of acquiring knowledge.
It is the act of the will that constitutes consent, and one cannot
will what he does not know. Moreover, a person, *who enjoys the
use of reason,* would be incapable of proper consent to marriage,
due to his mental condition, because he could not realize the substance of the marriage contract. The use of reason was the norm
used by the Roman Rota in former times due to the insecure
nature of psychiatry and psychology; but due to the growing

15. Van Ommeren, *Mental Illness Affecting Matrimonial Consents,*
CUA, 1961, p. 45.

refinement of both psychiatry and ecclesiastical jurisprudence we find that *"usus rationis non sufficit."* [16]

The investigation and scrutiny of insanity in matrimonial cases strictly speaking belongs to the experts in the matrimonial tribunals who gather their information from professional psychiatrists and other medical experts. However, every pastor or marriage counselor should be acquainted with some of the basic principles which surround these difficult cases of mental illnesses. There are some very good articles written in recent years on this subject.[17]

The Code of Canon Law contains no *explicit* substantive law regarding cases of insanity (*Amentia* - as it is called by the Rota). Canons 1081 and 1082,[18] however, contain *implicitly* the substantive law under which insanity cases are considered. These canons merely restate the natural law which is our source for an invalid marriage, due to insanity. Canon 1082 [19] states the need of using experts (psychologist and psychiatrist) in the adjudication of insanity cases. Articles of *Provida Mater Ecclesia*,[20] and the Allocution of Pope Pius XII recommended the

16. S. R. R. Dec. XXVI, 1934, p. 709.

17. *The Jurist*, Vols. XVI, 3, July, 1956; XX, 3, July, 1960; XXII, October 4, 1962. Bulletin of the Guild of Catholic Psychiatrists, Vol. VII, April, 1960: the following four articles:

1. Kubitschek, M. D., "Psychopathic Personality and Annulment," pp. 83-85.
2. Rt. Rev. John Hayes, "Mental Disease and the Ecclesiastical Courts," pp. 76-83.
3. J. W. Higgins, M.D., "Schizophrenia as a Consideration in Annulment of Marriage," pp. 87-96.
4. John R. Cavanagh, M.D., "Homosexuality as an Impediment to Marriage," pp. 96-110.

5. John R. Keating, "Marriage of the Psychopathic Personality," *Chicago Studies*, 1963.

6. Cuschieri, O.F.M., "Paranoia — Partial or Integral Insanity," *The Jurist*, IV, 69.

7. Rev. John Keating, "Marriage Nullity Trials," *Studia Canonicum*, Vol. IV, 1, 1970.

8. Lawrence G. Wrenn, "Annulments," Canon Law Society of America, 1970.

use of these experts. *At present the best source for processing and adjudicating insanity cases is to study the decisions of the Sacred Roman Rota.* Here we learn how to use and evaluate the opinions of the experts. *Since the latest decisions contain the best opinions, we should go to this source.*

Another common source of evaluating such cases, coming from the classical passage on insanity as invalidating marriage, is probably that of Cardinal Gasparri which is here summarized and which might be called the standard of canonical norm in treating insanity as it affects the validity of marriage:

Insane persons are divided into (a) *amentes* (furiosi), if the insanity deals with all things; or they are (b) *dementes* (monomaniacs) if the insanity pertains to one or other particular area.

A person who is *amens*, one whose insanity extends to all things, is incapable of contracting marriage (doctrine expressed in the Decretals)[21] and this *incapacity pertains to all types of contracts*, as well as to *every human act because the use of reason does not exist.*

It is the opinion of many authors, that marriage contracted during a lucid interval, would be valid; but generally speaking this marriage would be illicit due to the fact that this

18. Canon 1081: 1. Matrimony is effected by the consent of the parties legitimately expressed between persons capable according to law; which consent no human power can supply. 2. Matrimonial consent is *an act of the will* by which *each party gives and accepts a perpetual and exclusive right over the body,* for acts which are of themselves suitable for the generation of children.

19. In order that matrimonial consent may be possible it is necessary that the contracting parties be at least not ignorant that marriage is a permanent society between man and woman for the procreation of children.

20. Instruction, *Provida Mater Ecclesia*, August 15, 1936, AAS XXVIII, pp. 312-370.

21. Decretals, c. 24, X, De sponsalibus et matrimoniis, IV, 1.

insane person is incapable of educating the offspring of such a marriage.

Medical experts believe that an insane person (one insane from infancy) is not responsible (sui compos) even during lucid intervals, because during these intervals there remains a *certain latent insanity*. It is for these same reasons the civil law does not punish the insane for crimes committed, neither do they recognize any contracts which they have made during this interval. For this reason also the marriage is considered as doubtfully valid entered in during a lucid interval, and the defect of consent is presumed until the contrary is proved.

The circumstances of each case must be carefully weighed; if the interval of this lucidity is of long duration, the validity of the consent is upheld; otherwise, the decision should be for the nullity of the marriage.

However, if the insanity was of a temporary nature, and the medical experts concur that the person is cured, a marriage contracted either before or after this temporary insanity, is considered valid.

Insanity is not listed among diriment impediments to marriage (C. 1067-1080), nor among the defects of consent (C. 1081-93), except that which is found in Canon 1089: 3, regarding a proxy marriage when insanity has intervened. Undoubtedly, the codifiers considered insanity as a diriment impediment on a much broader scale, as seen implicitly in Canon 88: 2, and explicitly in Canon 1982.

If insanity (habitual mental disease) is considered as a diriment impediment, the natural integrity of the act of marital consent would not be the real criterion of a valid marriage. Here we concentrate not on *matrimonium in fieri* (*act of celebration*) but upon *matrimonium in facto esse* (*state of matrimony*). The person's mental state will be the cause of nullity, not necessarily because it incapacitates the act of consent during the actual wedding ceremony, but because it renders the person fundamentally unfit for the *state of matrimony*. He may have been able to give naturally sufficient consent during the ceremony, *but considering his natural disability*, was he an apt subject for (*matrimonium in facto esse*) the state of matrimony if, considering the peculiar nature of this mental disease, or given a true lucid interval, the person *could* and *did* elicit an integral *act of consent* capable of making a contract, but this naturally sufficient consent was inefficacious because this disability would prevent an effective exchange of the rights and obligations which are so important to marriage? Just as an *incurable impotent man*, who consents with a clear mind and with full deliberation, cannot contract a valid marriage because *he is incapable of giving an essential right and incapable to assume an essential obligation*, so too, *regarding the insane person*, who consciously, and with a clear mind and full deliberation gives consent, is naturally incapable of giving the essential right and assuming the essential obligations of marriage. For example, the sexual psychopath who is afflicted by a grave and incurable nymphomania may well know the substance and obligations of marriage and yet, may be incapable of contracting a marriage; the person is *psychically incapable* of assuming a perpetual obligation because he compulsively needs one consort after another; or he is *psychically incapable of an exclusive obligation*, because of the irresistible urge to indulge in extramarital affairs.

When we consider the distinction between *ius* and *usus iuris*, there might be an objection that this person can grant the right and assume the obligation, but on the other hand, propose not to observe their fulfillment, or, at least, he would know he will not fulfill them. As in the case, however, of the *incurably* impotent (of whom the same objection could be made), the response is that to grant a right or assume an obligation the person must enjoy liberty regarding the object of this right and obligation. The axiom *nemo potest ad impossibilia obligari* is equally applicable to the status of matrimony of the physically impotent and the psychically incompetent.

In nullity cases, juridically speaking, *amentia* would be likened to the diriment impediments, and especially to that of impotence which is governed by the natural law. The claim for nullity would be based upon a defect of personal capacity, sanctioned by an inhabilitating law of the natural law. The marriage would be null because the person would not be *iure habilis*.

The three main presumptions used in insanity cases are:

(a) *In dubium standum est pro valore matrimonii.*
(b) All men are sane unless the contrary is proved.
(c) When insanity is proved to have existed before and after a certain time, the presumption is that it existed during the interval. Of course, this presumption must be supported by other circumstances and evidence.

We have very few decisions from the Roman Rota on Insanity cases. Between 1937-1946, only twenty-two cases were decided. In the year 1943, only four cases were tried. Authors wonder why so few insanity cases reach the Roman Rota. The answer probably is that diocesan tribunals simply do not feel prepared to cope with the situation. Canonists and psychiatrists must try together to solve this important matter.

CHAPTER VII

FORM OF MARRIAGE

HISTORICAL SUMMARY

Canon 1094: Only those marriages are valid which are contracted before the pastor or the ordinary of the place, or a priest delegated by either of these, and at least two witnesses, but according to the regulations of the following canons, and with the exceptions mentioned in Canons 1098 and 1099.

As mentioned elsewhere, whenever two people (man and woman) contract a marriage without any formality and without any witnesses (clandestine marriage) but they mutually express their matrimonial consent externally, such a marriage is valid according to the natural law. In the early days of the Church, there were no general laws requiring that a marriage be celebrated before an authorized priest for validity, although the Church Fathers did forbid secret marriages and were insistent upon having all marriages contracted *publicly* and in *church.*

1. *Council of Trent* (1545-1563): This Council specified the form of marriage which is contained in the *Tametsi* decree. It stated that all marriages were invalid unless they were contracted before one's own pastor, or another priest delegated by the pastor or local ordinary *and* at least two witnesses.

Before the Council of Trent marriages contracted without a priest present were valid but illicit. After the Council of Trent, marriages contracted without a priest present were invalid where the *Tametsi* decree was published.[1] In the places where the decree was not promulgated, the marriage was valid even without the priest but this marriage was illicit. All baptized persons, including heretics, who were married in the place where the decree was published were bound by this form. Therefore, heretics marrying in such a place married invalidly. The pastor of the domicile or quasi-domicile of the parties to be married had *personal jurisdiction* over them whereby he was able to assist *validly* at any marriage of his subjects *anywhere*. (Today it is territorial, except in the case of danger of death C. 1044). The pastor also was able to delegate this same power to any other priest to assist at a marriage of his subjects anywhere.

2. *The Benedictine Declaration* (1741): Due to the fact that the *Tametsi* decree caused some hardship upon heretics marrying among themselves or with Catholics, Benedict XIV modified the *Tametsi* decree, exempting heretics from this legislation. *In the United States of America* the *Tametsi* decree or the *Benedictine Declaration* was in force only in places where it was published. A baptized person (Protestant or Catholic) who married a non-baptized person without a dispensation of disparity of cult married *invalidly*. (This was followed until 1918.)

3. *Ne Temere* (1908): In 1908 a new decree of Pius X, the *Ne Temere*, was published everywhere and bound every Catholic everywhere. Heretics were excluded unless they wished to marry a Catholic. The *Ne Temere* was incorporated into the New Code of Canon Law in 1918.

The Church claims the right of power to prescribe the form

1. Published in the Provinces of New Orleans, San Francisco, parts of Utah, Vincennes (Indiana) and St. Louis. It was not promulgated in the rest of the USA. Hence, a marriage contracted in the USA before 1908 in any other place without a priest—such a marriage was *valid*.

of marriage. According to Canon 1016, here the power extends to the entire contract which is subject to the natural and the divine law, leaving to the State the right of power over the civil effects alone.

Oriental Law: The form of marriage is precisely the same for the Oriental Church, with the exception that the marriage must be contracted with the so-called sacred rite, namely the *blessing of the priest*. Although this sacred rite is not a certain liturgical rite, but a simple blessing, nevertheless this blessing is required for *validity*.

PASTORS: Pastors mentioned in this canon include all clerics mentioned in Canons 451: 1; 216: 3; 451: 2; 1° and 2°. Canon 1095: 1, 1° must be observed regarding the canonical possession of a parish and the territorial limits.

WITNESSES: This canon mentions that *two witnesses must be present physically and morally (simultaneously) with the priest* and capable of giving testimony that a marriage was performed.

4. *Matrimonia Mixta* (March 31, 1970): This is a new legislation regarding mixed marriages. (Cf. Appendix and section on mixed marriage.)

ORIENTALS

The Form of Marriage in relation to *Ne Temere* and Orientals in the United States:

The Sacred Congregation of the Council, on March 28, 1908, stated that Orientals were only obliged to the decree *Ne Temere* when they married Latin Catholics. Generally speaking (with one exception) up to May 2, 1949, Oriental Catholics *marrying among themselves,* outside of their own Patriarchate, or an *Oriental marrying a non-Catholic,* were not held to the form of marriage (except Disparity of Cult cases).

The exception mentioned above refers to the Orientals (Ruthenians) of the Byzantine Rite who were bound to the form of marriage prescribed by the *Ne Temere* decree, not from 1908, but rather from August 17, 1914, when Bishop Ortynsky made a request of the Holy See that, for the sake of uniformity of discipline, the decree *Ne Temere* should be extended to all Uniate Greek Ruthenians in the United States (Decretum, *Cum Episcopo*, AAS, VI, 1914, 458-463). From this time on Orientals (Greek Ruthenians) were bound to contract marriage under the pain of nullity before a pastor or their ordinary or delegated priest and two witnesses as called for by the decree *Ne Temere*. This canonical form obliged those Ruthenians when they married among themselves and when they married with other Orientals who were heretics or schismatics. The Decree of 1914 refers only to the United States. Ruthenians of other countries became obligated to the *Ne Temere* at different times.[2]

A New Marriage Form for the Orientals

The II Vatican Council promulgated this new form on November 21, 1964; it went into effect in the United States on January 21, 1965.[3] This new marriage form is found in Article 18 of *Orientalium Ecclesiarum*, the Decree on the Eastern Catholic Churches of Vatican II. Article 18 states the following:

"To obviate invalid marriages when Eastern Catholics marry baptized Eastern non-Catholics, and in order to promote the stability and the sanctity of marriage, as well as domestic peace, the Sacred Council determines that the canonical form for the celebration of these marriages obliges only for liceity; for their validity the presence of a sacred minister is sufficient, provided the other prescriptions of law are observed."[4]

2. Cf. Pospishil, *Law on Marriage*, pp. 185-187, should such information be required, on the latter. / Marbach, F. Josepf, J.C.D., *Marriage Legislation for Catholics of the Oriental Rites in the U.S. and Canada*, Catholic Univ. Press, Washington, D.C.

3. Cardinal Joseph Slipy, the Byzantine Archbishop of Lwiw in the Ukraine who possesses quasi-patriarchal power and jurisdiction declared that the Decree would begin its legal force at a later date, namely April 7, 1965, due, probably, to the difficulties existing behind the Iron Curtain.

4. The translation of the text is taken from the Decree of the unofficial translation of the NCWC.

The introduction of this new marriage form for Orientals affects the validity of a marriage, therefore it is very important that the date (January 21, 1965) be kept in mind when dealing with cases involving *a Byzantine Catholic and a baptized non-Catholic of an Eastern rite*. Chancery and tribunal officials must keep this new legislation in mind when dealing with cases involving individuals of this category.

Liceity: The liceity of such marriages remains in effect as found in the former law (*Crebrae Allatae* - May 2, 1949) whereby censures and other penalties are incurred if the regular prescriptions of the law are not observed. Neither can ordinaries dispense from this marriage form whereby they would grant permission for a Catholic to contract marriage *solely* or *first* before a non-Catholic minister (*communicatio in sacris*). It must be noted that Pospishil gives his opinion and makes a fine distinction when he states that although *communicatio in sacris* is forbidden, nevertheless, after such a couple has exchanged the marriage vows before a Catholic priest, thereby becoming recipients of the sacrament of matrimony, the rites performed in the Eastern dissident church cannot lead to a sacrament; therefore this is an extra-sacramental *communicatio in sacris*, which is permissible according to the above mentioned principle.

A New Marriage Form for the Latin Church

The Decree *Orientalium Ecclesiarum*, Art. 18, was promulgated only for the Orientals, but the Latin bishops requested the same privilege for their subjects. It was granted three years later and went into effect March 25, 1967. Therefore this date is important because all marriages between a Latin Catholic and an Orthodox person in the Orthodox Church, *with* or *without* the Latin Ordinary's permission, is considered valid. The marriage would be considered only illicit if no permission was granted.[5]

5. Decree issued Feb. 28, 1967. — Cf. Appendix.

ORIENTALS

Before August 17, 1914:

1. Marriages Between two Oriental Catholics — VALID
2. Marriage between One Oriental Catholic and Orthodox — VALID
3. Marriage between One Oriental Catholic and Baptized Protestant — VALID
4. Marriage between One Oriental Catholic and Non-Baptized Protestant, Disparity of Cult (D.C.) — INVALID

August 17, 1914 to May 2, 1949:

1. Marriage between Two Oriental Catholics (One is of the Byzantine rite) — INVALID (DF)
2. Marriage between One Oriental Catholic (not of Byzantine rite) and Orthodox — VALID
3. Marriage between One Oriental Catholic (not of Byzantine rite) & (Baptized) Protestant — VALID
4. Marriage between One Oriental Catholic (not of Byzantine rite) & non-baptized person — INVALID
5. Marriage between Oriental Catholic and Orthodox — INVALID(DF)
6. Marriage between Oriental Catholic and Baptized Protestant — INVALID (DF)
7. Marriage between Oriental Catholic and non-baptized person — INVALID (DF)
8. Marriage between Two Orthodox — VALID
9. Marriage between One Orthodox and Baptized Protestant — VALID
10. Marriage between Orthodox and non-baptized person — INVALID (DF)

From May 2, 1949:

1. Marriage between Two Oriental Catholics — INVALID (DF)

2. Marriage between One Oriental Catholic and
   Orthodox   INVALID (DF)
3. Marriage between Oriental Catholic and bap-
   tized Protestant   INVALID (DF)
4. Marriage between Oriental Catholic and non-
   baptized person   INVALID (DC)
5. Marriage between Two Orthodox   VALID
6. Marriage between an Orthodox and baptized
   Protestant   VALID
7. Marriage between Orthodox and non-baptized
   person   INVALID (DC)

From January 21, 1965:

Marriage between One Oriental Catholic and
Orthodox   VALID

Marriage between One Latin and One Orthodox   VALID

When reference is made to Oriental Catholics above, this refers specifically to the Greek Ruthenians of the Byzantine Rite. We have six territories: Two Archeparchies (Archdioceses) and Four Eparchies (Dioceses): Archeparchy of Philadelphia, and Archeparchy of Munhall (Pittsburgh), Eparchies of Stamford, Conn.; Passaic, New Jersey; Parma, Ohio; Chicago, Illinois. According to the Catholic Directory of 1972, we have a total of over 600,000 Catholic faithful listed among these five dioceses. It is needless to say how important these facts of the validity or invalidity of marriage mentioned above since we have over a half million Byzantine Catholics in the United States. With people moving from place to place now adays, we will have more and more inter-ritual marriages and it is of utmost importance that all priests, especially pastors, should be prepared to meet these situations.

ORIENTAL RITE CATHOLICS IN THE UNITED STATES

The following Eastern Rite Catholics come under the jurisdiction of the Latin Ordinaries of the United States since they have no hierarchy of their own in the United States, except as noted below.

ARMENIAN

Our Lady Queen of Martyrs Church, Los Angeles, California
Holy Cross Church, Cambridge, Massachusetts
St. Vartan Church, Detroit, Michigan
Sacred Heart Church, Paterson, New Jersey
Our Lady of Loretto Church, New York, New York
St. Mark's Church, Philadelphia, Pennsylvania

BYELO-RUSSIAN

Christ the Redeemer Church, Chicago, Illinois

CHALDEAN

St. Addai's Church, Turlock, California
St. Ephrem's Church, Chicago, Illinois
Mother of God Church, Detroit, Michigan

MELKITE - Exarchate of Boston; Established, March 1966.

St. George's Church, Birmingham, Alabama
St. Ann's Church, Los Angeles, California
St. Mary's Church, Trinidad, Colorado
St. Ann's Church, Danbury, Connecticut
St. Ann's Church, New London, Connecticut
St. John Chrysostom's Church, Atlanta, Georgia
St. John the Baptist Church, Chicago, Illinois
The Annunciation Church, Boston, Massachusetts
St. Joseph's Church, Lawrence, Massachusetts
St. Basil's Seminary, Methuen, Massachusetts
Our Lady of Perpetual Help Church, Worcester Massachusetts
Our Lady of Redemption Church, Detroit, Michigan

Our Lady of Cedars Church, Manchester, New Hampshire
St. Ann's Church, Paterson, New Jersey
Virgin Mary Church, Brooklyn, New York
St. Nicholas Church, Rochester, New York
St. Basil's Church, Utica, New York
St. Joseph's Church, Akron, Ohio
St. Elias' Church, Cleveland, Ohio
St. Joseph's Church, Scranton, Pennsylvania
Our Lady of Mercy Church, Shenandoah, Pennsylvania
St. Basil's Church, Central Falls, Rhode Island
St. Elias' Church, Woonsocket, Rhode Island
St. George's Church, Milwaukee, Wisconsin

ROMANIAN

St. Michael's Church, Aurora, Illinois
St. Demetrius' Church, East Chicago, Illinois
St. Nicholas' Church, East Chicago, Illinois
St. Mary's Church, Dearborn, Michigan
St. John the Baptist Church, Detroit, Michigan
St. Mary's Church, Roebling, New Jersey
St. Basil's Church, Trenton, New Jersey
St. Theodore's Church, Alliance, Ohio
St. George's Church, Canton, Ohio
St. Helena's Church, Cleveland, Ohio
St. Basil's Church, Lorain, Ohio
Most Holy Trinity Church, Cleveland, Ohio
St. Mary's Church, Youngstown, Ohio
St. George's Church, Erie, Pennsylvania
St. John's Church, Farrell, Pennsylvania
St. Mary's Church, McKeesport, Pennsylvania

RUSSIAN

St. Andrew's Church, El Segundo, California
Our Lady of Fatima Church, San Francisco, California
Our Lady of Kazan Church, Boston, Massachusetts
St. Michael's Chapel, New York, New York

MARONITE - Exarchate of Detroit; Established, March 1966.

St Elias' Church, Birmingham, Alabama
Our Lady of Mt. Lebanon Church, Los Angeles, California
St. Anthony's Church, Danbury, Connecticut
St. Maron's Church, Torrington, Connecticut
Our Lady of Lebanon Seminary, Washington, Distr. of Col.
St. Joseph's Church, Atlanta, Georgia
Our Lady of Lebanon Church, Chicago, Illinois
Sacred Heart Church, Michigan City, Indiana
St. Joseph's Church, Waterville, Maine
Our Lady of Cedars Church, Boston, Massachusetts
St. Theresa's Church, Brockton, Massachusetts
St. Anthony's Church, Fall River, Massachusetts
St. Anthony's Church, Lawrence, Massachusetts
Our Lady of Purgatory Church, New Bedford, Massachusetts
St. Anthony's Church, Springfield, Massachusetts
Our Lady of Mercy Church, Worcester, Massachusetts
St. Maron's Church, Detroit, Michigan
St. Maron's Church, Minneapolis, Minnesota
Holy Family Church, St. Paul, Minnesota
St. Raymond's Church, St. Louis Missouri
St. George's Church, Dover, New Hampshire
Our Lady of Lebanon Church, Brooklyn, New York
St. Joseph's Church, New York, New York
Our Lady of Lebanon Church, Niagara Falls, New York
St. Joseph's Church, Olean, New York
St. Ann's Church, Troy, New York
St. Louis Gonzaga Church, Utica, New York
St. Maron's Church, Williamsville, New York
Our Lady of Cedars Church, Akron, Ohio
St. Anthony's Church, Cincinnati, Ohio
St. Maron's Church, Cleveland, Ohio
St. Maron's Church, Youngstown, Ohio
Our Lady of Lebanon Church, Easton, Pennsylvania
St. John's Church, New Castle, Pennsylvania
St. Maron's Church, Philadelphia, Pennsylvania
Our Lady of Victory Church, Pittsburg, Pennsylvania
St. Ann's Church, Scranton, Pennsylvania

St. George's Church, Uniontown, Pennsylvania
St. Anthony's Church, Wilkes-Barre, Pennsylvania
St. George's Church, Wilkes-Barre, Pennsylvania
St. George's Church, Providence, Rhode Island
St. George's Church, San Antonio, Texas
St. Anthony's Church, Richmond, Virginia
St. Elias' Church, Roanoke, Virginia
Our Lady of Lebanon Church, Wheeling, West Virginia

ORIENTAL LAW FOR MARONITES

Pope Paul VI, on January 10, 1966, erected the Apostolic Exarchate for the faithful of the Antiochene Rite of the Maronites in the United States. The seat of the exarchate is Detroit, Michigan. This exarchate is *ad instar* a suffragan of the Metropolitan See of Detroit, and the jurisdiction of the Exarch over the Maronites is not exclusive but is rather cumulative with the jurisdiction of the local Ordinaries; these latter, however, are to use their jurisdiction only in a secondary way. In places where the Maronites are without a parish or priest of their own rite, the Latin rite clergy shall assume their care until such time as they receive a priest of their own rite or a priest specially designated for them.[6]

VALID ASSISTANCE AT MARRIAGE

Canon 1095: 1. The Pastor and Local Ordinary Validly Assist at Marriage:

1° Only from the day on which they took canonical possession of their benefice according to Canons 334, §3 and 1444, §1 or entered upon their office, and provided they have not been excommunicated, placed under interdict, or, suspended from office or been so declared by a declaratory sentence;

6. AAS, 1967, pp. 529-530.

2° Only within the limits of their own territory, in which, they can validly assist at all marriages, *not only of their own subjects but also of non-subjects;*

3° Provided that they ask and receive the consent of the contracting parties without being coerced either by force or by grave fear.

2. The pastor and local ordinary who can validly assist at a marriage can also give another priest permission to assist validly at marriage within the limits of their respective territories.

3. Deacons: The power of the deacon to officiate at marriage celebration: A deacon who will not remain in this grade, but will advance to the priesthood, has those offices which are enumerated in n. 29 of the Dogmatic Constitution of Vatican II, *Lumen gentium,* and in n. 22 of the Apostolic letter *Sacrum diaconatus ordinem* of 18 June, 1967.[7] N. 22 states that it is the office of the deacon, but only insofar as the local Ordinary has commissioned him, to expedite a number of matters. Among these matters, in places where a priest is lacking (*ubi sacerdos deest*), the deacon may assist at and bless marriages in the name of the Church, by delegation of the bishop or the pastor, the norms of Canons 1095, #2 and 1096 being also observed. Canon 1098 remains in force, and what it says of the priest is to be understood also of the deacon. The clause *"ubi sacerdos deest"* mentioned above is *not* required for the validity of the delegation given to the deacon to assist at marriages.[8]

---

7. Pont. Comm. for Interp. Decr. Vat. II — AAS 60, p. 363.
8. *Ibid.,* AAS, 1969, p. 348.

PROPER DELEGATION

Canon 1096: 1. The permission to assist at a marriage granted
in accordance with Canon 1095, §2, must be
given expressly to a *certain priest for a certain
determinate marriage,* all general delegations
being excluded except to the regularly appointed assistants of the parish for the parish
to which they are attached, otherwise it is
invalid.

2. The pastor or local ordinary must not give
permission unless all the canonical requirements for proving the freedom of the parties
to marry have been fulfilled.

1. *Express delegation* (licentia) must be given to a certain
specified priest for a particular marriage. General delegation
is sometimes given to the assistants (vicarii cooperatores) for
the parish to which they are assigned.

2. *Valid Assistance*: Pastors or local ordinaries can validly
assist at all marriages *only within* the limits of their territory (in
danger of death 1043-44, of their subjects anywhere) not only of
their own subjects but also of those who are not their subjects.

3. *National Parishes*: Authors[9] are divided on this type of
parish. The Code did not change the status of such parishes
(S.C. of Conc. February 1, 1908). This Congregation stated that
such pastors who have no exclusive territory hold it together
cumulatively with another or other pastors. These might be
Italian, Slovak or German. One should acquaint himself with
the particular diocesan laws or the documents on the establishment of the parish or church. The Code did not change the

9. Woywood, *Canon Law,* p. 759. DeSmet, Leitner, Fanfani, Blat, Che-
lodi, Ayrinhac.

status of these parishes and the local ordinaries are not to make any changes without consulting the Holy See (C. 216).

Military Chaplains are such that they have this jurisdiction over military persons without regard to territory; they can assist at marriages of these persons anywhere without regard to territory.

Orientals: The law is practically the same. However, they cannot assist validly at a marriage of two Latin Catholics; neither may the Latin pastor or Latin local ordinary assist validly at a marriage of two Oriental Catholics. If the particular Orientals do not have a hierarchy in this country, the jurisdiction to assist at marriages belongs to the Latin local ordinary. The Holy See sanctions this in many instances (Cf. New Legislation for Orientals under C. 1094).

General Delegation to an assistant may come from (1) *Diocesan Faculties*: (2) from *The Pastor*: (3) or by *Letter of Appointment to a Parish* from the Ordinary.

Particular Delegation: This can be done by a (1) temporary administrator; (2) by the vicar substitute, (3) by the priest supplying for, and appointed by the pastor who for some reason or other leaves the parish suddenly, even without the approval of the ordinary as long as the notification is sent to the ordinary. All these faculties are given with the power to subdelegate; further subdelegation may not be involved unless granted by the pastor or the local ordinary. *Delegation is invalid,* if the pastor calls a monastery asking the prior or superior to send *someone* (not delegated) to perform a marriage in the parish. *This delegated power must be given to a priest.* It seems that it could also be given to a deacon just before ordination when the marriage is to take place after the ordination because this assistance at marriage is merely a quasi-jurisdiction, it is not the power of orders as such that is required to assist at marriage. Delegation must be expressed, orally or in writing; or by certain signs or facts surrounding the situation. Presuming delegation or assuming tacit delegation because one is a good friend of the pastor, etc., would render the marriage invalid. Oriental Law is the same unless a mixed rite is involved.

Inter-Ritual Marriages: We refer here to marriages between a Latin Catholic and a Byzantine Catholic. The previous requirement of seeking permission from the Apostolic Delegate for such marriages to take place in the rite of the bride has been changed. These cases are provided for by Canon 88, 3 of the Oriental Code, *Crebrae Allatae,* and Canon 1097, 2 of the Latin Rite Code. An interpretation from the Cardinal Pro-Prefect for the Sacred Congregation for the Doctrine of the Faith, Feb. 1, 1967 states that the local Ordinary can now dispense from these provisions. In other words, the local Bishop is now competent in inter-ritual marriages, to grant permission for the marriage to take place in the rite of the bride. For example: John, a Byzantine Catholic is going to marry Mary, a Latin Catholic. According to the law, this marriage should take place in the Byzantine Church because the husband is Byzantine. However, the bride prefers to have the marriage in her Latin Church. The Latin pastor may get this permission from his Latin Ordinary to do this; he need not apply to the Apostolic Delegate as it was done in the past. Neither must he apply to the Oriental Ordinary. The Latin Ordinary has this faculty. This works both ways; the Oriental Ordinary has the same privileges for a Byzantine bride and Latin groom, should they seek such a privilege.

Canon 1097: 1. The pastor or the local Ordinary may *assist* at a marriage:

    1° After they have legitimately ascertained according to law, the freedom of the parties to marry;

    2° After they have ascertained moreover, that one

of the contracting parties has a domicile or quasi-domicile, *or a month's residence;* or in the case of a vagus (itinerant) who is actually staying in the place where the marriage will be contracted.

3° Provided that, if the conditions mentioned in n. 2 are wanting, the permission is had from the local ordinary of the domicile or quasi-domicile or place of a month's residence of one of the contracting parties, unless it is a question of itinerants (vagi) who are actually traveling and have no place of sojourn anywhere, *or unless some grave necessity occur which excuses from asking the permission.*

2. In every case let it be taken as the rule that the marriage should be celebrated before the pastor of the bride-to-be unless a just reason excuses therefrom; marriages, however, between Catholics of different rites are to be celebrated before the pastor of the groom and according to the ceremony of that rite, unless some laws provide otherwise.

3. A pastor who assists at a marriage without the permission required by law, has no right to the stole fee and must return it to the proper pastor of the parties.

This canon deals with the *liceity, not the validity.* Should such permission be lacking, the marriage is valid but illicit. It is the pastor and local ordinary who are obliged to see that the individuals are free to marry. The proper pastor of the investigation is usually the pastor of the bride; the pastor of the groom could do this also, but it belongs to the bride's pastor.

Month's Residence: When circumstances warrant it, one month's residence is sufficient. This brief stay is equivalent to a domicile or quasi-domicile, and this residence need not be made physically for 30 continuous days; a *morally* continuous month suffices before marriage is contracted.

Non-Subjects: To perform a marriage validly and licitly of a non-subject, a pastor should have the permission of the proper pastor with (1) the pastor of the bride-to-be, or (2) the pastor of the groom.

Permission is not needed for itinerants (vagi) who have no domicile or place of permanent residence; therefore, there is no one from whom to get the permission. However, the pastor should consult the local ordinary before assisting at such a marriage (C. 1032). Permission is not needed in case of necessity.

Case of Necessity: If a business man, or a government employee, or soldier, is leaving on an urgent business or other business and there is no time to get in touch with the proper pastor, (all things being equal) all the canonical aspects cleared, the pastor may go ahead with the marriage.

It must be kept in mind that all pastors can assist at all marriages of *non-subjects* in their own territory (C. 1096) validly, also licitly, if they have the proper pastor's permission (*not delegation*) unless they are vagi or in case of necessity.

Orientals: Conditions for lawful assistance are the same as in the Latin Code. However, a Latin pastor can assist at a marriage of an Oriental man and Latin woman validly but illicitly, because such a marriage belongs to the pastor of the groom. The Latin pastor would have full right if the groom was of the Latin rite. The marriage must take place in the parish of the groom when there is a marriage between a Latin and an Oriental. In the case of an Oriental woman of the *Byzantine Ruthenian rite and a non-baptized person*, the Byzantine bishop is the only one competent to grant the dispensation and the marriage is to take place in the Byzantine Church. Otherwise, the dispensation would be invalid and the marriage would also be invalid (*Diriment Impediment*).

Witnesses at a Catholic or Non-Catholic Marriage

Members of the Orthodox Church and also Protestants of other denominations may act as bridesmaid or best man at a wedding in a Catholic Church. A Catholic too can be best man or bridesmaid at a marriage properly celebrated among our separated brethren or celebrated in any Protestant Church.[10]

LACK OF FORM CASES

Since the so-called "Lack of Form Cases" are on the increase in the United States, as many as 800 in one large diocese in one year, which causes so much alarm, the Fathers of the Ecumenical Council gave some consideration as to whether a change should be effected regarding the form of marriage. Some countries such as Germany and Holland are having high casualty rates in this regard. In dealing with the Universal Law - Canon Law - it is the opinion of most canonists that the Church could allow some special way in handling these situations, but it would not be feasible to make the law whereby the universal Church would be obligated. It is the general consensus of opinion among canonists, especially those of the United States, that the form of marriage be retained despite the fact that we have many cases coming to the attention of our Tribunals. To do away with the present legislation of the form of marriage would only increase the number of ligamen cases and we would be in a worse state than the first.

Because of the prevalent unfortunate situation, every priest should be acquainted with the essential items that are considered

10. *Directory for Ecumenism* of the Secretariate for Christian Unity, May 14, 1967, nos. 49-58.

in the Lack of Form cases. Ordinarily this is a case which is handled in the administrative process in the Tribunal. Some of the essential items would be:

1. That at least one of the parties was held to the Catholic form of marriage at the time of the marriage;
2. That the marriage did not take place before a Catholic priest;
3. That the marriage was not later validated or sanated in some church.

The following documents in general are necessary to establish the Lack of Form case:

1. The petition which should clearly state the facts of the case.
2. A recent copy of the baptismal record of the Catholic party.
3. A First Communion record *or* Confirmation record *or* proof of Catholic parentage or training when the marriage took place before January 11, 1949, for a Latin Catholic.
4. A certified copy of the marriage certificate.
5. A decree of the civil divorce or annulment.
6. There should be a sworn testimony of the Catholic party that the marriage was not validated.
7. The testimonial of character.

CASE

Lack of Form (C. 1097)

On August 14, 1928, John Beck married Mary White before Rev. George Black of the Christian Alliance Church. John is a member of the Evangelical Church in Albany, New York. John claims that his wife was unfaithful. They lived together from 1928 until 1932. They were divorced in August, 1950. One child was born of this union. Mary White is married again.

John Beck wishes to marry again. The woman he plans to marry is Mary Day, a Catholic of St. John's parish. She has been a parishioner at St. John's since 1943. This church wedding which he is planning is merely a validation because he and Mary Day were married by a Justice of the Peace. John Beck was a baptized Catholic before 1928.

1. What is necessary for the pastor of St. John's to do in the investigation of this case?
2. List the necessary documents which must be obtained before handling this case.
3. How would you handle this case?

EXTRAORDINARY FORM OF MARRIAGE

Canon 1098 1. If it is impossible without grave inconvenience to have or reach the pastor or local ordinary, or a delegated priest, who can assist at the marriage in accordance with canons 1095-96:

1º In danger of death, marriage is valid and licit when celebrated before the witnesses alone; and even *outside the danger of death,* provided it be prudently foreseen that these circumstances (difficulty to get an authorized priest) will last for a month.

2º In both cases, if another priest who can be present is available he must be called and must assist at the marriage, together with the witnesses, without prejudice however to the validity of the marriage contracted before the witnesses alone.

1. *In Danger of Death*: The reasons would be the same as those enumerated in Canons 1043-44-45.

Inconvenience: This could be bad highways, rough seas, distance (e.g., in mission territories - Brazil, India), too great expense (on part of the people or priest); sickness, bad weather (ice and snow in northern countries); great fear of being apprehended (e.g., living in communistic territory); during persecutions, floods, disasters, etc. One is not obliged to use the telephone or telegraph. The inconvenience could be either physical or moral and could be on the part of either the priest or the parties wishing to contract marriage.[11] If there is any diriment impediment, without a priest, nothing is provided whereby this impediment could be dispensed, i.e., when two witnesses are had. If any priest is present, he could invoke Canons 1043-44 and absolve and dispense the couple from the impediment.

Outside the Danger of Death: When it is foreseen that they will not be able to approach a priest for a month, the parties may contract marriage before two witnesses. However, if they wish to marry and wish to have it recognized by the civil law (because of property rights, etc.) they would be justified to go to the Justice of the Peace or any civil magistrate (as the judge), who is entitled to assist at marriages. If any of these would be unavailable the parties would be justified to go to any minister (who would not act as a minister of religion) who would merely perform the ceremony without any religious ceremony, according to his right given him by civil authorities.[12]

2. *In both cases, in danger of death and outside the danger of death,* if another priest (not authorized as such) can be had, he may assist at the marriage as an official witness. Further, he may use the faculties of Canons 1043-44-45 as a norm for dispensing from impediments of marriage, if necessary. The general rule is that *in danger of death or outside of danger of death as mentioned* in the conditions above, a priest should be called if it is possible; otherwise, the two witnesses would suffice for a valid and licit marriage.

PERSONS BOUND BY THE FORM

Canon 1099: 1. The aforementioned law on the form of marriage

11. Code Commission, May 3, 1945.
12. Woywood, *op. cit.*, p. 777.

obliges the following:

1° All persons baptized in the Catholic Church and those who have converted to it from heresy or schism, even if the former or latter afterwards fall away, whenever they contract marriage among themselves.

2° The same aforementioned persons when they contract marriage with non-Catholics, either baptized or non-baptized, even when a dispensation has been obtained from the impediment of mixed religion or disparity of cult.

3° Orientals, if they contract with Latins bound by this form.

2. Without prejudice to the prescriptions of paragraph 1, n. 1, non-Catholics whether baptized or non-baptized, if they contract among themselves, nowhere are bound to observe the Catholic form of marriage.

The law is clear in itself. When non-Catholics marry among themselves, it makes no difference who assists at the marriage, minister, Justice of the Peace, etc., this marriage is considered valid. The clause "likewise exempt are persons born of non-Catholic parents, even though they have been baptized in the Catholic Church, who have grown up from infancy in heresy or schism or infidelity, or without any religion, when they contract with a non-Catholic party" was abrogated by the *Motu Proprio* of Pope Pius XII, August 1, 1948, and took effect January 1, 1949. The phrase: *children of non-Catholics* refers canonically to children of apostates.[13] Children of non-Catholic parents and those of apostate parents, even though they be *baptized in the Catholic Church*, were not obliged to the Catholic form of marriage, if they grew up from infancy *without any religion*, and married non-Catholics.

13. AAS XXI, 1929, p. 573; AAS XXII, 1930, p. 195.

Without any Religion: What is meant here? If one receives instructions for First Communion, or if one knows the Our Father and Hail Mary, or if one went to church occasionally, would we consider this as sufficient to constitute *some religion*, some religious training, which would oblige one to the form of marriage? This is the question that puzzled canonists since 1918 to 1949. Since Jan. 1, 1949, *anyone baptized in the Catholic Church* regardless how much religious training he had, or if he had none whatsoever, *is bound by the form of marriage*. One can readily see the importance of this date in reference to the people mentioned in this canon.

Case: John and Mary came to their pastor to see if they could be married. John was married before and was divorced. He and his wife had been baptized in the "Church with the Lighted Cross" (non-Catholic). He knew nothing of his wife's background, but upon investigation it was found that his wife was born in a Catholic hospital and had an emergency baptism. Her mother, a Catholic, died at childbirth. Since the marriage of this baptized Catholic took place after 1949, even though she had no religious instructions in the Catholic religion, (she was brought up by her Lutheran grandparents as a Lutheran) her marriage to John was invalid because of Lack of Form *due to the revision in the code* in 1949. If this revision or deletion had not taken place, her marriage would have been valid. John and Mary were permitted to marry.

RITE

Canon 1101: 1. The Pastor shall take care that the parties receive the solemn Nuptial Blessing which may be given them even after they have lived for a long time in the married state, observing the special rubrics.

2. The solemn blessing can be given either in person or through a representative, by that priest

alone who can validly and licitly assist at the marriage.

NUPTIAL BLESSING

In a Catholic marriage, the wedding ceremony takes place not at the beginning (as was customary), but *after the Lord's Prayer in the Nuptial Mass*. In the marriage of two Catholics, the nuptial blessing is always given, even if, for good reasons, the marriage takes place outside the Mass, in which case the Nuptial Blessing is given following the Blessing and Exchange of Rings. The Nuptial Blessing is always given for both a Catholic and a Mixed Marriage, even when it takes place during Lent or Advent (Decree MR. 23/969, March 19, 1969, S.C.R. Card. Gut). It may be given more than once, and even for a mixed marriage.

MIXED MARRIAGES

Canon 1102: 1. In marriages between a Catholic and a non-Catholic party, the questions regarding the consent must be asked according to the prescriptions of Canon 1095, p. 1., n. 3.

2. But all sacred rites are prohibited; if however, it is foreseen that greater evils were likely to result from this prohibition, the ordinary can permit some of the usual ecclesiastical ceremonies, excluding always the celebration of Mass.[14]

ORIENTALS

THE NUPTIAL BLESSING OR CROWNING

14. Decree March 18, 1966, no. 4. As an exception the Local Ordinaries may permit the celebration of a mixed marriage using the Sacred Rites with the usual blessing and discourse.

Interpretation issued by the *Pontifical Commission for the Redaction of the Code of Oriental Canon Law* on May 3, 1953.[15]

> *Question: Is the word "blessing" in can. 85 #2 to be understood as a simple blessing, or is a certain liturgical rite required?*
>
> *Answer: Affirmative in respect to the first part, negative to the second.*

1. MARRIAGE FORMS IN GENERAL

1. In discussing ecclesiastical marriage forms of the past often not sufficient attention is paid to the fact that they must be distinguished in accordance with the legal sanctions which were attached to each of them. Although in centuries past a marriage entered with willful disregard of an obligatory ecclesiastical marriage form was gravely sinful, the marriage itself could have been valid.

The marriage ceremony in the Ancient World was a public contract also, and an occasion for a religious rite. However, no public official, religious or secular, was commissioned to represent the state. The Church of the Apostolic era had therefore no special interest in strictly demanding that the marriage contract be concluded in the church and in a liturgical rite, particularly when the parties alone were the ministers of the sacramental action. Nonetheless, it was ruled very early that no marriage should be celebrated without the bishop (St. Ignatius the Martyr to St. Polycarp, 107 A.D.). This does not mean the establishment of an ecclesiastical form, but merely that the presence or approval of the bishop should be secured.

Tertullian (197-217) spoke of a liturgical rite of marriage, and ecclesiastical legislators of the following centuries are even more explicit; without it they considered a marriage contracted outside the Church invalid. Later centuries made it even clearer:

15. AAS, 1953, p. 313.

who ever married without an ecclesiastical rite committed a sinful act, which sometimes was even punished by an excommunication *latae sententiae,* but the marriage was thereby not invalidated. This was an obligatory ecclesiastical marriage form, which was not, however, sanctioned with invalidity of the marriage contract.

In some parts of the Oriental Church the liturgical marriage form was made obligatory for the marriages only of the nobility or freemen while serfs could marry without the ceremony of coronation.

The last stage of the development of the marriage form, i.e., when it became obligatory and its neglect invalidated the marriage contract, was reached in the Latin rite Church with the Council of Trent (Decree *Tametsi*). However, even here a limitation remained: *Tametsi* was not in force everywhere, but solely in certain places. Only the Motu Proprio *Ne Temere* (1907) and the CIC (1917) made the obligatory marriage form with a sanction of invalidity applicable everywhere for Latin rite Catholics. This strict obligatory form was established also for all Oriental Catholics by the motu proprio Cr. All. (1949).

Canon 1112:2 of the Latin Code is not included in the Oriental legislation. If a priest of the Latin rite lawfully assists at a marriage of an Oriental Catholic and a non-Catholic (either baptized or non-baptized) he must follow the Latin rite liturgical formula according to Canon 1102:2, and not that of the Oriental ritual (C. 85). Likewise, if a priest of the Oriental rite lawfully assists at a marriage of a Latin rite Catholic and a non-Catholic (baptized or non-baptized), he must follow the Oriental ritual according to Canon 85 of the Oriental law and not of Canon 1112:2.

2. "If the religious form (blessing or crowning) is required for validity of a marriage, it must be proved that such legislative authority had been granted by the Church, either by specific enactment or by tacit recognition of a legal custom. Neither of these has ever been done." [16] "The argument has been brought

16. Pospishil, *Law on Marriage,* pp. 135-136.

forward that the obligatory marriage form among dissident Orientals may have been in existence before the schism and therefore continues its legal force which it acquired then. However the studies of E. Herman, S.J., on the historical evolution of the marriage form within the many Oriental groups, the Byzantine rite, showed the conviction that the act of exchanging consent must be accompanied by a religious, liturgical rite, was not customary all the time or did not apply to all classes of the faithful and was never a general practice in all Byzantine territories. The same may be said, but more strongly, for the other Oriental rites.[17]

"It might be advanced," says Pospishil, "that the Oriental dissidents by themselves could evolve a legal custom introducing an obligatory marriage form sanctioning marriages contracted in defiance of it be null and void, but this would have to be proved in each single community; the argument can never be raised higher than to a mere hypothesis. Practically it was never adopted or followed by any office of the Catholic Church, and will not contribute to the solution of problems in practice, that is, will not overcome the presumption enunciated in Canon 3 Cr. All. (C. 1014) *in dubio standum est pro valore matrimonii,* in doubt the validity of the marriage must be upheld.

As to the blessing itself, required by Canon 85, 2 as an essential part of the Oriental marriage form, the Pontifical Commission for the Redaction of the Oriental Code resolved that *any blessing suffices as far as the validity is in question,* and no specific liturgical act is required. For the lawful assistance at marriage the respective liturgical formularies must be followed. Many dissident Orientals consider the solemn coronation of the spouses, which consists in an imposition of wreaths or crowns on their heads by the priest, the essential form of marriage, an assumption not substantiated by historical documentation, even though the coronation ceremony belongs to the age old custom

17. Herman, E., S.J., "De Benedictione nuptiali quid statuerit ius Byzantium sive ecclesiasticum sive civile," found in *Orientalia Christiana Periodica,* 1938, pp. 189-234.

of the marriage rite.[18]

In other words, the Oriental law requires the simple blessing of the priest assisting at marriage; it is essential but only for *liceity;* it would be unlawful if it were not given, but the marriage would still be *valid.*[19]

REGISTRATION OF A MARRIAGE

Canon 1103: 1. After the celebration of marriage, the pastor or one who is taking his place shall, as soon as possible, enter the names of the contracting parties and witnesses, the place and date of the celebration of the marriage and other items according to the method prescribed in the ritual books and by his local ordinary; and this must be done even though another priest, delegated by the pastor or by the ordinary, assisted at the marriage.

2. Moreover, according to Canon 470, §2., the pastor shall also note in the baptismal register that the party has contracted marriage in his parish on a certain date. If the party was baptized elsewhere, the pastor of the marriage shall send notification of this marriage to the pastor of baptism either himself or through the episcopal Curia, in order that the marriage may be recorded in the baptismal register.

3. Whenever the marriage is contracted according to Canon 1098, the priest, if he assisted at it, otherwise the witnesses are bound in solidum with the contracting parties to take care that the marriage be recorded as soon as possible in prescribed books.

18. *Ibid.*
19. Pospishil, *loc. cit.*

The Council of Trent (Sess. XXIV, c. 1) commanded pastors to have a book in which to enter marriages which took place in their parishes and include the names of the parties and the witnesses, the day and the place of the contract. We find the same prescriptions in the Roman Ritual [20] giving the forms to be used and stressing the fact that the parish priest should enter the marriage which took place as soon as possible. It further prescribed that he put this in his own handwriting, even when another priest (if he was delegated by him to the ordinary) took care of the marriage. The law of 1908 contains the same prescriptions and added new ones. This law stressed the fact that it was a grave obligation on the part of the parish priest to have the marriages that took place in his parish to be registered into the marriage record as soon as possible. It also stressed the fact that *one must be careful to avoid omissions and inaccuracies. The record must contain the names of the contracting parties, place and date of the marriage, and other particulars. The priest who officiated, if he was delegated, the dispensations that were obtained, the promises that were made in a mixed marriage, the publication or omission of banns.* If for some reason the marriage was declared null later on, this fact should be recorded also (C. 1918). A marriage should be entered into the baptismal record of the parties, if any of them were baptized in another parish. According to the new baptismal record, there is a margin left for such notations. This notation notification could be sent directly or through the Chancery Office, (Instr. 1941), to get better results it is best to send it through the Chancery or episcopal curia, if the marriage was celebrated according to the norms of Canon 1098. If a priest was present at such a marriage, it is his obligation to send in the information. If no priest was present, the obligation rests with the witnesses and the parties themselves. The record of all marriages should be kept in order to prevent bigamy or fraudulent unions. The Catholic Church has this wonderful system because by cross-checking a pastor can very easily find out whether a person was married before or not. All one has to do

20. Roman Ritual Trt. 7, Ve. Sap. Matt. c. 2.

is to consult the baptismal register, or the baptismal certificate, which must be issued at least within the last six months, and presented to the pastor who is going to marry the parties; the baptismal record should contain all the items which are found in the baptismal records. Sometimes there is a double record: in the baptismal and the matrimonial register.

MARRIAGES OF CONSCIENCE

Canon 1104: Only for a very grave and a very urgent reason and by the local ordinary in person, not even the Vicar General without a special mandate, can it be permitted that a marriage of conscience be contracted, that is, that a marriage be celebrated without the publication of Banns and in secret according to the norm of canons which follow.

A marriage of conscience is one in which a marriage is contracted without the publication of banns, in which the priest and witnesses who assist at the ceremony, are bound to strict secrecy. After careful investigation, the local ordinary may permit a marriage of conscience. In such a case the information regarding the parties must be gathered secretly without revealing the identity of the parties. The reasons for such marriages of conscience might be, e.g., (1) a widow who has to raise a number of children and conduct a business (which forbids marriage); if it were known that she was married it would put the business in jeopardy; or perhaps a person who is in the Army and is forbidden to marry while he is in this position, has a grave reason to get married. In conditions such as these, marriages of conscience are permitted.

Canon 1105: The permission to celebrate a marriage of conscience imposes a promise and grave obligation to observe the secret on the part of the priest assisting, the witnesses, the ordinary and his successors, and also the other contracting party as long as one does not consent to the divulgation of the marriage.

Canon 1106: The obligation of this promise on the part of the ordinary does not extend to a case in which any scandal or grave injury to the sanctity of the marriage is imminent as a result of the observance of secrecy, or of the children born of such a marriage, or have them baptized under fictitious names, unless in the meantime notifying the ordinary within 30 days of the birth of the children, giving notice of birth and baptism of the child, and the true indication of the parents, or if the parents neglect the christian education of the children.

Regarding the permission for a marriage of conscience, the local ordinary must insist on the obligation of secrecy about this marriage and all those connected with its celebration. He is also bound implicitly to the secret in such a way that it is a conditional promise, for if there is some danger to the common good, or if some evil should follow from such a marriage, he would be bound to reveal the secret. This is the local ordinary's prerogative. Children that are born of marriages of conscience at times must be given fictitious names; precautions must be taken that the names of the parents do not appear on the baptismal register, nor the proof of the legitimacy of the children. All this information is kept in the secret archives of the Chancery.

Whenever the ordinary permits a marriage of conscience to a couple who are forbidden to marry by civil law because of some impediment of civil law, all the necessary precautions and care must be taken that this does not become known publicly, because the state can impose a fine or imprisonment upon the priest assisting at such a marriage. Some marriages are permissible under the laws of the Church but might be forbidden by some civil laws; therefore, it is necessary to handle this matter with great caution. In the final analysis, marriage is governed objectively by the divine law and the Church who is the custodian of the divine law.

Canon 1107:   Marriages of conscience should not be recorded in the usual matrimonial and baptismal register, but in a special book to be kept in the secret archives of the curia mentioned in Canon 379.

Some kind of notification should be made in the church of baptism; perhaps this should be put in the secret archives of the respective chancery.

TIME

Canon 1108:   1. Matrimony can be contracted at any time of year.

2. Only the solemn nuptial blessing is forbidden from the first Sunday of Advent to the day of the Nativity of our Lord inclusive, and from Ash Wednesday to Easter Sunday inclusive.

3. However, ordinaries of places can, observing the Liturgical laws, permit the nuptials even during the above mentioned time, for a just cause and admonishing the parties to abstain from excessive festivity.

1. *Marriage may be celebrated at any time of the year.*
2. It can also be celebrated any time of the day unless the ordinary has some diocesan legislation, enacted for some good reason, forbidding marriage at a certain time or on a certain day. *This particular law would only be for liceity, not for validity.* The ordinary must obtain a special indult from the Holy See to enact a law forbidding it under the penalty of invalidity.

PLACE

Canon 1109:   1. Marriage between Catholics should be celebrated in the parish church; it may however take place in another church or oratory whether public or semi-public, only with the permission of the local ordinary or the pastor.

2. Ordinaries can permit that marriage be celebrated in a private home only in an extraordinary case and always on condition that there be a just and reasonable cause; but ordinaries must not permit it in churches or oratories of a seminary or of religious women, unless in case of necessity and with proper precautions.

Canon 1113:   Parents are bound by a most grave obligation to provide for religious and moral as well as for the physical and civil education of their children and also to provide for their temporal welfare.

Parents must attend to their welfare that (1) they receive catechetical instructions, (2) they receive the sacraments often, especially to make their Easter duty each year, and (3) they attend a Catholic school.

LEGITIMATION

Canon 1114:   Children who are conceived or born of a valid or putative marriage are legitimate, unless *at the time of conception,* the use of the marriage theretofore contracted was forbidden to the parents because of solemn religious profession or the reception of a sacred order.

PATERNITY

Canon 1115:   1. The father is he who is indicated by a lawful marriage unless the contrary be proven by conclusive arguments.

2. Children born at least six months after the celebration of marriage or within 10 months after the date when conjugal relations ceased are presumed to be legitimate.

Canon 1116: By the subsequent marriage of the parents whether true or putative, whether newly contracted or validated, even though it was not consummated, the offspring become legitimate provided the parents were legally capable of contracting matrimony together at the time of conception, or of pregnancy, or of birth.

Canon 1117: Children legitimated by a subsequent marriage, as regards canonical effects, are equal to legitimate children, unless the contrary is expressly provided.

---

n.b. See p. 67 - Legitimation

CHAPTER VIII

CONSEQUENCES OF MARRIAGE

RATUM ET CONSUMMATUM MARRIAGE

Canon 1118: Marriage which is *ratum et consummatum* cannot be dissolved by any human power nor by any cause except death.

This canon is precise and clear indicating that marriage cannot be dissolved by the parties themselves (*intrinsic indissolubility*); neither can a marriage be dissolved by any human power by secular or religious authorities (*extrinsic indissolubility*).[1] Natural law is the basis for indissolubility as an essential property of marriage whereby every marriage is indissoluble but not absolutely. *Extrinsic indissolubility* is possible when the marriage is *non consummatum*. A ratified and consummated marriage is one in which two baptized persons (Catholic or non-Catholic) perform the human action of copula whereby there is the penetration of the vagina by the male organ and the emission of true semen therein; hence, such a marriage is indissoluble and even beyond the power of the Supreme Pontiff.

The ultimate reason for this inflexibility may be found in the mystical signification of Christian marriage; according to St. Paul (Eph 5: 32), marriage between Christ and his Church. Now this reproduction is achieved in its perfection in

1. The existence of this power was clearly and explicitly taught only in the 13th century and, with the exception of cases of Solemn Religious Profession, only in the 15th century was the power knowingly used. Pope Martin V (1417-31) and Pope Eugene IV (1431-47).

marriage between baptized persons which has been consummated. Common sense teaches us that by the use of the conjugal right, marriage receives a sort of completion; something irreparable has taken place; the affective and verbal self-surrender has been supplemented by an actual physical one which justifies the expression, very significant in itself, of "consummated marriage." *It is consummated in the symbolical and mystical order,* in which it represents the indefectible union between Christ and his Church. In a perfect representation of this union, the indefectibility of the union must have its own symbol; and it has it in the absolutely indissoluble marriage.[2]

It is interesting to note that the question here is not the controversy of fact but the controversy of the question of law (*questio iuris*) and from time to time authors boldly step forward with their opinions. We find one such opinion in *Ephemerides Theologicae Lovanienses*.[3] "Does it follow then that what the Church has bound today she can loose tomorrow through the exercise of the same power of the keys? . . . . Inasmuch as all marriages are contracts, even though some of them are sacramental and consummated, they all come under the power of the keys . . . . In *actu primo*, therefore, even ratified consummated marriages form no exception to this unlimited power of the Church. In *actu secundo*, however, these marriages are extrinsically indissoluble *de iure divino* simply because the *Church has used her divinely given binding power upon them instead of her loosing power* . . . . Having once committed herself to its intrinsic indissolubility, there need be no fear that at some future time she may reverse herself and dissolve a marriage of this kind."

According to this opinion, a ratified and consummated marriage was within the ambit of the ministerial power of the Church; in other words, such marriages are, by divine law, extrinsically indissoluble, simply because up to the present day, the *Church has always used her binding power rather than her loosing power*. It is the opinion of authors [4] that there is noth-

2. Vermeersch, *What is Marriage?*, no. 68, p. 26.

3. O'Connor, W. R., *The Indissolubility of a Ratified, Consummated Marriage*, Ephemerides, Theologiae Lovanienses, XII, 1936, pp. 720-722.

4. Abate, Antonius, O.P., *The Dissolution of the Patrimonial Bond in*

ing against holding the opinion that the Church by some dint of the same ministerial power by which today she declares indissoluble a *ratum et consummatum marriage* of two baptized, can tomorrow change her attitude and allow dissolution.[5] Although in recent years the Church has granted a dissolution of the matrimonial bond in cases where, in the past, she never conceded a dispensation should be a caution to us regarding such a warning to us not to make or formulate categorical assertions. It is only through, or after some practical experience with actual cases that we know the precise limits of the ministerial power derived from the divine law. However, it is possible to believe that in some future date the Church can intervene in a ratified and consummated marriage, not by extending its power, but by specifying and revising the notion of non-consummation extending this term also to the case where conjugal copulation, though having taken place, has, because of permanent sterility, never attained the primary end of marriage, namely, the generation of offspring.

"It is certain that consummation, like sacramentality, does not add any fuller perfection to the indissolubility of the validly contracted bond. What it does is to *actuate* in a more adequate manner, the symbolism existing in a marriage between the baptized. The marriage that is solely sacramental represents the union of Christ with the soul through grace, a union which can be destroyed by mortal sin. The marriage crowned by consummation, however, represents the unbreakable union of Christ with human nature. It is only on account of this element that the ratified and consummated marriage is asserted to be absolutely indissoluble, both extrinsically and intrinsically."

Essential Facts in Dealing With non-Consummated Marriages

1. There is no *consummation of marriage* unless there is the actual penetration of the vagina by the male organ and the emission of the *true semen* in it. There is no consummation if this is lacking.

Ecclesiastical Jurisprudence, Desclee, N.Y., pp. 25-29.

Bride, A., "Le Pouvoir du Souverain Pontif sur Le Marriage des infideles," *Revue de Droit Canonique,* X-XI, 1960-61, pp. 98-99.

5. *Ibid.*

2. There is no true consummation if contraceptive devices are used. However, each case must be thoroughly investigated and studied before making a decision. Anyone interested in such a case may consult this author regarding an actual case handled favorably by the Holy See. Publication protocol of the Holy See prevents the publication of it here.

3. A marriage is considered as non-consummated if intercourse takes place *only* before a marriage.

4. The investigation of the fact of *non-consummation of marriage* and of the *existence of a just cause for granting a dispensation belongs solely* to the Sacred Congregation of the Sacraments. Therefore, no ordinary may constitute a tribunal and conduct a test trial with the questioning of the parties and witnesses in the form of a judicial process until he has received express authorization to do so from this Sacred Congregation.

5. *What right then, or what is the source of power which the Church exercises to dissolve such marriages, since marriage is naturally indissoluble by the parties themselves or by any other human power?*

Marriage is *intrinsically indissoluble* but *extrinsically dissoluble* in certain cases. Theologians have discussed this question for a long time whether the dissolution of the marriage bond by religious profession depends upon the *natural law*, the *ecclesiastical law*, or the *positive divine law*. The Church has never given an official pronouncement on this matter. The Council of Trent condemns anyone who claims that the Church has no such power. The history of this case and the reasons which prove that the Supreme Pontiff has this power has been under discussion by theologians. The conclusion of these discussions end in saying that this matter has reference to Christian morality and that the Supreme Pontiff cannot err in matters of faith and morals; therefore, we can reasonably conclude that the Pope has this power.

DISSOLUTION OF THE MARRIAGE BOND

Canon 1118: A valid marriage which is *ratum et consummatum* cannot be dissolved by any human power or any case except death.

Canon 1119: A non-consummatum marriage between baptized persons, or between a baptized and a non-baptized person, is dissolved by solemn religious profession, and by a dispensation granted by the Apostolic See for a just cause, at the request of both parties, or either party, even though the other be unwilling.

1. Canon 1119 deals with two methods in dissolving a *ratum et non-consummatum* marriage, namely, (a) by Solemn religious profession and (b) by dispensation of the Holy See. Consummation is the conjugal copula or intercourse, that is the physiological elements: penetration of the vagina by the male organ and the emission of the true sperm in it. A marriage that is *ratum et consummatum* (C. 1118) cannot be dissolved. For "What God has joined together, let no man put asunder."

2. *Solemn Religious Profession* dissolves a *non-consummatum marriage* not only for a Christian but also for the non-Christian (unbaptized).

3. *Dispensation of the Holy Father*: The Pope can dissolve a *ratum et non-consummatum* marriage of Christians by papal dispensation, if it can be proven to the matrimonial court that the marriage was not consummated. Such cases are long and very involved.

THE PAULINE PRIVILEGE

With almost fifty percent of the population in the United States practicing no religion, and another twenty-five percent belonging to the Jewish faith or the non-Catholic religions, we have a total of seventy-five percent of the population from which the Pauline cases arise. Therefore, it can be said that this is fertile ground for souls who are searching for the truth and are trying to find their way into the Catholic Church. Some of these ship-wrecked cases, through divorce and remarriage, may cause some difficulties before being admitted; there are also others who find the doors open through the Privilege of the Faith.

Canon 1120: 1. Legitimate marriage between unbaptized persons, even though it has been consummated, is dissolved in favor of the faith by the Pauline Privilege.

2. This privilege does not apply in a marriage between a baptized and an unbaptized person

entered into with the dispensation from the impediment of disparity of cult.

1. Canons 1120 to 1126 deal with the Pauline Privilege, although Canon 1025 (Constitutions) deals with marriages between unbaptized parties (a requisite in the Pauline Privilege); nevertheless, some of the other requisites of the Pauline Privilege are lacking. Canon 1127 deals with the privilege of the Faith in doubtful cases, that is, when a doubt arises in a Pauline Privilege category.

2. When we speak of the privilege of the Faith, we do so in generic terms for the privilege of the Faith is a *genus*, whereas the Pauline Privilege and the Petrine Privilege are the *species* of this *genus*.

3. *Pauline Privilege*: This is a privilege whereby a legitimate marriage between two unbaptized persons, even though it is consummated, is dissolved in favor of the Faith.

4. *Requisites for the Pauline Privilege*: To utilize this privilege, it is required that (1) two persons be unbaptized at the time of the marriage; (2) that one of these persons be validly baptized after that marriage; (3) that the baptized person interpellate the other unbaptized party according to Canon 1121; (4) when the new marriage is contracted the former marriage is automatically (*ipso facto*) dissolved.

5. *Petrine Privilege*: This is a privilege whereby the Roman Pontiff dissolves a legitimate consummated marriage between a

baptized person and an unbaptized person in favor of the Faith.

8. *Baptism of Heretics*: Regarding the valid baptism of heretics, it is morally certain that this baptism would be a sufficient foundation to use this privilege. However, the Church does not use it. It is a difficult procedure to handle such a case. It would simplify matters if the heretic became a convert to the Catholic religion. In such a case, we could call it the dissolution of a "natural bond" of marriage rather than the Pauline Privilege.

7. *Departure of the Unbaptized*: This departure must be proved by (1) interpellations (C. 1121 to 1122) from the circumstances whereby a dispensation is granted from making the interpellations. The departure of the unbaptized party must not be the fault of the converted party after baptism. The Pauline Privilege gives the new convert the right to marry a Catholic. However, in recent years, the Holy See has granted permission to marry another infidel or a baptized non-Catholic.

THE INTERPELLATIONS

Canon 1121: 1. Before the party who has been converted and baptized can validly contract a new marriage, he or she must, except as provided in Canon 1125, interpellate the unbaptized party:
(1) whether he or she is also willing to be converted and to receive baptism;
(2) or at least be willing to live peacefully without offense to the Creator.

2. These interpellations must always be made unless the Apostolic See shall have declared otherwise.[6]

Canon 1122: 1. The interpellations are to be made regularly,

6. Pope Paul VI has declared otherwise. Cf. *Pastorale Munus* I, 23 in the Appendix.

at least in a summary and extrajudicial form, by authority of the ordinary of the converted party, and the same ordinary shall also grant the unbaptized party, if he or she asks for it, an extension of time to think over the matter, warning the same party however that in case there is no reply within the specified time, a negative reply will be presumed.

2. Interpellations, even when made privately by the converted party himself, are valid, and indeed even licit in case the form above prescribed cannot be observed; but in this case they must be proved for the external forum by at least two witnesses or by some other lawful manner of proof.

Canon 1123: If the interpellations have been omitted by declaration of the Holy See, or if the unbaptized party has expressly or tacitly given a negative answer, the baptized party has the right to contract a new marriage with a Catholic person, unless since baptism he or she has given the unbaptized party a just cause for departing.

Canon 1124: The baptized even though since baptism he or she may have lived in matrimonial relations with the unbaptized party, does not thereby lose the right to contract a new marriage with a Catholic, and can therefore make use of this right in case the unbaptized party changes his or her mind and departs without just cause or ceases to cohabitate peacefully without offense to the Creator.

---

1. *Departure of the unbaptized party:* This is understood if, when he does cause offense to the Creator by giving scandal (moral departure), or threaten the party with physical harm or causes life to be miserable, e.g., by quarrelsome dispositions, outbursts of anger, causes perversion, forces the person to ona-

nism or commits some grave sin, the baptized convert may make use of the privilege.

2. *Infidel wishes baptism but not cohabitation with the baptized convert:* In this case we consider the matter a physical departure; however, it would be best for the convert to use this privilege before the other spouse is baptized; otherwise this would result in a *ratum* marriage causing complications and another intervention with the Holy See. Sometimes it happens that the infidel party (while separated and married) receives baptism (heretical sect) while the Pauline privilege case is being expedited, unknown to the newly baptized convert; when the interpellations are made, this is then discovered. The case becomes a *ratum* matter and is referred to the Holy See. We could also have a physical departure of the infidel when, for example, one is given a long prison term. An infidel who already married for the second time is considered as a physical departure.

3. *Dispensation from the interpellations*: Ordinaries did not have this faculty from their Quinquennial faculties, but have them now from Pope Paul VI: *Pastorale Munus*.

4. *Time of interpellations*: After the baptism and before the conversion of the other party. If the interpellations were made before the baptism, the action would be valid provided that the non-baptized party did not change his mind.[7] Moreover, in a summary or extra-judicial form, the ordinary must give an extension of time if the infidel asks for it according to C. 1122.

5. *Factors of Importance*:
(1) If the unbaptized person gives the necessary guarantees to let the newly baptized convert practice his religion freely, etc., and later violates this promise, the Catholic party is not obliged to live with that party and may get a divorce provided that the interpellations are made, or again a dispensation is obtained.

7. *Pastorale Munus* I, 23, grants faculties to the Ordinaries, "permitting them, for a grave cause, to make the interpretations *before the baptism of the party who is being converted* to the faith; also dispensing from the same interpellations before the baptism of the party . . . when the interpellations cannot be made or it would be useless."

(2) It must be kept in mind that the legitimate marriage is not dissolved at the time of baptism of one party, but only after at the very moment of the new marriage of the convert.

(3) If the case is such that the interpellations cannot be made because it would be useless to make them, or the party cannot be found, or because the party is already married, *nevertheless, the invalidating canonical law* would render the new marriage invalid if they are not made. Canon 1121 is clear: "that the interpellations must always be made *unless the Holy See declares otherwise.*" *Pastorale Munus* changed this, since this faculty has been granted to ordinaries. We have canonists who discuss this speculative question whether the interpellations can be omitted if the party is already married or cannot be found. Practically the interpellations are useless in this case. Nevertheless, we must submit to the law and let the *Ordinary declare otherwise.*

INVESTIGATING THE NON-BAPTISM OF BOTH PARTIES

In dealing with a Pauline Privilege case, one must investigate and obtain conclusive evidence with moral certainty of the non-baptism of both parties of this legitimate marriage. Proving negative facts is very difficult, yet by a process of elimination this can be done as follows:

1. Check the religious affiliation and background of the parents or guardians. We have a very good and strong presumption of non-baptism of the party, if the parents belong to a *sect which rejects baptism,* if the parents belong to a sect which *believes only in adult baptism* (they reject infant baptism), or if the parents have *no religious affiliations whatsoever.*

2. If some of the children were baptized and the party claims no baptism, inquiry should be made why baptism did not take place. Also check the belief or practice of the parents regarding the baptism of their children. A search for possible records of baptism in the church or churches in the place of domicile.

3. Besides inquiring from the parents, one should check with the sisters, brothers, relatives and friends as to the possible baptism.

PAULINE PRIVILEGE EXTENDED

Canon 1125: Those things which pertain to marriage in the Constitutions: *Altitudo* of Paul III, June 1, 1537; *Romani Pontificis* of Pius V, August 2, 1571; *Populis* of Gregory XIII, January 25, 1585, which were decreed for particular territories are *extended to other regions that have the same circumstances.*

In addition to the provisions of Canons 1120-1124, we have an extended privilege in Canon 1125, which can be used in regions in which particular circumstances exist. It may also be said that Canon 1125 is practical application of Canon 1127.

I. Constitution - *Altitudo,* Paul III:

(1) If a convert becoming baptized had several wives, but does not remember which he married first may, after his conversion to the faith, choose anyone and marry her, excluding all the others.

(2) If he remembers the first one he married, he must keep her and dismiss the rest. He cannot use the privilege of this Constitution. He may then use the Pauline Privilege if she is not baptized, but if she refused to live with him peacefully without offense to the Creator, he may use the Pauline Privilege.

Some of the important factors of this Constitution are:

(1) This constitution contains a dispensation (*ipso jure*) from the impediment of consanguinity and affinity.[8]

(2) No dispensation is needed from the impediment of disparity of cult; however, the *cautiones* required by the divine law are imposed.

(3) No interpellations are necessary.

II. Constitution - *Romani Pontificis,* St. Pius V:

8. Ordinaries of Place-Now have the faculty from *Pastorale Munus,* Dec. 3, 1963.

(1) If a man, before receiving baptism, chooses from among his wives the one who wishes to be baptized with him and keep her to the exclusion of all the rest, even though she was not the first one he married, he may do so.

(2) No interpellations are made whatsoever.

III. Constitution - *Populis*, Gregory XIII:

Local Ordinaries,[9] pastors and confessors of the Jesuits *can dispense from the interpellations in Pauline Privilege cases, and provided that a summary and an extrajudicial investigation took place, when the party cannot be interpellated; or was interpellated and did not make known these intentions within a certain specified time*:

(1) whenever his whereabouts is unknown;
(2) whenever his whereabouts is known but cannot be reached;
(3) whenever his whereabouts is known but he is inaccessible;

(4) whenever the interpellations have been made and no answer is given.

Many authors agree that the ordinary of the pastor can *use this faculty* in favor of his subjects *anywhere,* and also for non-subjects within their own territory. Since this privilege comes from ordinary power, it can be delegated to others.[10] All religious orders who held the communication of privileges may use this privilege. For the confessors of the Jesuits and others (religious orders) this faculty is not restricted to the internal forum; it may be used in the external forum.

When the newly baptized convert obtains his dispensation from the interpellations, the Constitutions permit him to marry. This marriage is valid even if the former party appears on the scene and gives the excuse that there was no opportunity to answer.

9. Mathis & Meyer, *Pastoral Companion*, p. 283.
10. Winslow, Vromont, n. 355, pp. 75-82.

A dispensation from a legitimate consummated marriage between two infidels, which later became a ratified marriage but was not consummated after the ratification is also included in this Constitution *Populis* of Gregory XIII.

Theoretical Factors: Some authors claim that these Constitutions are an extension of, and an application of the Pauline Privilege; while others claim that it is really a *special vicarious power of the Supreme Pontiff,* apart from the Pauline Privilege, and because the latter Constitution dispenses with the interpellations.[11]

The circumstances considered here need not characterize a whole territory, but could be applied to individual cases. It would be sufficient in the case of a couple who is separated (when the other party cannot be found) that the ordinary or the pastor could utilize this Constitution in such a case.

When speaking of polygamy, it need not be simultaneous because successive polygamy would be sufficient. For example, we have cases in the United States in which non-baptized people get divorced and marry many times successively. This Constitution could be used in this particular case. Furthermore, these powers enumerated in Canon 1125 are actually *common law itself* and can be used without consulting the Holy See, when one is assured that all the conditions are verified. It is most unfortunate that this Constitution is not utilized more here in the United States by the ordinaries and pastors to whom it is directed.[12]

Canon 1126: The bond of the former marriage contracted in infidelity, is dissolved *only* at the time when the baptized party contracts a *new marriage* validly.

If the newly baptized convert does not get married, the former marriage is considered valid; neither can the other (infidel) party marry validly again because of ligamen.

11. Ayrinhac-Lydon, p. 32.
12. Winslow, p. 55.

THE PRIVILEGE OF THE FAITH

Canon 1127: In doubt, the privilege of the Faith enjoys the favor of the law.

Dissolving Non-Sacramental Marriages and Privilege of the Faith:

Strictly speaking, the privilege of the faith signifies a faculty granted to a convert from infidelity through the vicarious power of the Roman Pontiff, whereby after the reception of baptism, the convert may contract a second marriage if the infidel party departs. In this sense, the privilege of the faith is synonymous with the Pauline privilege. Non-Sacramental marriages can be dissolved according to Canons 1119, 1120 and 1125, and the granting of dispensations in cases not directly contained in the Pauline privilege. Here, too, contrary to what seems to be the widespread misconception, Canon 1127 cannot be applied in a case in which a party who is certainly unbaptized with one who is certainly baptized in heresy. Canon 1127 deals with the question of doubt; in this case there is no question of doubt. The validity of this marriage as well as the baptism of one party is certain. Today the privilege of the faith, has been broadened to include the vicarious power of the Pope over such consummated legitimate marriages. This dispensation from the bond of marriage is given in circumstances not covered directly by Canons 1120 and 1125.

1. This power is exercised first in the three constitutions mentioned in Canon 1125 and all the conditions required for a Pauline Privilege were absent. This is especially true of the Constitution *Populus,* of 1585 of Gregory XIII.

2. In the Helena Case of Montana, 1924: A non-baptized man who contracted marriage with a baptized non-Catholic woman before a non-Catholic minister, the Holy Office petitioned the Holy Father to dissolve the natural bond of this marriage in favor of the faith. This marriage was dissolved. This case differs from the Pauline Privilege because the latter (Pauline privilege) deals with a valid marriage of two non-baptized persons; it also differs from the cases considered by Canon 1127,

which deals in doubtful cases in favor of the faith. For example, whenever there is a doubtful baptism involved. It is clear that the dissolution of the Helena Case is due to the power of the Roman Pontiff, since a valid sacramental marriage which is consummated cannot be dissolved by any human power (Canon 1118), we can conclude as certain that a valid marriage between a certainly baptized person and a non-baptized person is not a sacrament and for grave reason the Holy Father can dissolve such a marriage.

3. In the Fresno Case, the Roman Pontiff dissolved a valid marriage of a baptized Catholic with a non-baptized person, contracted with a dispensation from disparity of cult; since this is not a sacramental marriage but a natural contract, there is no intrinsic difference between these cases and those of a baptized non-Catholic and a non-baptized person. This latter dispensation is a departure from the former policies. The Church had this power; nevertheless, was reluctant to act in these cases. The reason for this reluctance in which a prior marriage was celebrated after the granting of a dispensation from the impediment of disparity of cult is that some authors claim the Church would undo what she herself sanctioned to do previously. However, these are dogmatic truths; and basically the dogmatic aspects also have practical application. In the hierarchy of values, a sacramental union is to be preferred to a non-sacramental union. *Salus animarum'* is the principle involved. A marriage of a Catholic contracted with a non-baptized person with a dispensation given by the Church for the disparity of cult is no more a sacrament than a marriage contracted by two non-baptized persons, since we cannot have half a sacrament. Moreover, it is no more sacramental than a marriage between a baptized non-Catholic and an unbaptized person. The granting of a dispensation by the Church for such a marriage does not render it intrinsically different. It is understood that some who are concerned with such problems do not look with favor upon granting such dispensation for reason of scandal, laxity on the part of Catholics; but it may be that the meaning of the phrase *in favorem fidei* is sometimes misunderstood.

We cannot deny that the privilege of the faith means in some cases that a person who is baptized enjoys more favors in

the Church than an unbaptized person. Moreover, the privilege
also means that a person who receives baptism acquires a more
favorable position legally than he had formerly. According to
an Allocution of Pope Pius XII to the Sacred Roman Rota,
he remarked that in approaching this type of case, we are not
to be too lenient, nor too strict. The *via media* should be chosen,
first things should be put first; *salus animarum* is to be preferred
to the letter of the law. In the words of St. Paul, "The letter
killeth, the spirit quickeneth." Pope Pius XI, who was a great
defender of Christian marriage, has revealed in *Casti Connubii*,
that he too was greatly concerned with the sacrament of marriage but was never reluctant to use the privilege of the faith
when cases were presented to him. Therefore, *salus animarum*
should be the principle governing such cases.

Pastoral Aid or Consideration of a Non-Sacramental Marriage and What Is Necessary in Gathering Documents

1. A history of the case. This history should set forth all
the facts, showing who is the baptized party, who the unbaptized
party, the time of the marriage, the history of their marital
difficulties, the time, place, and petitioner of the divorce. The
certificate of marriage and divorce must be sent in. If the parties
desire to keep the original certificates, then a certified copy
should be obtained from the County Clerk. The complete history
should be written on a separate sheet of paper.

2. The full name and address of the petitioner.

3. The names and addresses of the parents of the petitioner.

4. The name and address of the unconverted party.

5. Names and addresses of the parents of the unconverted
party.

6. The names and addresses of people who can give testimony about the baptism or absence of baptism of either party,
specifying for which party the witness appears. The witnesses
for the unbaptized party should be the parents and relatives who
lived in the vicinity during the infancy of the person, and who
know the whole life of the person. In case an authentic baptismal
record can be furnished no witnesses need be brought forward
to substantiate the baptism.

7. Names and addresses of several people, preferably Catholics, who can testify concerning the truthfulness of the above mentioned witnesses, especially concerning those who testify to show the non-baptism of one of the principals.

8. The Catholic baptismal record of the convert.

9. The names and addresses of at least seven witnesses who can give testimony to show that the couple had no marital relations after the baptism of the spouse who had never been baptized. This is very important when the convert is the one who had not been baptized previously.

10. The name of the pastor.

11. The name or names of the priest who gave the instructions to the convert.

NON-CATHOLIC CAN ACT AS PLAINTIFF IN A MARRIAGE CASE

The Instruction *Provida Mater,* Aug. 15, 1936, 35, 3, states that non-Catholics, whether baptized or not, cannot act as plaintiffs in marriage cases without recourse in each case to the Congregation of the Holy Office. However on January 20, 1970, a letter from the Apostolic Pro-Nuncio to Canada to Archbishop Plourde expressed the opinion of the Signatura that marriage cases initiated by non-Catholic plaintiffs may be heard by a diocesan tribunal since non-Catholics, whether baptized or not, no longer need to request the ability to act as a plaintiff in marriage cases because of the promulgation of the apostolic constitution *Regimini Ecclesiae Universae.*

In a letter from the Congregation of the Doctrine of the Faith to the Bishop of Portland, dated October 15, 1968, it was stated that the Ordinary who is competent to process a case in the first instance can allow a non-Catholic the faculty to stand in court. A similar letter is found under c. 1646 in Volume VI of the Canon Law Digest, New York: Bruce, 1969, page 827. Dated February 12, 1966, it is a private reply from the Congregation of the Doctrine of the Faith that "the Ordinary who is competent to draw up the process in the first instance can grant to the petitioner the faculty to sue in court even though the person is a non-Catholic, and this is true also in a case of nullity."

CHAPTER IX

SEPARATION OF MARRIED PERSONS

GENERAL PRINCIPLES

Canon 1128: MARRIED PERSONS ARE OBLIGED TO OB-
SERVE THE COMMUNITY OF CONJUGAL LIFE UN-
LESS A JUST REASON EXCUSES THEM.

The Church admits separation of spouses for reason of
(1) adultery, (2) heresy or schism, (3) grave bodily or spiritual
danger, (4) mutual consent.[1]

ADULTERY

Canon 1129: 1. Whenever one party is guilty of adultery, the
other party, the bond remaining intact, has a
right to terminate the community of life even
permanently, unless he consented to the crime,
or was the cause of it, or condoned it expressly
or tacitly, or himself committed the same crime.

2. Tacit condonation is had, if the innocent party,
after learning of the adultery, of his own accord receives the other with conjugal affection:
Condonation is presumed, unless the injured
party within six months expels or deserts the
adulterer, or brings a legal accusation against
him.

---

1. Gasparri, *De Matrimonio*, II, n. 1363.

To separate because of adultery the act must be (1) formal, (2) complete, (3) morally certain, and it must not be attributed in any way whatsoever (refusal of the marital debt, desertion, etc.,) on the part of the other party.

The tacit condonation must be spontaneous, it must not arise from fear or danger of grave inconvenience. After six months, if the party does not separate or bring legal action, condonation is presumed, unless the contrary is proved.

THE RETURN OF THE GUILTY PARTY

Canon 1130:   The innocent party who has separated legally, whether by judicial decree or on his own authority, is never bound to admit the adulterous partner again to conjugal life, but he may either receive or recall the party, unless the latter, with the consent of the innocent party has in the meantime embraced a state of life incompatible with the married state.

SEPARATION

Canon 1131: 1. If the other party has joined a non-Catholic sect; or educated the children as non-Catholic, or is leading an ignominious and criminal life; or is causing grave spiritual or corporal danger to the other; or makes the common life too difficult by cruelty; these and other things of the kind, are so many lawful reasons for the other party to depart, on the authority of the local ordinary, and also on his own authority if the reasons are certain and there is danger in delay.

2. In all these cases, when the cause of the separation has ceased to exist, the common life is to be restored; but if the separation was decreed by the ordinary for a definite or indefinite time, the innocent party is not bound to the common life unless by decree of the ordinary or upon expiration of the time.

It is always best to handle separation cases through the local chancery because here the experts can evaluate the cases and situations surrounding the trouble. Here the parties are interrogated privately and separately. Reconciliation is always the objective, especially if there are children involved. In too many instances these cases go on too far to salvage them. The pastor should know his people and should enter into these conflicts and try to settle them. He is considered the pastor of souls and it is his obligation. If he gets the case in its early stages, chances are that he will be contributing much not only to the family but also to society in general.

Separation can also be made on the party's own initiative, if the legal cause is certain and there is danger of delay. Here again many times the innocent party is upset and is not able to evaluate the circumstances. In all cases and whenever possible, they should take the case to a priest; all priests should make themselves available for such cases and situations. A priest who would be deliberately avoiding such cases would be guilty of a grave sin of omission; after all, he is the shepherd of his flock and has a given responsibility before God.

CHILDREN OF SEPARATED PARTIES

Canon 1132: When the parties are separated, the children are to be educated by an innocent party, or, if one of the parties is a non-Catholic, by the Catholic party, unless in either case the local ordinary has declared otherwise for the benefit of the children themselves, always keeping in mind their Catholic education.

The statistics of today [2] show that there are 10 million divorced people in the United States; there are 400,000 divorces a year; 55,000 of these are Catholics (divorced).

In some of the dioceses there is no established procedure to handle separation cases. It is usually left up to the pastor, but if the pastor also is indifferent, little is done and disaster follows. It is the prerogative of every ordinary in his administrative and judicial capacity to adjudicate marriage cases. Better administration would result. Because divine and ecclesiastical law is never specific on the nature and indissolubility of marriage, these laws must be kept.

JUDGES, LAWYERS AND DIVORCE

I. The Judge

Every judge before entering upon the duties of his office usually takes an oath or affirmation, swearing (or affirming as the case may be) in some such terms as these that he will support the Constitution of the United States and the Constitution of the state in which he will preside, and will faithfully discharge the duties of judge in the particular court to which he is assigned, according to "the best of his ability." *Could a judge in conscience take such an oath if he knows that he cannot grant a divorce decree in the manner in which the state understands it?* We can assuredly answer in the affirmative that he could take such an oath; this is so because every oath taken by any man is understood in such a way that there is no intention to violate the law of God. It would be blasphemy to think otherwise. Moreover, there is no civil law which requires that the judge must share the intention of the legislator—the lawgiver. Consequently, when the judge grants a divorce he is not coerced or forced in any way *to intend* to dissolve the bond of marriage, in any way. He must stress the civil effects, however, in the decree or in the admonishment. Despite all this, the State, the public, and the divorced parties will look upon the decree as a means of breaking this bond of marriage. Nevertheless, the judge has the right to grant the divorce, if statutory evidence warrants it and there are *grave reasons* for his action and cooperation.

2. Flemming, Thos., "The divorced ones," *This Week Magazine*, Jan. 26, 1964. Statistics here presented from good Catholic source.

What would be considered a grave reason *for a judge to cooperate in such a case? Judges are public officials who are working for the common good.* In looking further, what does a judge do but hear the case presented to him in court; he weighs it on the "scale of justice"; and, in turn pronounces the verdict according to all the evidence which is presented to him. It would be wrong to ask all upright and conscientious judges to give up their offices in order to prevent them from granting a divorce decree. The judge on the bench holds a very important position. In this position he can offer his advice, counsel and possibly the ways and means for proper reconciliation. It is a known fact that many such judges have been very successful in this way. The judge is doing a service to the common good and at the same time is preventing a greater evil which is a justifying reason for permitting the judge to cooperate *materially* in granting a divorce.

It must be kept in mind, however, that a judge should never be guilty of *formal* cooperation in granting a separation or divorce decree; he must never act as if the case really pertains solely to the competency of the civil court; otherwise, he would be considered as *formally* cooperating and really usurping the power of the Church. This would be true in the case of a complete divorce, annulment, a separation maintenance, or even if he is denying such a petition. This would also be true even if the Church already declared that the marriage in question was null and void, because of some impediment of the natural or divine law. Every judge whether he be Catholic or non-Catholic should endeavor to persuade and assist the parties in becoming reconciled for the common good and the lessening of evil in the world.

II. The Lawyer

The lawyer is in a different category than the judge. A lawyer is called a private attorney because he is just that. As a private professional individual he has an option to take or refuse a case that comes to his attention; whereas, a judge is a *public official* in a public office and has no choice in the matter. He must act on the cases that are presented to him.

According to Canon 31 of the Statutes of Professional Ethics issued by the American Bar Association, we find: "No lawyer is obliged to act either as advisor or advocate for every person who may wish to become his client. He has the right to decline employment. Every lawyer upon his own responsibility must decide what business he will accept as counsel, what cases he will bring into court for plaintiffs, what cases he will contest in court for defendants. The responsibility for advising as to questionable transactions, for bringing questionable suits, for urging questionable defense, is the lawyer's responsibility He cannot escape it by urging as an excuse that he is only following his client's instructions. The ecclesiastical norm of moral conduct is the same regarding divorce and separation. *By the very fact that the lawyer represents and speaks for his client, he may licitly do only what his client may licitly do in regard to divorce and separation.* The lawyer is considered by the public as the "alter ego" of the client. Moreover, he is the necessary cooperator with the client in the case which he petitions or defends. As a result, in these divorce and separation cases, he is the cooperator, at least materially, in all the evil that would follow from the divorce, as for example, the unjust usurpation of competency in marriage cases on the part of the State, and in the violation of the divine law on the indissolubility of a valid marriage. However, just as the judge may be morally justified in cooperating materially with such evils, so also may the lawyer if he has a proportionately grave reason for such cooperation in the case. This will be determined on what the client may do licitly in regard to seeking a civil divorce or separation.

A person may licitly seek a civil divorce in the following circumstances: (1) when the Church declares a marriage null and void which is nothing more than dissolving the civil effects of an invalid contract; (2) when the Church decides that there is sufficient reason for a permanent or indefinite separation in a valid marriage and merely permits the civil divorce to protect the civil rights of the party. Two conditions must be verified by the client: (a) that there is a just cause for the separation and (b) that the party obtain the permission of the ordinary of the place to bring the matter to the civil court to obtain separate maintenance. If all of these conditions are fulfilled the lawyer may licitly represent his client. If the client is seeking the real dissolution of a valid marriage in order to remarry, the lawyer cannot represent him. Neither could he take it because another lawyer will take the case. The lawyer must be objective in dealing with his clients. Subjectivism has no place for the good lawyer. He must obey *his conscience,* not that of his client.

CHAPTER X

CONVALIDATION OF MARRIAGE

SIMPLE CONVALIDATION

Canon 1133: 1. For the convalidation of a marriage which is invalid because of a diriment impediment, it is required that the impediment cease or be dispensed, and that consent be renewed at least by the party who is aware of the impediment.

2. This renewal of consent is required by ecclesiastical law for the validity of the marriage even though both parties gave their consent in the beginning and have never revoked it.

CONVALIDATION

    ORDINARY (simple)
        DIRIMENT IMPEDIMENT
        DEFECT OF CONSENT
        DEFECT OF FORM

    EXTRAORDINARY i.e., SANATIO IN RADICE
        CONVALIDATES
        has retroactive effect

Diriment Impediment: This impediment must first cease or be dispensed before convalidation takes place by renewal of consent. This renewal of consent is required by ecclesiastical law. It is not required by the natural law. For example, a non-baptized person marries and later is divorced, but marries again. This person has a ligamen (bond) impediment and his second marriage is considered invalid while he is living with his second wife. His first wife dies but he continues to live with his second wife. Since his marriage is governed by the natural law, he need not renew consent; but if he were a Catholic, he would have to renew his consent since it is required by Canon Law. When it is impossible to get a non-Catholic party to renew the consent again and from the circumstances of the case we find that the children are being brought up Catholic, one can apply the *Sanatio* in this case, as explained later on.

Some Valuable Suggestions

1. A pastor should never be too hasty in getting a marriage validated.

2. A pastor should never be too quick to tell the parties that their marriage is invalid.

3. When it is discovered that there is no hope to validate the marriage, they should separate, but if the parties are in good faith, in extraordinary circumstances, we should let them go.

RENEWAL OF CONSENT

Canon 1134:   The renewal of consent must be a new act of the will having for its object the marriage which is known to be invalid from the beginning.

MANNER

Canon 1135:   1. If the impediment is public, the consent must be renewed by both parties in the form prescribed by law.

2. If the impediment is occult and known to both parties, it is sufficient that both parties renew their consent privately and secretly.

3. If it is occult and not known to one of the parties, it is sufficient that only the party who is aware of the impediment renew his consent privately and secretly, provided the other party perseveres in the consent once given.

When the impediment is occult and known to both parties, they need not go before the priest (C. 1094) but should renew their consent *explicitly*, externally, and through a mutual act. The conjugal act would not necessarily supply this; however, if they agreed to this way of giving mutual consent, this act would suffice.

If the impediment is occult and known to only one of the parties, all that is required is to make an internal act of the will; the confessor who might be handling the case, would simply ask the party to express his consent explicitly.

Canon 1136: 1. A marriage which is invalid for want of consent is validated if the party who had not consented, *consents now*, provided the consent given by the other party continues to exist.

2. If the lack of consent was merely internal, it is sufficient that the party who had not consented, give his consent interiorly.

3. If it was external also, it is necessary to manifest it externally also, either in the prescribed form by law, if the lack of consent was public, or in some other way privately or secretly, if it was occult.

Here we have three types of lack of consent cases: (1) internal, (2) external but occult, and (3) external and public. If the person withheld his consent by a positive act of the will regarding, e.g., the conjugal right or the essential properties of marriage, the MARRIAGE WOULD BE NULL. But this fact could never be proved in the external forum. Since this fact comes up in the confessional, the confessor should have the party elicit the consent then and there explicitly.

If the party withheld the consent by an external act, which would be impossible to prove in the external forum, he need merely to express his consent externally, not necessarily publicly.

If the lack of consent is both public and external, it must be renewed in the same manner, otherwise the marriage would be invalid.

Canon 1137: A marriage which is invalid for lack of form must be contracted again in the form prescribed by law in order to be made valid.

SANATIO IN RADICE

Canon 1138: 1. The "healing in the root" of a marriage is its convalidation involving, besides the dispensation or cessation of an impediment, a dispensation from the obligation of renewing the consent, and retroactivity through fiction of law, as regards canonical effects, to the past.

2. Convalidation takes place at the moment when the favor is granted, but retroaction is understood as going back to the beginning of the marriage, unless there are express provisions to the contrary.

3. The dispensation from the law concerning renewing the consent can be granted even without the knowledge of one or both parties.

A sanation implies three different items: (1) a dispensation or cessation of an impediment; (2) a dispensation from the law (C. 1094) which requires the renewal of consent; and (3) retroactivity.

NATURE OF THE SANATION

When a marriage has been contracted invalidly due to some impediment or for lack of the proper form; the consent which was given in the invalid marriage must continue or persevere. The dispensation of the sanation removes the impediment, if there is any, and the necessity of observing the form of marriage, or renewing the consent. The original consent which had no effect canonically, is now canonically made effective.

By retroactivity we mean that when the sanation is given, by fiction of law, the marriage is considered as valid from the very beginning. The dispensation *sanates* it. Children who were born illegitimate to such an invalid marriage are hereby legitimated canonically even as far as the canonical effects are concerned.

Our most common case is where there is a mixed marriage: when the non-Catholic party refuses to come to the church to have his marriage validated because he claims that he was married once; nevertheless, he does not disturb the Catholic party, he allows the practice of their religion and the Catholic education of the children. He will not go before a Catholic priest to renew his consent. Since this creates a problem, the church allows this dispensation in favor of the Catholic party in order to receive the sacraments, when the request is made to *sanate* the marriage.

TYPES OF SANATIONS

We have two kinds of sanations:

(1) *Perfect*: If there is a dispensation from renewing the consent by both parties and this makes it retroactive.

(2) *Imperfect*: If any of these items is absent, the sanation is imperfect:

   (a) *when one party only renews the consent;*
   (b) *when a sanation is given after the death of the party,* the bond of marriage is not there, but the

other effects can take place by fiction of law, e.g., legitimation.

(c) *if the retroactive effect does not go all the way but only partially.*

Canon 1139: 1. Any marriage which was contracted with the consent of both parties which was naturally sufficient but juridically ineffective because of a diriment impediment of ecclesiastical law or because of the defect of form, can be sanated, provided that the consent perseveres.

2. But a marriage that was contracted with an impediment of divine or natural law, even if the impediment has since ceased to exist, *cannot be sanated by the Church,* even from the time of the cessation of the impediment.

According to this Canon, whenever an impediment ceases, the consent must be given again. Gasparri claims that the sanation could be given up to the time that the impediment ceased. But the Church does not do so. The Code does not say that it cannot. We have evidence of such cases being granted by the Holy See.[1]

CONDITIONS FOR SANATION

Canon 1140: 1. If the consent is lacking on the part of both parties or in either party, the marriage cannot be sanated "in the root," regardless whether the consent was lacking in the beginning or was originally given and later revoked.

2. If consent was lacking in the beginning, but was afterwards given, a sanation can be given from the moment when the consent was given.

Canon 1141: A sanation in root can be granted only by the Apostolic See.

1. Gasparri, *De Matrimonio,* II, nos. 1215-19; Cappello, *De Matrimonio,* n. 854.

When the Code of Canon Law is revised at some future date, this Canon will be revised, because this faculty has been granted on a permanent basis to all bishops throughout the world. They need no longer go to Rome for these faculties.

With the Motu Proprio, *Pastorale Munus,* of Pope Paul VI, Nov. 30, 1963, *"all bishops, both resident and titular, have the special privilege to grant this sanation, provided that the consent perseveres, in marriages that are invalid because of minor impediments, or defect of form, even if there is a question of mixed marriage, but in this last case, Canon 1061 of the Code must be observed."* #21. #22: They can also grant *"the sanation in radice provided that the consent persevered in a marriage that is invalid because of the impediment of disparity of cult, even if they are invalid because of the lack of form, as long as Canon 1061 of the Code is observed."* (Canon 1061 deals with the necessary promises).

The widespread proposal by some of the hierarchy to abandon the law which requires the promises from non-Catholics has had very little impact upon the Holy Father since he included and stressed this factor in his Motu Proprio that *these promises must be given.* There does not seem to be any reason to exempt the non-Catholics from these important promises which are indirectly bound to the divine law.

SECOND MARRIAGES

Canon 1142: Although a chaste widowhood is more honorable, nevertheless, second and further marriages are valid and licit, without prejudice to the provision of Canon 1069, p. 2.

Canon 1143: A woman who has received the nuptial blessing once cannot receive it again in a subsequent marriage.

There is an interesting history on this phase of marriage.[2]

2. Perrone, *De Matrimonio Christiano,* Vol. III. Chardon, *Histoire des*

BROTHER AND SISTER ARRANGEMENT

(The Last Resort)

We find very little written about the Brother and Sister arrangement among the authors. Yet such arrangements have been made for almost two thousand years since the time of Christianity. Of course, it is only within recent years that this method has been adopted on a wider and bigger scale whereby the external forum has a better control of this age-old arrangement. Although we still have some of the clergy who frown upon this arrangement, nevertheless, it is a universal solution to many unfortunate cases. It requires very little reasoning to understand that such an arrangement is possible and feasible. To illustrate a case, a woman who lived in an invalid marriage for years and after ceasing marital relations for some ten years, asked a priest why she could not receive the sacraments. She explained that she was married by a justice of the peace; there were no children of the marriage and she lived in a large city where no one knew of her status. She further stated that for the past ten years she was living as any housekeeper does. She wondered why she could not go to the sacraments under these conditions after reasoning the matter out. She asked for the priest's advice. Her case was none other than those we handle now as a Brother and Sister case. It did not require much reasoning for this simple woman to draw the practical conclusion.

More and more cases of this kind are coming to our attention. We must be prepared to meet them. *Salus animarum!* With the necessary and proper precautions we can be of immense assistance to many souls who are in an invalid marriage but, for some reason or other, cannot separate. *For the best method, in handling such cases, is through the diocesan chancery or tribunal.* Here the experts could scrutinize the case with care and greater success than would the parish priest who might not be fully aware of the dangers which lurk in handling such a case. Scandal is the great factor that must be considered here.

Some dioceses are not too anxious to handle these cases through diocesan channels in which case, the parish priest is at

Sacrement du Marriage. Martene, *De Antiquis Ecclesiae.* St. Basil, *Ad Amphilochium ritibus*, C. 1, (Ayrh).

a loss on what to do. In 1950 when this kind of case was being discussed and brought out into the open, we found that some bishops frowned upon this arrangement. Today we have thousands who have found their salvation through this particular channel. A few years ago a book was published by a Catholic woman with an *imprimatur* explaining the "brother and sister" case which she discovered after searching for a solution of her own marital problem for many years.[3] With this information which was made public, there is no way in which this system can be suppressed. It is no longer the secret it once was; therefore, those priests who cannot handle this case through their diocesan chancery or tribunal, and are forced to take care of the matter themselves could use the following formula:

BROTHER AND SISTER ARRANGEMENT

After Careful Investigation of the Case One Must be Sure That:

1. Validation of the marriage is impossible.
2. Separation of the parties is extremely difficult (children and property).
3. Scandal will not result from this arrangement.
4. Danger of incontinence is removed (advanced age, illness or serious operation).

QUESTIONNAIRE FOR THE MAN

1. Name ....
2. Address ....
3. Date of Birth .... Place of Birth ....
4. Religion ....
   If (Catholic), when did you go to the Sacraments the last time?........
   ....
   If (non-Catholic) what church do you attend?.....................................
   Where? ....
   Do you wish to become a Catholic?..
5. Did you ever ask for such permission before?.....................................
   When?........................... Were you ever refused?...........................

3. McAuley, Clair, *Whom God Hath Not Joined*, Sheed & Ward.

Explain? ....

6. Where were you married?...
   When? .... Before whom? ....

7. Did many people know at that time that your marriage was invalid?
   .... How many? ....

8. How many children were born of this marriage?.................................

9. How long have you lived in this town?...

10. How many neighbors and friends know that your marriage is invalid?
    List them on a separate sheet. ....

11. How many relatives and friends know that your marriage is invalid?
    List them. ....

12. How many know that your marriage cannot be validated?...................
    List them. ....

13. Is it at all possible for you to separate?...
    If not, why? ....

14. What type of illness do you have?..

15. How many times were you married before?...

16. What is the date and place of your wife's death?................................

17. Her name (if living) .... Religion?......................
    Catholic? .... Non-Catholic? ....

18. When were you married? .... Where? ....
    By whom? ....

19. How many children were born of this marriage?................................
    List them. ....

20. Why did you separate? ....

21. Where did you get your divorce? ....
    When? .... Where? .... By whom? ....

22. Give the name and address of your former wife ....

23. Did she remarry?................. When?.................... Where?....................

24. If you had more than one wife, list them ....

25. Are you sure that you can keep your promise to live as brother and
    sister? .... Why are you so certain? ....

26. Have you ever tried to live in such a manner?..................................
    How long have you tried this?...

27. Would you be able to support your wife if she would separate from
    you? ....

28. Would there be scandal, if she separated (if people considered you
    married)? ....

29. If the answer is no, check on the financial standing. ....

30. Where will you go for confession and communion?................................
(Here the priest would advise the party or parties where to go without causing any scandal)
31. Do you realize that you will have to forfeit your right to Christian burial? ....

QUESTIONNAIRE FOR THE WOMAN

This questionnaire could be the same as that for the man except to change the wording where this will be necessary.

PROMISES

(Have both read the following together)

I. We, the undersigned, knowing full well that our marriage is invalid in the sight of God, and realizing that it is sinful to live in the manner of husband and wife, and realizing that it would be difficult for us to separate, WE HEREBY BEG FOR PERMISSION TO LIVE TOGETHER AS BROTHER AND SISTER and to BE READMITTED TO THE SACRAMENTS OF THE CHURCH. (Leave out last part for Non-Catholic.)

OATH

(This will be made by each party separately in the others presence.)

II. I .... realizing full well the sacredness of an oath, and my obligation *before God, touching the Holy Gospels, I solemnly swear;*

1. THAT I WILL NOT ATTEMPT TO LIVE AS HUSBAND AND WIFE WITH MY PRESENT CONSORT.
2. THAT I WILL SEPARATE, AND REFER THE MATTER TO THE (BISHOP) OR PRIEST BEFORE I RECEIVE THE SACRAMENTS AGAIN.
3. THAT I WILL RECEIVE THE SACRAMENTS ONLY IN THE CHURCHES WHERE MY MARITAL STATUS IS UNKNOWN TO THE PARISHIONERS.
4. TO EXPLAIN MY STATUS TO MY REGULAR CONFESSOR AND WILL REPORT TO HIM REGULARLY.

5. THAT I WILL TAKE EVERY PRECAUTIONARY MEASURE TO AVOID SCANDAL IN USING THIS PRIVILEGE, SO HELP ME GOD AND THESE HOLY GOSPELS WHICH I TOUCH.

Signatures   .... (Man)

                                .... (Woman)

                                .... (Priest)

DATE: ....

SEAL:

THE GOOD FAITH SOLUTION

Intolerable Marriage Situations: The Conflict between the External and the Internal Forum.

The Code of Canon Law has numerous laws that govern and protect the institution of Christian marriage. The procedure of handling informal and formal marriage cases are all found in the laws on marriage in Canons 1012-1143, 1552-2194, the Instruction *Provida Mater Ecclesia* (1936) and the *23 Provisional Norms on Procedure* (1970). The purpose of this legislation is to protect and promote the values of Christian marriage. As members of the Catholic Church, these laws must be upheld if we are to be faithful to Christ and his Church, at least in our present understanding of what Christian marriage is.

Since the codification of Canon Law in 1918, drastic changes have taken place throughout the world especially in the last five or ten years. These changes occurred in the development of jurisprudence regarding the grounds of annulment of marriage, such as psychic-incapacity, alcoholism, sociopathy, homosexuality, etc. Annulments on such grounds are granted today; ten years ago this was an impossibility.

No law is ever perfect because the human law maker of church laws is subject to imperfections. We must admit that we live in an imperfect and a changeable world. Even St. Thomas admitted this when he stated: *"because the human acts with which law deals are surrounded with particular circumstances which are infinitely variable, it is impossible to establish any law that suffers no exception; law makers observe what generally happens, and legislate accordingly; in some instances, to observe the law would violate the equality of justice and hurt the very welfare which law is meant to serve."* This is also the reason why we have such things as *epikeia*, rescripts and dispensations of all sorts. So too, we must look to new insights not only from theological and scriptural sources but also from the secular sciences, such as sociology, psychology, anthropology, etc., which are so intimately connected with human beings, it would be a mistake to overlook them in pursuance of truth and equity.

Everyone is aware of the changes that have come about and are continuing since Vatican Council II. The recent legislative norms to come from the Holy See (1970) are the *Twenty-Three Norms of Procedural Law*. Since they are only provisional is an indication that the law-giver is acting with caution and therefore are given by way of experimentation, which is a great step forward in the field of justice. So too, the long awaited answers to our present day intolerable marriage situations are being given to a hungry and large segment of our Catholic population through the "Good Faith Solution."

Before venturing into this category, for the sake of the would-be critic who will claim that the private good must suffer to preserve the common good, we reply that a balance must be maintained between the common good of the society and the justice and rights due to any individual within that society. Even Christ, who had a great respect for Jewish law and order, as well as the common good, made many exceptions to that law when human beings were suffering. For example, he healed the sick on the Sabbath, which was directly opposite to the Jewish law, and caused great scandal among the people. In reference to the common good, did he not suggest that we leave the ninety-nine and go in search of the one that was lost? Or, the woman who was caught in adultery was to be stoned to death according to the law, but Christ stepped in on the scene and opposed the law; and, instead of reprimanding the adulteress Samaritan woman, he talked to, and accepted a drink from her; this certainly was against the Jewish law.

Pope John XXIII also spoke clearly on this issue and about the definition of the common good in which we see the ultimate concern must be the welfare of the person, namely: "the sum total of those conditions of social living whereby men are able to achieve *their own* integral perfection more fully and more easily."

Marriage as we know it, is indissoluble. This we uphold; but there must be a marriage first in order to speak of indissolubility. We cannot take apart something that has not been molded together. We have seen many marriages that have failed because they were not true marriages to begin with. According to our marriage laws, marriage is a public act, not a private act. Marriage enjoys the favor of the law by legal presumption, and therefore considered valid until someone can prove it to be invalid.

If an ecclesiastical annulment could be obtained more reasonably than the present code of law permits, the problem would be lessened. The following illustration will show the conflict which can arise between a just law and the private good of an individual conscience:

Mary Jones was abandoned by her husband shortly after their marriage. He left telling her that he only married her to give the baby a name and that he never intended to remain with her permanently. In this case, Mary would have good grounds for an ecclesiastical annulment, but she must prove these facts in an ecclesiastical court. According to the law, she would have to bring two or more witnesses to establish conclusively that her husband lied to the priest before the marriage when he was asked: "Do you intend a permanent union?" The difficult burden of proving that he lied at the time of the marriage falls on her. Mary was deceived by her husband, but she is not able to produce the necessary evidence to convince the Church officials of the invalidity of her marriage. She can find no witnesses; she can offer no legal proof. Tribunal officials are satisfied that they have done all they can under the circumstances. Mary finds herself stranded to the frightening alternatives of living alone for the rest of her life (according to the law), or of marrying again outside the Church. She wants neither. She is doomed.

Later on, however, Mary falls in love and is married outside the Church; she is denied the sacraments because she is considered a sinful woman. Is she really a sinful woman? Is this second marriage really an invalid marriage? This is the question.

Ayrinhac-Lydon give their version of this dilemma in the following example, which fits our case: "The conflict would be more serious if the man who simulated consent had afterwards, being really free, contracted a valid marriage with another woman. In the external forum the first woman would be considered his legitimate wife; he would be bound to live with her and forbidden to have relations with the second one. In conscience, before God, the second woman would be his real wife, and there would be no possibility of revalidating the first marriage." [4]

The dilemma is self-evident. Our attempt is to maintain a healthy attitude towards the laws governing marriage and to look into the possibilities that would allow for a just and reasonable way of handling these situations where we find the legal system of the Church inadequate, unprepared or incapable of handling it. We must look elsewhere for the solution. In the past years, the Canon Law Society of America and Canada, theologians and canonists have looked elsewhere in their search for an answer. We have also learned that for many years this solution was obtained through the internal forum from the Sacred Penitentiary and for this reason is called the "Internal Forum Solution." However only a few priests knew about it or did anything about this problem. Today it is referred to as the Canonico-Moral solution, or pastoral solution, and is being used in many dioceses throughout the United States. It has been used, e.g., by the Chicago Tribunal for 20 years under three different Cardinal Archbishops. [5]

Our problems concern primarily the conflicting situation between *truth internally known* and truth *externally unknown;* secondly, it concerns the difficulty that arises from apparently genuine irregularity on the one hand, and a desire to be in line with the community, on the other. In other words, the problem concerns primarily the conflicting situations that arise when a marriage is invalid before God but it cannot be proved to be so before a human tribunal. Secondly, it concerns the situations when a marriage was a sacrament before God and the community, and the person now desires to receive the sacraments while remaining faithful to his second marital union. This is really the case of those who are divorced and remarried and are now anxious to return to full communion with the Church but cannot do so either because their first marriage was invalid, but invalidity cannot be proved, or because the first marriage, valid as it was, ended in divorce and there is now another marital union.

4. Ayrinhac-Lydon, *Marriage Legislation*, 1959, N.Y.
5. *The Jurist*, Vol. XXIX, Oct. 4, 1969, p. 428.

The Good Faith Solution

The Good Faith Solution is operative under four conditions:

1) *There must be an insoluble doubt about the validity of the first marriage.* The doubt must be founded on (a) the statement of the petitioner indicating invalidity; (b) at least a few references to invalidity from one or two witnesses; (c) good circumstances to indicate invalidity. After a thorough discussion with the party of the previous marriage, there must be some solid doubt in the mind óf the petitioner. If necessary the priest or counselor may help the person arrive at such a conclusion. An effort should be made to establish the doubt from all three sources, but if one or the other are missing one could still pursue to the needed solution.

(2) The present (second) marriage must have stability. A stable marriage is the most important factor to a future healthy growth of the family. When a stable marriage exists the priest or counselor would be reluctant to ask people to break up their marriage as a condition to enter the Church. As for a brother-sister relationship, this is clearly unrealistic among the great majority of people.

(3) Assurance must be sought from the principals of the marriage in possession that they were in "Good Faith" at the time they entered this marriage. Did they feel that they were violating God's law in entering a second marriage? Or did they feel that this was a real marriage in the eyes of God upon which they could ask and expect God's blessing? In almost all cases where the parties are non-Catholic, good faith seems to exist on the part of both parties. We might find an exception where one of the parties would be the cause of the break-up of the first marriage.

(4) One must be careful that no scandal would result should this second marriage be allowed to continue. This information can be obtained from the pastor of the parties or from the individuals themselves.

People in general do not know all the complexities of canon law; therefore the priest or counselor must be patient in handling any marriage case. We must take people where they are; considering their background, education, environment, etc. We must remember that there is no ideal man. Since every human being is unique, so every marital situation is to a certain extent unique also. For the convenience of those counselors who wish to understand the "Good Faith" solution in greater depth, the following list of books and articles are given here:

Bibliography of Books and Articles on The Good Faith Solution

Basset, William, *The Bond of Marriage*, Univ. of Notre Dame Press, 1968.

Bresnahan, James F., "Problems of Marriage and Divorce," *America*, May 25, 1968, pp. 706-709.

Carey, Raymond G., "The Good Faith Solution," *The Jurist*, Vol. XXIX, Oct. 1969.

Catoir, John T., "Church and Second Marriages," *Commonweal*, April 14, 1967, p. 113. "What is the Marriage Contract?" *America*, Vol. 118, no. 7, p. 229.

Constitution on the Church in the Modern World, nos. 12, 17.

Council Daybook, Vatican II Session 4, pp. 71-72, An Address by Archbishop Elie Zoghbi.

Doherty, Denis, "Problem of Divorce and Remarriage," *Marriage* 28, 1966, pp. 12-18.

Häring, Bernard, *The Law of Christ*, Newman Press, 1966, Vol. III, p. 327.

Hertel, James R., O.D.M., *When Marriage Fails*, Paulist Press, Paramus, N.J.

Hertel, James, "Save the Bond or Save the Person," *America*, Vol. 118, n. 7, Feb. 17, 1968, pp. 217-220.

Hurley, M., S.J., "Christ and Divorce," *Irish Theol. Quarterly* 35, 1968, pp. 58-72.

"Indissolubility of Marriage, The," *The Theological Tradition of the East*, pp. 97-116.

Kelleher, S.J., "The Problem of the Intolerable Marriage," *America*, September 14, 1968, pp. 178-182.

Krebs, A. V., "American Catholic Marriage and the Church," *America*, Feb. 1969, p. 228.

Mahoney, John, "Do They Intend Marriage," HPR, 67, 1966.

Monden, Louis, S.J., *Sin, Liberty and Law*, Sheed & Ward, N.Y. 1965, pp. 135-136.

Montserrat, J. — Torrents, *The Abandoned Spouse*, Bruce, 1969.

Pope John XXIII, *Pacem in Terris*, no. 58.

Pospishil, Victor J., *Divorce and Remarriage,* Herder and Herder, N.Y., 1967, pp. 40-73. / "The Damned Millions: The Problem of Divorced Catholics," HPR, 1968, pp. 95-104.

"Sacraments: An Ecumenical Dilemma, The," *Concilium* 24, Paulist Press, N.Y., 1967, pp. 113-138.

Shaner, Donal, *A Christian View on Divorce,* E. J. Brill 1969, Leiden, pp. 14-25.

Sullivan, Jos. Deuel, "Divorce and Psychological Change," *Cath. Theol. Soc. of America Proceedings,* Vol. 22, 1967, pp. 245-252.

The Jurist, January 1970 contains these excellent articles:

  (1) "Intolerable Marriage Situations: The Conflict between the External and Internal Forum," by Ladislas Orsy, S.J.

  (2) "Law, Conscience and Marriage," by Peter Huizing.

  (3) "Internal Forum Solutions to Insoluble Marriage Cases," by Bernard Häring.

  (4) "The Pastoral Care of Those Involved in Canonically Invalid Marriages," by Anthony Kosnik.

  (5) "Toward 'An Immediate Internal Forum Solution' For Deserving Couples in Canonically Insoluble Marriage Cases," by Leo C. Farley and Warren T. Reich, S.J.

"The Tragedy of Broken Marriages," *Jubilee,* March 1966, p. 48.

APPENDIX

PASTORALE MUNUS

The Motu Proprio, *Pastorale Munus* of Pope Paul VI, given December 3, 1963 grants special faculties and privileges to all local ordinaries on a permanent basis.

The bishops, though hindered by many obstacles, have nonetheless given an example of special charity in all times and dedicated themselves to the pastoral office to which Jesus Christ assigned the very important task of teaching, of leading to holiness, of binding and loosing.

With the increase through the centuries of the Church's concerns and labors, the Apostolic See has always replied promptly and eagerly to the requests of the bishops regarding pastoral care and not only has it added to the extraordinary authority and jurisdiction of the heads of dioceses but also endowed them with singular faculties and privileges which appropriately met current needs.

Now, moreover, while the second session of the Second Vatican Ecumenical Council approaches its end and since we wish nothing more dearly than to express to the council Fathers the very great esteem we have for all the venerable brothers in the episcopacy, it seemed good to us to accept their requests willingly and grant them things which may place their episcopal dignity in the proper light and at the same time render their pastoral function freer and more effective. We think this is very fitting to our office as universal Shepherd. In bestowing these things most willingly on the bishops, we at the same time request that they all, moved by the breadth of flaming charity and joined closely with Christ and with us, His vicar on earth, should seek through their collaboration to lighten *that care for all the churches* (cfr. 2 Cor. 11, 28) which weighs upon our shoulders.

Since it is a matter of faculties of the utmost importance, we grant them in such a way that they cannot be delegated by the bishops except to a coadjutor, auxiliaries and vicar general, unless expressly noted in the concession of an individual faculty.

According to the prevaling norm of law, however, such faculties, which we declare belong by law to residential bishops, also belong by law to vicars and prefects apostolic, permanent apostolic administrators, abbots and prelates *nullius*, who in their territory enjoy the same rights and faculties that residential bishops have in their own dioceses. And although vicars and prefects apostolic cannot appoint a vicar general, they nevertheless can legitimately delegate to their vicar delegate the faculties treated here.

And so, having maturely considered everything from our reverence and charity toward each bishop of the Catholic Church, of our own initiative (motu proprio) and by our apostolic authority we decree and establish that from the eighth of December of this year 1963, the bishops may immediately and legitimately use and enjoy the following faculties and privileges:

I. *Faculties* which by right belong to a residential bishop from the moment that he takes canonical possession of the diocese. Unless it is expressly stated in the faculties, he may not delegate them to others except to coadjutor and auxiliary bishops and a vicar general.

1. Proroguing for a just case, but not beyond a month, the lawful use of rescripts or indults which were granted by the Holy See and have expired, without a request for their renewal having been sent at the proper time to the Holy See. There is an obligation to apply at once to the Holy See for the favor, or to seek a reply if the petition has already been submitted.

2. Permitting priests, because of scarcity of clergy and for a just cause, to celebrate Mass twice on weekdays, and even three times on Sundays and Holy Days of obligation, provided genuine pastoral necessities so demand.

3. Permitting priests, when celebrating two or three Masses, to take liquids even though there be not an interval of an hour before the next Mass.

4. Permitting priests, for a just cause, to celebrate Mass at any hour of the day and to distribute Communion in the evening, with due observance of the other prescriptions of law.

5. Granting the faculty to priests who suffer from poor eyesight or are afflicted with some other infirmity, to offer daily the votive Mass of the Blessed Virgin or the Mass of the dead with the assistance, according to their needs, of a priest or deacon and with due observance of the Instruction of the Sacred Congregation of Rites of April 15, 1961.

6. Granting the same permission to priests who are totally blind provided they are always assisted by another priest or deacon.

7. Granting priests the faculty to celebrate Mass outside a sacred place, but in a reputable and decent place, never in a bedroom, on an altar stone: in an individual case for a just cause but habitually only for a graver cause.

8. Granting also the faculty to celebrate Mass for a just cause at sea and on rivers, with observance of the required precautions.

9. Granting the faculty to priests, who enjoy the privilege of the portable altar, that, for a just and grave cause, they may use, instead of an altar stone, the Greek antimension, or the cloth blessed by the bishop, in the right corner of which are placed relics of the holy martyrs authenticated by the bishop, with due observance of other requirements of the rubrics, particularly regarding altar cloths and the corporal.

10. Granting to infirm or elderly priests the faculty of celebrating Mass at home, but not in a bedroom, daily and even on the more solemn feasts, observing the liturgical laws, but with the permission of sitting if they are unable to stand.

11. Reducing because of a decrease in income, as long as the cause obtains, Masses from a legacy (which per se remain

fixed) at the rate of the stipend lawfully in effect in the diocese, provided that there is none who is obliged and can rightfully be expected to increase the stipend; likewise, of reducing the obligations or legacies of Masses which burden benefices or other ecclesiastical institutes, if the income of the benefice or institute becomes insufficient for the suitable sustenance of the beneficiary and for fulfilling the works of the sacred ministry attached to the benefice or for attaining in a fitting manner the proper end of the ecclesiastical institute.

12. Granting to chaplains of all hospitals, orphanages and prisons the faculty, in the absence of the pastor, to administer the sacrament of Confirmation to the faithful in danger of death, with due observance of the norms of the Sacred Congregation of the Discipline of the Sacraments established by the decree, "Spiritus Sancti munera" of September 14, 1946, for priests administering the sacrament of Confirmation.

13. Granting to confessors the faculty, in individual cases, of absolving any of the faithful in the act of sacramental confession from all reserved sins, with the exception however of the sin of false denunciation in which an innocent priest is accused of the crime of solicitation before ecclesiastical judges.

14. Granting confessors distinguished for knowledge and prudence the faculty, in individual cases, of absolving any of the faithful in the act of sacramental confession from all censures, even reserved, with the following exceptions: (a) "ab homine" censures; (b) censures reserved in a most special way to the Holy See; (c) censures which are attached to disclosure of the secret of the Holy Office; (d) the excommunication incurred by clerics in sacred orders and all presuming to contract marriage with them, even only civilly, and actually living together.

15. Dispensing for a just cause from the defect of age for ordination provided that it does not exceed six full months.

16. Dispensing from the impediment to orders by which the sons of non-Catholics are bound as long as the parents remain in error.

17. Dispensing those already ordained, for the purposes both

of celebrating Mass and obtaining and retaining ecclesiastical benefices, from any of the irregularities, whether ex delicto or ex defectu, provided that scandal does not arise thereby and provided that the ministry of the altar is correctly performed, with the exception of those mentioned in Canon 985: 3 and 4 of the Code of Canon Law. In the case of the crime of heresy or schism, there must be a prior abjuration in the hands of the one absolving.

18. Conferring sacred orders outside the cathedral church and "extra tempora," including weekdays, if this is useful from a pastoral point of view.

19. Dispensing for a just and reasonable cause from all the minor matrimonial impediments, even if there is question of mixed marriages, but with observance in this latter case of the prescriptions of Canons 1061-1064 of the Code of Canon Law.[1]

20. Dispensing, when a just and grave cause urges, from the impediments of mixed religion and disparity of worship, even in the case of use of the Pauline Privilege, with observance of the prescriptions of Canons 1061-1064 of the Code of Canon Law.

21. "Sanandi in radice," provided the consent perdures, marriages that are invalid because of a minor impediment or defect of form, even if there is question of mixed marriages, but in this case there must be observance of Canon 1061 of the Code of Canon Law.

22. "Sanandi in radice," provided consent perdures, marriages that are invalid because of the impediment of disparity of worship, even if they are also invalid because of a defect of form, with observance of the prescriptions of Canon 1061 of the Code of Canon Law.[2]

23. Permitting for a grave cause, that the interpellations of an infidel spouse may be done before the baptism of the party who is being converted to the faith; and dispensing, also for a grave cause, from the same interpellation before the baptism of the party who is being converted: provided, in

1. Cf. C. 1063, New Decree on Mixed Marriage.
2. Cf. C. 1063.

this case that it is clear from a summary and extra-judicial process that the interpellation cannot be made or it would be useless.

24. Reducing, for a just cause, the obligation by which cathedral chapters and colleges of canons are obliged to perform ritually the daily Divine Offices in Choir, by granting that choral service may be satisfied either only on certain days or merely by a certain determined part.

25. Entrusting, where necessary, certain canons with the tasks of the sacred ministry, of teaching or of the apostolate, with a dispensation from choir, while preserving the right of receiving the fruits of the prebend, but not the distributions, whether *inter praesentes,* as they are called, or daily.

26. Commuting for reason of weak eyesight or other cause, as long as the condition persists, the Divine Office into daily recitation of at least a third part of the Rosary of the Blessed Virgin Mary or other prayers.

27. Deputing in particular cases, or for a time, the vicar general or another priest with ecclesiastical dignity, to consecrate portable altars, chalices and patens, according to the rite prescribed in the Pontifical and using the Holy Oils blessed by the bishop.

28. Allowing minor clerics, lay Religious and also pious women to wash with the first ablution, palls, corporals and purificators.

29. Using the faculties and privileges, while observing their extent and intent, which religious communities having a house in the diocese enjoy for the good of the faithful.

30. Granting to priests the faculty by which, with the rites prescribed by the Church, they may erect the Stations of the Cross, even in the open air, with all the indulgences that have been granted to those who make this pious exercise. The faculty cannot be exercised in parochial territory where there is a house of religious who by apostolic grant enjoy the privilege of erecting the Stations of the Cross.

31. Admitting illegitimate sons into the seminary if they show the qualities required for admission into the seminary, provided it is not a question of offspring of an adulterous or sacrilegious union.

32. Granting permission that, for a legitimate cause, ecclesiastical goods may be alienated, pledged, mortgaged, leased, redeemed from a long-term lease, and that ecclesiastical moral persons may contract on indebtedness to an amount proposed by the national or regional conference of bishops and approved by the Holy See.

33. Confirming even to a fifth triennium the ordinary confessor of Religious women if another provision cannot be made because of the scarcity of priests suitable for this office, or if the majority of the Religious, even those who in other matters do not have the right to vote, agree in secret ballot to the confirmation of the same confessor. Another provision must be made for those who disagree, if they so desire.

34. Entering, for a just cause, into the pontifical cloister of monasteries of nuns situated in his diocese, and permitting for a just and grave cause, that others be admitted into the cloister, and that the nuns go out from it—for a truly necessary period of time.

35. Dispensing, on the petition of the competent superior, from the impediments which prevent those who have adhered to a non-Catholic sect from being admitted into Religion.

36. Dispensing, on the petition of the competent superior, from illegitimacy of birth, those to be admitted into Religion who are destined for the priesthood, and also others who are forbidden admission into Religion by a prescription of the Constitutions. In neither case can adulterous or sacrilegious offspring be dispensed.

37. Waiving in whole or in part, on the petition of the competent superior, the dowry which postulants should bring to be admitted to a monastery of nuns or another religious community, even of pontifical right.

38. Permitting religious to transfer from one to another community of diocesan right.

39. Dismissing from the diocese, in the presence of a most serious cause, individual Religious, if their major superior has been warned and has failed to provide; moreover, the matter is to be referred immediately to the Holy See.

40. Granting, also through other prudent and capable men, to the individual faithful subject to himself, the permission to

read and retain, with care however less they fall into the hands of others, prohibited books and periodicals, not excepting those which purposely defend heresy or schism, or attempt to overturn the very foundations of religion. However, this permission can be granted only to those who need to read the forbidden books and periodicals either to attack them, or to meet properly their own obligations or to follow lawfully a course of studies.

II. *Privileges,* which, besides those enumerated in their titles in the Code of Canon Law, belong to all bishops, residential or titular, as soon as they have received the authentic notification of canonical election.

1. Preaching the word of God—everywhere in the world, unless the Ordinary of the place expressly denies it.
2. Hearing the confessions of the faithful and of Religious women anywhere in the world, unless the Ordinary of the place expressly denies it.
3. Absolving any of the faithful anywhere in the act of sacramental confession, from all reserved sins, except however the sin of false denunciation in which an innocent priest is accused of the crime of solicitation before ecclesiastical judges.
4. Absolving any of the faithful anywhere in the act of sacramental confession from all censures, even reserved, excepting however: (a) censures "ab homine"; (b) censures reserved in a most special way to the Holy See; (c) censures which are attached to disclosure of the secret of the Holy Office; (d) the excommunication incurred by clerics in sacred orders and all presuming to contract marriage with them, even only civilly, and actually living together. Residential bishops can also use this faculty for their subjects in the external forum.
5. Reserving the Blessed Sacrament in their private oratory provided that the prescriptions of the liturgical laws are fully observed.
6. Celebrating Mass at any hour of the day, for a serious reason, and distributing Holy Communion even in the evening, obll norms enjoined.

7. Blessing anywhere by a single sign of the Cross, with all the indulgences usually granted by the Holy See, rosaries and other beads used for prayers, crosses, medals, scapulars approved by the Holy See and imposing them without the obligation of inscription.

8. Blessing for the faithful, who because of infirmity or other lawful impediment cannot visit the sacred Stations of the Cross, images of the Crucified with an application of all the indulgences attached by the Roman Pontiffs to the devout exercise of the Way of the Cross.

We with pleasure grant these faculties and privileges to Our Brothers in the Episcopacy with the intention and purpose we have noted above: that all these may particularly be for the glory and advantage of the Church of Christ to whom We and Ours are indebted for all things.

Notwithstanding anything to the contrary, even worthy of special mention.

Given at Rome, at St. Peter's, on the 30th of November, 1963, the first of Our Pontificate.

PAUL PP. VI

N.C.W.C. News Service

A PRESUMPTION OF DEATH CASE [3]

With the solution of an unusual presumption of death case, the hope arose that its publication might encourage others with similar cases to pursue them to a decision by the competent ecclesiastical authority. Since many difficult cases of this kind may have been solved already in the various chancery offices, this

---

3. By Bernard A. Siegle, T.O.R., J.C.D.

one is submitted for consideration only as an example. It may serve also as an indication of the various and extensive means of investigation which may be employed.

Part I consists of general observations on the canonical doctrine governing the settlement of presumption of death cases; Part II describes the efforts made in the case of John H. White to discover his whereabouts or to uncover proof of his death; and Part III is the decree issued at the conclusion of the investigation.

I. The Presumption of Death

His Holiness, Pope Pius XII, of blessed memory, in speaking to the personnel of the Roman Rota in 1942 regarding moral certitude, reminded them for the second time that absolute certainty is not necessary to pronounce a judgment. "In many cases," he says,

> "it is humanly unattainable. To require it of the judge and of the parties would be demanding something which is unreasonable; it would put an intolerable burden on the administration of justice and would seriously obstruct it. The other extreme of quasi-certainty or common speech is also to be avoided. Between the two extremes of absolute certainty and quasi-certainty is the moral certainty which is usually involved in the cases submitted to your court. Moral certainty is necessary and sufficient for the rendering of a judgment, even though in a particular case it would be possible directly or indirectly to reach absolute certainty. Only thus is it possible to have a regular and orderly administration of justice, going forward without useless delays and without laying excessive burdens on the tribunal as well as on the parties.
>
> *Sometimes moral certitude is derived only from an aggregate of indications and proofs, which, taken singly, do not provide the foundation for true certitude, but which, when taken together no longer leave room for any reasonable doubt on the part of men of sound judgment.*

In any event, this certainty is understood to be objective, that is, based on objective motives. If after serious consideration and study, a grade of certitude is attained which corresponds to the requirements of law and to the importance of the case, there should not be insistence, to the serious inconvenience of the parties, that new proof be adduced so as to attain a still higher degree of certitude. To require the highest possible certainty, notwithstanding that a sufficient certainty already exists, is without justification and should be discouraged." [4]

The moral support of the Holy Father gave me the courage to work on this case which fell to my lot. There were no wars, earthquakes or floods as some would have it in order to work on such a case. Of the many canonists consulted on this voluminous case, there were as many different opinions as to how this could be handled. Some thought it best to drop the matter, others suggested sending it to Rome, again others thought it was a challenge and that it should be handled through the chancery here in the United States. It was finally decided to handle it here.

To begin with, we know that a valid marriage of Christians consummated by the conjugal act cannot be dissolved by any human authority for any reason; death alone can dissolve the bond.[5] Consequently, once a party to such a marriage desires to marry again, he must present proof of the death of his former spouse. A death certificate by the competent ecclesiastical or civil authority usually suffices.

Wars, shipwreck, earthquakes, plane crashes and other disasters cause the disappearance of persons about whom nothing is heard. And it then happens that the other spouse desires to marry again on the assumption that his or her partner is dead.

To the pastor and officials of the diocesan curia these cases offer a challenge because they can become complex. We read often in the press of men reportedly dead and later found to be alive. Cases of this kind do serve as a warning not to proceed too hastily in allowing a second marriage. On the other hand, they are no license for the officials of the curia to file away the

4. Allocution to the Roman Rota—AAS XXXIV, 1942, p. 338.
5. C. 1118.

case and do nothing about it. Postponing or delaying solution of the cases presents a hardship to the surviving spouse.

Before a marriage is celebrated, it must be ascertained that there is no obstacle to its valid and licit reception.[6] Moreover, canon 1069 declares that "marriage is rendered invalid by the bond of a previous marriage, even though not consummated, except in the case of the privilege of the faith. Even though the first marriage be null or dissolved for any reason whatsoever, it is not lawful to contract another marriage before the nullity or dissolution of the first be established legitimately and certainly."

No new instructions on this subject were issued after the promulgation of the Code and, although the Code itself contains no explicit or implicit reference to the Instruction of 1868, it does contain an implicit reference to the proof of death cases in canon 1069, § 2, when it requires certainty of the dissolution of the first marriage before a second marriage can be allowed. The Instruction of 1868 explains how this certainty is to be acquired, and consequently it would seem to hold even today in such cases. All doubt in the matter is dispelled by the practice of the Roman Curia. The Sacred Congregation of the Sacraments directed the bishops on various occasions to use the instruction of 1868; in two post-Code Rota cases in which the question of the proof of death was taken up reference was made to this instruction.

The Instruction of 1868 consists of a preamble and eleven paragraphs. However, there are two main ideas which permeate the Instruction: first, that the unity of marriage must be protected, especially against fraud and deception; and secondly, that everything possible must be done to give a person the opportunity to exercise the freedom of re-marriage after the death of the former spouse. *The Holy See did not wish to have people forced to remain celibate after the death of the first spouse, and for this reason was desirous of having cases of doubtful death settled as quickly as possible without recourse to the same Holy See.*

Because of the desire of the Holy See to settle such cases as soon as possible, they are ordinarily handled and settled through the administrative process.

6. C. 1019, § 1.

Primarily, it is a part of the process for the ascertainment of the *status liber* of a prospective contractant of marriage. And all agree that this process is essentially administrative. The authorization granted by the Code in Canons 1019-1034 is sufficient to empower the Ordinary or his delegate to handle such cases. Even when cases of this nature become so extremely difficult and complicated that they are referred to the Holy See, the process nevertheless remains administrative, as is evident from the method employed by the S. Congregation of the Sacraments in handling such matters.[7]

If the Ordinary wishes, he may remand cases involving the question of presumed death to the judicial tribunal for formal trial. However, it is to be borne in mind that administrative procedure is the normal, ordinary method for handling such cases even though some authors strongly recommend the formal judicial process. Briefly, in these cases formal procedure is always optional; but not absolutely necessary.[8]

It must be understood from the beginning that the certitude required in doubtful cases of presumed death is not metaphysical certitude (which one chancery official demanded but was rebuked by the Holy See for demanding), nor physical certitude, but moral certitude.

II. Acquisition of Moral Certitude in the Presumption of Death of John White

On the morning of January 11, 1945, at 9 o'clock, John White, husband of Mary Jones White, left his residence to submit an application in the office of the War Manpower Com-

7. S. Cong. de Sacraments, Mohilovien, 16 Decembris, 1910, AAS III, (1911), pp. 26-29; 18 Decembris, 1914, AAS VII, (1915), pp. 40-44; 29 Aprilis, 1915, AAS VII, (1915), pp. 235-236; 25 Iunii, 1915, AAS VII (1915), pp. 476-479; 25 Februarii, 1916, AAS VIII, (1916), pp. 151-153; 19 Ianuarii, 1917, AAS IX, (1917), pp. 120-122; 18 Novembris, 1920, AAS XIV, (1922), pp. 86-97.

8. Doheny, *Canonical Procedure in Matrimonial Cases*, II, p. 596.

mission, Pittsburgh, Pennsylvania. That was the last time that Mrs. White saw her husband. To determine the decedent's whereabouts, his wife has used all possible means to locate her husband, as follows:

(a) Notified the Police department as well as the Missing Persons Bureau in Pittsburgh, Pennsylvania;

(b) Secured the aid of the District Attorney's office, where detectives took a personal interest in trying to locate the missing man;

(c) Requested the help of American Legion. This was given in the form of searching parties who combed the countryside and the city of Pittsburgh for weeks in an effort to find John White;

(d) Had his description broadcast over the radio, on which a special effort was made to locate him. His wife also appeared on the radio broadcast known as "We the People," where the fact of presumed decedent's disappearance and description was broadcast over the entire network of the Columbia Broadcasting System. At this time this program enjoyed great popularity and its audience ran into the tens of millions;

(e) Had the fact of his disappearance and his description published in all the local papers;

(f) With the help of the American Legion, over a 100,000 dodgers were published with John White's description and the facts of his disappearance. These were sent to every American Legion post and official organization in the United States, Hawaii, Alaska and Canada;

(g) Notified the fact of the disappearance to State Police at Harrisburg who made arrangements through their facilities to contact every law enforcement agency in the United States including the State Police and State Patrols of every state; and

(h) Filed notification of his disappearance (his description and fingerprints) at the Federal Bureau of Investigation during the entire time of the search.

Since it would be impossible to give all the details of the case in this article, it is hoped that a general summary will suffice. One of the factors indicated in the Instruction of 1868 which must be considered is: "The moral character of the allegedly deceased person: his mode of life, whether he was pious and religious, and whether he had love for his wife." The individuals interrogated included Mary Jones White, the wife of the presumed decedent, four of his sisters—three older and one younger than he (one is a Sister of Mercy), an older brother, two intimate friends, and the supervisor of the American Legion. Most of the conjectures and presumptions as prescribed by the Instruction were obtained from the answers to over two thousand questions which were asked of these individuals.

All witnesses unanimously testified to John White's very good moral character. One of the sisters related that he stayed with her for three years before his marriage and that during that time he never missed Mass on Sundays and holy days, and made retreats. He had his own business which he sold when he went into the service. When he was discharged, he found it impossible to resume the same business because the essential items needed were not available. He tried in vain to find work even though jobs were plentiful. This was probably due to the fact that he had only one eye. Employers considered this factor an obstacle in their places of employment, because of the dangers it presented and the compensation entailed in case of an accident. He lived on his wife's investments and always felt that he was a burden; because of this he became very despondent. On several occasions he mentioned that he would like to end it all, and even hinted to friends that he might jump in the river. His brother and sisters agree that both spouses were in love and never had any major quarrels. White realized that his wife was doing more for him than any woman ordinarily would do in such a case. His brother related that Mrs. White was intellectually above his level, honest, sincere, and ready to help him in any circumstance.

Last will and testament: Three months before his disappearance John White made out his will. A person does not ordinarily make out a will unless he foresees something in the future. The will was made out leaving everything to his wife and son. This Last Will and Testament proves that White was on good terms with his wife and was concerned about her and about his son.

Family appraisal: John White's brother and all of his sisters gave a praiseworthy account of their sister-in-law, Mrs. White, and testified that they got along very well together. They also testified that if he were normal, he certainly would not be absent from his home so long. He loved his wife and son, he enjoyed his home, and he was a family man. The fact stands that he disappeared, yet no reason whatsoever could be established for his absence, except the aforementioned matters: that he was despondent and made threats concerning his life.

Army life: While in the Armed Forces for four months and nine days, John White spent over two months in the hospital getting treatments. He gave indications that he enjoyed getting these treatments at army expense. The authorities, aware of his physical condition, honorably discharged him "for the convenience of the government" after this short time in the service. He returned home and was unable to find work. In 1943 he married Mary Jones; in 1944 a son was born to them.

Married life: From the day that he married until the time of his disappearance in 1945, White did not have a permanent job. In one instance, when he was evaluated with 15 other salesmen, he had the lowest rating as a salesman. He acted very queerly in the presence of his friends, at times making threats to take his own life. His relatives and friends noticed he did not act like himself at all, but seemed as if in a daze or in a fog.

White had many fainting spells at home, and also had a strange fear when people called at his home. He would say: "Don't tell anyone I'm home." He tried to do carpentry work, but his hands would swell up causing him great pain. He would stay in bed with his swollen hands propped up by pillows.

Auto accident: Five days before his disappearance, White had an accident with his car. During a cold foggy day, when the roads were covered with ice and snow, as he was going down one of the hills in Pittsburgh, he crashed into a tree. A short time afterwards one of his friends who was passing by stopped and asked him if he was hurt or needed any help. White was silent and wouldn't speak—after asking him several times and getting no answer the friend became angry and went away. It was only later that White's friend realized that he must have been in a state of shock. Upon arriving home, White told his wife about his accident, but refused to have her call a doctor. He was afraid of doctors. The car was towed to the garage in the meantime. From the damage to the car, it was determined by experts that White must have been injured seriously. The entire front of the car was demolished. After the accident, he was not himself; it seems that his mental condition was getting worse because he had fainting spells quite frequently and he could not sleep well at night.

His disappearance: About five days after the accident, John White gave his wife the impression that he was going out to look for a job. He was asked to do some shopping while away, but his wife found that he left without taking his wallet containing all his papers necessary to get a job; he had only a few dollars with him.

White was asked to mail a letter for his wife while he was out. It was discovered later that he mailed this letter at a post office near one of the rivers in Pittsburgh. This is the last place in which he was known to be.

Medical report: Since White feared doctors, he had no personal physician from whom we could obtain a report. His army medical report was important to this case. To obtain a medical report from any branch of the service is very difficult. According to official policy it is issued to the person concerned and no one else. In this particular case, Mrs. White requested public officials of Congress who tried to get this report but failed. After about eight months of writing and taking other measures, we obtained a copy of the army medical report. This report revealed that White had severe pruritis ani and underwent surgery, while in the service. He also had acute catarrhal nasopharyngitis. According to the physician's interpretation, this malady is of such a nature as to cause mental derangement in an individual in due time. In White's case, the time given was five to six years. His automobile accident only aggravated the circumstances. This medical report threw great light on the case and proved why his behavior was so unusual.

Social security: The Social Security Board was asked to check their files, and they disclosed that no one under the name of John White was receiving wages in the United States. After the court declaration of the presumed death of John White, his wife was informed that she could receive benefits as the widow of a person who was carrying social security. She had no difficulty and received the benefits during this entire period.

Coroners: All the coroners of all the counties bordering the entire course of the Ohio river down through the Mississippi river to the Gulf of Mexico were contacted to determine whether any of the bodies they picked up in the spring of 1945 resembled John White. All answers were in the negative. The presumption held in this case is that White ended his life in the river which was close to the post office from which he mailed his wife's letter. The coroners report that none of the bodies picked up met the description of John White. There was only one body in Kentucky that remained unidentified; this also did not fit his description too well. It could have been our missing person but some doubt remained because the body was in the state of decomposition and only a general observation was possible by the coroner. From the description given, this did not seem to be the one we were seeking, although there were a few indications it could have been John White.

Amnesia: The question came up that perhaps White was an amnesia victim. It is a general policy of all institutions to check their inmates when they are admitted. Most institutions are crowded and should a total stranger seek admittance, investigation usually follows to determine the state or district to which he belongs. No institution likes to handle another territory's subjects; hence, through the police and other agencies, especially the Federal Bureau of Investigation, investigations are made and the subject is returned to his proper jurisdiction.

Federal Bureau of Investigation (F.B.I.): John White's fingerprints were filed with the F.B.I. from the time of his disappearance. In all the years of search, no information ever came to this agency.

U.S. Coast Guard and Corps of Engineers of U.S. Army: A theory was held that it is possible for a body to fall into the river and yet never rise to the surface. The U.S. Coast Guard and the Corps of Engineers of the U.S. Army of Pittsburgh were consulted on this matter. It was asked whether a drowned person in a river could be caught in such a way in the locks among debris and tree branches and remain there to corrupt, decompose or disintegrate so that the constant rush of the water would leave no way of identifying the body. It was the opinion of these agencies that such a thing was possible. According to their statements: "It is true that the system of locks, dams and other man-made permanent structures, when added to the natural underwater obstacles which are found in river streams, sometimes make the recovery of a body seem impossible."

In conclusion, then, if John White wished to disappear and did disappear, his mental and physical condition would eventually have led him to some institution for medication and help. If he was an amnesia victim, he could not have escaped the net set out to find him and the surgical operation in the Army and the seriousness of his condition limited his ailment to only a few years. After a ten year period of absence, thorough search and investigations, the firm conviction was reached that John White was dead.

III. Decree of Presumed Death

Tribunal of the	Jones — White
Diocese of	De Obitu Coniugis

DECREE

In the year of our Lord 1954, on the 27th day of August, from the Hall of Sessions of the Tribunal of the Diocese of ...., the undersigned Officials of the Diocese of ...., acting in the present instance as the delegate of His Excellency, Most Reverend ...., Bishop of ...., renders the following decision as the culmination of an investigation into the alleged death of John White, the husband of Mary A. Jones.

Species Facti: Mary A. Jones, the petitioner, contracted marriage with John H. White, a widower, both Catholics, before Reverend .... at .... on May 8, 1943. The parties had a happy conjugal life and their union was blessed with one child. At the time of the marriage, John H. White had just been discharged from service with the Armed

Forces. He had been sick much of the time he was in service. Prior to entering service, he had liquidated his business and after his discharge and following the marriage he found it difficult to obtain steady work. He manifested an increasing despondency over his failure to obtain satisfactory employment and at times hinted at suicide.

On January 11, 1945, John H. White left his wife in their home in Pittsburgh, ostensibly to go out and look for work. That is the last that has ever been heard or seen of him. For years his wife, Mary A. Jones, conducted an intensive search for him, all to no avail.

After seeking in vain a declaration of presumed death from the ecclesiastical authorities in the localities where she had a domicile, Mary A. Jones took up residence in the Diocese of .... and petitioned the undersigned Officials, as delegate of the Most Reverend Bishop, for a decision in the matter of the presumed death of her absent husband, John H. White.

In Iure: Canon 1118 states that: "Valid marriage ratified and consummated can be dissolved by no human power and by no cause other than death." Because of this law of God and Church, canon 1019, § 1, legislates that "before a marriage is celebrated, it must be ascertained that there is no obstacle to its valid and licit reception." Moreover, canon 1069 declares that "marriage is rendered invalid by the bond of a previous marriage, even though not consummated, except in the case of the privilege of the faith. Even though the first marriage be null or dissolved for any reason whatsoever, it is not lawful to contract another marriage before the nullity or dissolution of the first be established legitimately and certainly."

From the foregoing it is clear that, whenever doubts arise in cases of presumed death, the proper investigations must be made with conscientious diligence. A new marriage may not be permitted until there is moral certitude of the death of the former consort. The decision as to whether there is moral certitude concerning the alleged death of one of the consorts rests with the Bishop of the diocese or with his delegate. The norms to be followed in investigating cases of presumed death are usually those outlined in the Instruction of the Sacred Congregation of the Holy Office promulgated in the year 1868. However, the authority of the Bishop or his delegate to decide these cases is not derived from the Instruction of the Holy Office, as some authors erroneously seem to think, but from the powers clearly conferred upon the Bishop in the different canons of the Code (Canons 1019-1034).

The following are the principal points emphasized in the afore-mentioned Instruction of the Holy Office:

(a) The prolonged absence of a consort, the mere lapse of time, or the presumptions of death recognized in civil law are not considered sufficient proof in Canon Law. This holds true even if the civil authorities accepted the presumption of death and even permitted the surviving consort to remarry, after an edictal citation by the civil authorities and notifications in public newspapers.

(b) An authentic death record must be sought.

(c) If no authentic document of death is available, this deficiency should be supplied by the depositions, under oath, of trustworthy witnesses testifying from their own personal knowledge, who knew the deceased and who are in agreement as to the place, cause of death, and other important circumstances.

(d) If actual ocular witnesses of death are not available, hearsay evidence may be taken, provided it is reasonable and above suspicion.

(e) Experience frequently proves that not even a hearsay witness can be found. In such a case the proof of death must be arrived at from conjectures, presumptions, indications, and diverse circumstances, carefully and accurately verified by thorough investigation. And thus from a multiplicity of findings, moral certitude may be attained or a prudent judgment may be formed affirming the death with probability, after the nature and importance of the circumstances have been duly evaluated and their relationship to the fact of death established.

Wherefore, in individual cases it must be left to the prudent decision of the Bishop or his delegate to determine the amount of proof deducible from all the conjectures taken together.

In Facto: Nothing has been heard from or concerning John H. White from the time of his disappearance on January 11, 1945.

Every conceivable effort has been made to locate him, without success. There are no visual witnesses to his death. There is not even one who testifies that he or she heard of his death from another. All we can go on, unless Mary Jones is to be kept waiting forever for a decision as to her free state, is presumptive evidence.

First of all, let it be stated at the outset that all the evidence in this case establishes beyond a shadow of a doubt that, if John H. White were today alive and able to do so, he would have returned to his wife and child. All the evidence agrees that a definite mental change occurred in John H. White after his discharge from the Army. Before he had been jovial and humorous and normal in every respect, but afterward he acted depressed, listless, melancholy, etc. His moral character was of the best. He was regular in his religious duties and he went beyond the level of mere obligation in religious matters, being accustomed to make retreats. His domestic life was above reproach. He loved his wife and "adored" his child. There were no quarrels of any kind. He had a happy home life. Hence there is no logical explanation why he should discontinue that happy home life, unless he were either dead or completely out of his mind.

It is to be noted particularly that on three occasions John H. White, in remarks made to his wife, declared that he was meditating suicide as a "solution" to his problem. He declared that he was no help to his wife and child and that they would be better off without him. This mental depression increased and was quite acute in the days immediately preceding his disappearance. His condition was undoubtedly aggravated by an automobile accident in which he was involved and in which he wrecked the car he was driving.

Several things about White's disappearance indicate that he made deliberate preparation to depart and not return. He left his wallet at home, something which he never did before. He could have taken twenty dollars with him but took only two dollars and left the larger sum for his wife and child. He had access to money in the bank, but never tried to withdraw any of it. He took no belongings with him, no extra clothing. In fact he was wearing a shoe from which portions of the leather had been cut and which was hardly suited for survival in January weather. He had a letter to be mailed and this was posted in a section of Pittsburgh which is near the river and was far off the route to the employment office to which he declared he was going. It might be noted that his meditations on suicide tended toward "jumping into the river."

Even supposing there had been any rift between John White and his wife, it might be expected that he would at least contact his relatives sometime during his long absence, since he was on the best of terms with them. Yet we have obtained the testimony of all of them and they agree in the belief that he is dead. All the relatives are convinced that if he were living he would contact some one of them.

It should also be observed that on October 6, 1944, a few months before his disappearance, John White drew up a will in his own handwriting, leaving all his possessions to his wife. This would tend to indicate that he was on the best of terms with her. If such had not been the case, certainly he would have changed the will prior to his disappearance, that is, supposing that he planned to disappear.

It should be stressed that, in the present case, efforts far beyond the average were made to locate the missing person. A dodger, with his picture and description, was circulated among all the American Legion Posts in the United States and its possessions. Institutions of all kinds around Pittsburgh and throughout the country were contacted. State and local police officers were notified. The F.B.I. in Washington was alerted. A radio program, which has a nation-wide audience, featured this disappearance on one of its programs. This alerted millions of people throughout the country to the plight of Mrs. White and the absence of her husband.

We feel likewise that it should be stressed that all of this investigation was done *tempore non suspecto,* that is, at a time when Mary White, fully in love with John White, had no notion of another marriage but was intent upon effecting the return of her absent husband.

It should be stressed likewise that the F.B.I. Office in Washington had the fingerprints of John H. White from his service with the armed forces and that these fingerprints were on file in Washington throughout the entire period of his disappearance, even up to the present time. This fact is possibly the most important single item in the chain of proof which leads one to the conclusion that John H. White must be presumed dead.

Furthermore, White was in love with his wife and child: he had every reason to return to them unless prevented. He could be prevented only by his death or by being out of his mind. We have given considerable thought to this latter alternative, namely, whether John H. White is simply living somewhere out of mind and unaware of his own identity. We feel morally certain that such is not the case, for the following reason. If John White were in such a deteriorated mental or physical condition as to be unaware of his own identity, and wandering about the country, we feel that unquestionably he would by now be an inmate of some institution. It is not likely at all that he would be abroad and on his own in such a condition. And if he were such an inmate, the first thing that the officials of the institution would do would be to try to ascertain his true identity. His fingerprints would have been taken long ago and sent to Washington for comparison with the file of fingerprints of known individuals. In that case his true identity would have been established, since the fingerprints of John White have been on file in Washington throughout the whole period of his disappearance.

It might likewise be argued that if White had died and had remained unidentified, the prints of the corpse would have been taken and sent to Washington for identification. That consideration is true and merits our attention. There is also the possibility that the corpse, when recovered, might have been in such a state of decomposition that identifiable fingerprints would have been unavailable. This may very well have been the case if John White had carried out his idea of relieving his wife and child of the "burden" by jumping in the river. With this in mind, Mary White and her associates caused all the coroners on the Ohio river down to the point of its junction with the Mississippi river to be notified and alerted for possible discovery of John H. White's body.

This phase of the investigation must also be noted. It disclosed that several bodies which had been recovered in various stages of decomposition during the winter of 1945 from the river could not be identified.

A final consideration seems in order. It is the custom of any public institution which receives an unidentified individual to ascertain his name and address in order that he may be transferred to an institution of the city, county or state where his true residence is located. His identification is usually established through fingerprints and it is to be stressed that the prints of John H. White were on file with the F.B.I. in Washington from the earliest days of his disappearance. We believe, therefore, that if John White were alive today and a public charge in any institution, whether in his right mind or out of his mind, his true identification would be known.

WHEREFORE, having conscientiously gathered all the evidence available and having weighed all the facts and circumstances in the case, having only God before our eyes, acting as a delegate of His Excellency, the Most Reverend .... Bishop of .... we hereby declare and decree that John White, husband of Mary Jones, is to be presumed dead and that the said Mary Jones, insofar as her union with John White is concerned, is now free to contract marriage with Robert Smith, a Catholic, always, however, with the understanding that if our presumption should prove untrue and it should develop that John H. White is actually alive, the said Mary Jones will be obliged in conscience to leave Robert Smith and return to John White.

Given at ...., from the Hall of Sessions of the Tribunal, this 27th day of August, A.D. 1954.

PRESUMPTION OF DEATH CASE - (1963)

John Black, a Catholic, attempted marriage with *Dora Jones, a baptized Lutheran* and wished to have the marriage validated in the Catholic Church. However, *Dora Jones* was married to one - *A George Smith in 1912* and was divorced about 1926. She testified under oath that her brother-in-law (who was an exemplary Catholic and who died about 15 years ago) told her that he met a friend who seemed to have known her husband and that this friend stated that *George Smith, her husband,* was dead for some time. When she heard about this, she did nothing to have her marriage validated or check this hearsay evidence. (As a non-

Catholic this was not unusual.)

Her present Catholic husband, *John Black,* is eighty-five years old and is in ill-health. A certain diocesan tribunal began immediately to conduct an investigation to determine whether this George Smith was actually dead. No living relative of his or anyone else could be found to testify regarding his death. Nor could his wife furnish any information and is really disinterested in the matter to the extent that she does not want to be bothered with further investigations. However, due to the old age and ill-health of the second husband, Mr. Black, has been granted permission for a *frater-soror* arrangement.

If *George Smith* were still alive, he would now be 75 years old and he was known to have been an habitual drunkard. All this information and hearsay evidence gave the tribunal enough moral certitude to solve the case. Since the Holy See was competent to handle such cases and grant the *documentum libertatis* for these parties to marry validly in the Church, the case was sent to the Holy Office. A reply was sent back to this particular tribunal granting the permission to validate this marriage. It was signed by Cardinal Ottaviani.

THE DIOCESAN TRIBUNAL

The common complaint among laymen who have a marriage case is that the pastor or assistant does not understand them or their case. They fail to realize that the life of a pastor is one of manifold dimensions: instructing, administering the sacraments, building, financial worries, etc., so much so that it is impossible for him to be an expert in the matrimonial field. The pastor of souls is not expected to understand all the details of matrimonial procedure, nevertheless, there are certain fundamental principles that every priest should know and understand in matrimonial procedure. The following is a brief resumé of some of these fundamentals:

Personnel

The personnel of the diocesan tribunal are the following: Officials, Judges, Promoter of Justice, Defender of the Bond, Notary, Procurator and Advocate.

The Officials

The bishop or archbishop is the Presiding Judge of the tribunal; however, according to the Canon Law prescription the bishop appoints one to take his place. This person is called the Officialis who shares with the bishop all the powers on judicial matters. Therefore, the Officialis is also the Presiding Judge of the Tribunal and in this capacity he functions as one person with the bishop. He may also exercise the delegated powers which the bishop grants to him upon his appointment.

The Judges

Besides the Presiding Judge, Canon Law requires that the Ordinary appoint other Judges to the Tribunal who help to decide the cases that come to their attention. Three Judges are required for deciding formal cases. Some cases of a criminal nature require five judges. (If judges are selected in a Synod, they are called Synodal Judges; if chosen outside the Synod they are called pro-synodal judges. They should not number more than twelve in a diocese).

The Promoter of Justice

The Promoter of Justice may be considered the diocesan attorney. He has the responsibility to uphold the common good. Thus, if it is known publicly that a certain marriage is invalid, and that scandal has resulted from the parties cohabiting, it is the duty of the Promoter of Justice to petition the nullity by bringing forth witnesses and other proofs to substantiate his claim; or, he can enter a cause for nullity to a Tribunal when the parties involved are prohibited by law from acting as Plaintiffs (e.g., non-Catholics) and the Promoter of Justice is convinced that the public good requires the intervention of the Tribunal. Moreover, among his other duties, he must follow the progress of a case during a trial and see to it that the proper procedure is followed in the case. Usually this office is filled by the Defender of the Bond.

The Defender of the Bond

The Defender of the Bond is the attorney for the Church; his office is similar to that of the State Attorney or Prosecuting Attorney in a criminal case. He is a very important member of the Tribunal. He is the defender of the law, insofar as he sees to it that the law is always upheld. For example, when a certain marriage is attacked to be invalid, he defends the marriage bond by the application of the proper canons. He also prepares the questionnaires for the examination of the witnesses. These questions, in turn, are proposed to the witnesses by one of the judges (or by the Auditor-appointed by the Officialis) in the judicial examination. He also points out the flaws in the evidence offered by the plaintiff, by calling witnesses of his own, etc.

The Notary

The Notary is an official who, in a formal trial, puts into writing the replies of the witnesses. He must put to writing either the exact words of the witnesses or the substance of them as dictated by the judge or auditor. The Notary keeps a record of the entire trial. His name and seal attest to the authenticity of a very judicial act or deposition. If his signature is not on the judicial act, this act is considered null. It is also advantageous for the Notary to take shorthand.

Procurator-Auditor

The Procurator or Auditor is appointed by the Ordinary, to serve as lawyers for the parties in the case. One is appointed for each of the parties - namely, the Plaintiff and Defendant. If the Defendant does not select one, the Presiding Judge will appoint one or leave the defense to the Defender of the Bond.

The Procurator-Auditor assists in contacting witnesses; he takes the necessary steps during the trial to promote the cause of the client, without however, jeopardizing the truth in any way; when the case is closed he will, by a written brief, seek to advance the case of his client. This brief will be answered in writing by the Defender of the Bond. If necessary he may write a second brief which is handled in the same manner. The Procurator-Auditor may leave the defense of the marriage to the Defender of the Bond.

MARRIAGE PROCEDURE

The fourth Book of the Code of Canon Law gives the procedure on handling marriage cases. Some are simple, others are complicated and require more study. In summary, we have the following types of procedure:

I. Simple Administrative Procedure

This procedure is called simple because there is *no court procedure* of any kind here. It consists merely in a judgment made by the Ordinary or his delegate based upon the documents or affidavits presented. For example, in deciding questions of nullity based on the *lack of canonical form* (Defect of Form). Pauline Privilege cases are decided in the same way. Here again the Ordinary or his delegate makes a judgment on the proof of both parties in the marriage in question based on the evidence presented them.

II. The Formal Procedure

The formal process is more complicated than the others. The case is usually admitted for trial by three judges. In all such cases, (1) careful investigation must be made to determine whether a particular court is competent [9] to handle it; (2) the judges must determine whether there is a case according to the law (an impediment) as a basis of nullity in this particular case; (3) that there is a possibility of proving the case by competent witnesses, documents, testimony, etc. Following the acceptance of the case and after the Procurators are appointed, the session is held for "joining the issues" (litis contestatio). At this meeting the Presiding Judge (Officialis) together with the Defender of the Bond and the Procurator of the parties, determine the exact point in question to be solved in the case.

The testimony of the parties and the witnesses are then taken. All the witnesses are heard in the presence of the three judges of the court (or auditor), the Defender of the Bond and Notary. When all the testimony has been taken and all the proofs submitted, the case is declared closed. Afterward, the Procurator and the Defender of the Bond must submit their written briefs. These together with all the testimony gathered, are submitted to the three judges. (Copies are made for each of the judges).

The decision of the Judges is based entirely upon the facts contained in the case. Judges are reminded here to remember the well-known axiom "*Quod non est in actis, non est in mundo.*" If the Judges uphold the validity of the marriage, their decision will be considered: "Negative." If the Judges declare the marriage null, the decision of the Judges will be considered: "Affirmative."

In either the affirmative or negative decision, the case is not considered settled as yet, because the law requires two concordant decisions.

For example, (1) the decision of the Judges is "Affirmative" the law requires the Defender of the Bond to appeal the case to the higher court (Court of Appeal or Court of Second Instance). If this Appellate Court likewise gives an "Affirmative"

9. Competent Court — A Tribunal is competent if it (1) is the diocese in which the marriage in question took place or (2) is in the diocese of the defendant, or (3) in the case of a mixed marriage, is in the diocese of the Catholic party; and (4) a woman who has separated with ecclesiastical approval may choose the diocese in which she is; otherwise, she must follow the domicile of her husband. There are some other exceptions.

decision, the marriage case in question is considered null and the case is considered as settled. If, (2) the decision of the Judges of the First court is "Negative," the plaintiff has the right to appeal the case to the Court of Appeals, but is not obliged to do so. He may abide by the decision. If the Plaintiff does appeal, his case to the Appellate Court and this Court would reverse the decision (i.e., First Court: "Negative" - the Second Court: "Affirmative"), the case has to be appealed further (for two concordant decisions) to the Court of Third Instance, namely, to the highest court, the Roman Rota.

III. Summary Procedure

The Summary process, in brief, means that the testimony is heard by the Ordinary or his delegate after the Defender of the Bond has reviewed the case and the parties to the marriage in question have been notified or cited. This procedure is used in all cases that come under Canon 1990, namely, disparity of cult, Order, solemn vows, ligamen, consanguinity, affinity and spiritual relationship. If any of these cases become too complicated, then it is processed according to the Formal Procedure mentioned above. The Defender of the Bond has the right to appeal the decision of the Judge to the court of appeal. Courts of appeal are selected by the Holy See for each diocese. The court is also called the Appellate Court.

IV. Special Procedure

The Special Procedure pertains to cases which are sent to Rome for a decision:

I. *Non Consummation Cases*

1. The Ordinary must first obtain the necessary permission from the Holy See to begin such a case.
2. This obtained, the formal process is followed, with the exception that the procurators are not appointed for the parties in this case.
3. The decision is not made by the local Ordinary or Tribunal, but the case is sent directly to Rome and the decision is made by the Sacred Congregation.

II. *Privilege of the Faith*

These cases also follow this formal procedure, except that (1) the Defender of the Bond need not be present at the hearings of the witnesses; however, he prepares the necessary questionnaire in the case, (2) neither Judges nor Procurators are appointed, and (3) the decision is not given by the Ordinary or the Tribunal but by the Sacred Congregation.[10]

NEW NORMS OF PROCEDURE FOR MATRIMONIAL CASES

The Canon Law Society of America initiated a study on procedural law (1968) whereby Tribunals in the United States would operate in a manner that would be meaningful and effective for the benefit of Christian people in the circumstances of our present age. It was presented to the National Conference of Bishops for approval; it was adopted by this body and submitted to the Holy Father with the request that the rules be authorized for use in the United States.

In response to the request from the National Conference of Catholic Bishops at its plenary session of November 1969, the Holy See issued a series of twenty-three norms to be used on an experimental basis for three years beginning July 1, 1970, for matrimonial cases. The following are the norms with a brief commentary, preceded by the rescript from the Council for the Public Affairs of the Church:

The Rescript

CONSILIUM PRO PUBLICIS ECCLESIAE NEGOTIIS

N. 3320/70

Attentis precibus Conferentiae Episcopalis Statuum Foederatorum Americae Septemtrionalis, quibus petitur ut, consideratis peculiaribus sui territorii necessitatibus, normis quibusdam, quae precibus adnectuntur, ad expeditiorem reddendum causarum de nullitate matrimonii cursum, in eodem territorio, tribunalia utantur, Ss.mus Dominus Noster PAULUS Papa VI

---

10. Marriage cases, Detroit, 1960, A Practical Guide prepared by the Archdiocese of Detroit.

supradictis precibus annuere dignatus est, ad triennium et experimenti causa, concedendo facultates omnes necessarias et opportunas et derogando, quatenus opus est, iuri vigenti; cauto tamen ut de cetero, cum praedictis normis totus processus non exhauriatur, serventur iuris canonici praescripta. Idem Summus Pontifex statuit ut supradictae normae a die 1 Iulii 1970 valere incipiant.

Velit autem Praeses Conferentiae expostulantis mittere quotannis Supremo Tribunali Signaturae Apostolicae relationem de causis in unoquoque Tribunali propositis, vel desertis, vel appellatis.

Ex Aedibus Vaticanis, die 28 Aprilis a.D. MCMLXX.

J. CARD. VILLOT
Praefectus Consilii pro Publicis Ecclesiae Negotiis

PROCEDURAL NORMS

Norm 1

The Diocesan Tribunal will consist of judges, a defender of the bond, a promoter of justice and notaries and all will be appointed to their offices by the Ordinary. The judges, defenders of the bond and promoter of justice shall be priests; all, however, shall be endowed with those qualities required by law.

Norm 2

The Ordinary will appoint a chief judge who will direct the work of the Tribunal and assign judges and defenders of the bond for individual cases.

Norm 3

A collegiate Tribunal must be constituted for each case. The Episcopal Conference, in accordance with faculties to be sought from the Holy See, may permit the competent ecclesiastical Tribunal to derogate from this norm for a specified period of time so that a case may be handled by a single judge.

The conditions are that: 1) there be a grave reason for granting the derogation; and 2) no formal opposition be expressed prior to the definitive sentence by either the judge, the defender of the bond, the promoter of justice or either of the parties.

Norm 4

If both parties are desirous of a declaration of nullity, one advocate may represent both. Unless a party decides otherwise, the advocate in first instance will also be the advocate in second instance. Advocates representing the parties will be those approved to work with marriage cases by the Ordinary or his delegate.

Norm 5

The notary for the Tribunal will preserve a written record of all procedural and substantive acts, with special regard to names, dates and places as well as the authenticity of documents and depositions. While acts not authenticated by the notary are null, it suffices that copies of these acts be authenticated by a single statement of the notary at the termination of the case.

Norm 6

The Ordinary will provide sufficient judges, defenders and advocates so that all petitions for declaration of nullity may be accepted or rejected promptly and decisions given within six months following acceptance of the petition.

Norm 7

The first competent Tribunal to which a party presents a petition has an obligation to accept or reject the petition. The competence of a Tribunal of first instance shall be determined by the residency of either party to the marriage, the place of the marriage or the decree of the judge to whom the petition is presented that his Tribunal is better able to judge the case than any other Tribunal. In this last instance, however, the judge may not issue such a decree without first obtaining the consent of his Ordinary and the consent of the petitioner's Ordinary and chief judge.

Norm 8

Any spouse, without qualification, may seek a declaration of nullity of his marriage. To do so, he will employ the services of an advocate. The petition for the declaration of nullity indicating the basis for nullity and the sources of proof is to be accepted or rejected by the judge within the thirty days following the presentation and after consultation with the advocate and defender. Recourse against the rejection of a petition may be made to the Tribunal of second instance. Within thirty days of recourse, rejection of the petition is to be sustained or the case is to be remanded for prompt instruction by the Tribunal of first instance.

Norm 9

The promoter of justice may petition that a marriage be declared null when he decides this will be for the public good.

Norm 10

If he is available and cooperative, the respondent will be given the opportunity to choose an advocate prior to the determination of the precise basis of nullity. If the respondent is not available and cooperative, the judge will proceed to this determination in accordance with the following rule.

Norm 11

Within a month after the acceptance of the petition, the judge, after consultation with the advocate and defender, will determine the precise basis or bases for the nullity of the marriage, the documents to be obtained, and the witnesses to be heard. During the course of the trial the judge may add an additional basis or bases for nullity.

Norm 12

At any time in the course of the trial, the petitioner may request that the case be transferred from one competent tribunal to another competent tribunal. This permission will be granted provided that a grave reason warrants it, that the defender of the bond has been heard and that it is agreeable to the other party, the Ordinary *a quo* and the chief judges of both tribunals.

Norm 13

The testimony of the principals and the witnesses will be taken by the judge as soon as available, either at the Tribunal or elsewhere. A person will be asked to take an oath before testifying unless the judge determines otherwise. The advocate (unless the judge determines otherwise) and the defender have the right to be present at the hearing of the principals and witnesses. In the event that the advocate is present, the defender of the bond must always at least be cited. The questions proposed by the judge will be based upon the information and questions supplied by the advocate and the defender. The principals and witnesses may also be questioned directly by the advocate and the defender under the direction of the judge. When a judge is personally unable to take the testimony of a witness, he will appoint a competent delegate to do so.

Norm 14

Following consultation with the advocate and defender, the judge will determine the significance of the unwillingness of a principal and/or witnesses to testify and will, if necessary, proceed to the conclusion of the case without their testimony.

Norm 15

The advocate and the defender may examine the acts of the case at any stage of the process unless in particular cases the judge decides otherwise.

Norm 16

The judge will carefully weigh the depositions of each witness. Testimonials concerning the credibility of the principals and witnesses will be required if, in the opinion of the judge, they seem necessary or useful.

Norm 17

In cases involving physical or psychic impotence and lack of consensual capacity, the judge, after consultation with the advocate and the defender shall designate one or more experts to study the acts of the case and submit a written report thereon. When advisable, this expert will examine the party or parties to the case and will include in his report the results of his examination. The oral testimony of the expert is to be taken only if his report requires clarification or implementation. Following consultation with the advocate and the defender, the judge may appoint additional experts.

Norm 18

When, after consultation with the advocate and the defender, the judge has decided that all necessary and available evidence has been obtained, the principals will be permitted to read the acts unless, in the opinion of the judge, there is danger of violation of the rights of privacy. The judge will consider the requests by the principals for further instruction before bringing the case to a conclusion.

Norm 19

The advocate and the defender will submit written briefs independently within one month after all evidence has been presented and will be given the opportunity of a rejoinder to be made within two weeks.

Norm 20

Following whatever consultation with the advocate and the defender which is allowed by law and which he deems necessary, the judge will render a decision within one month after the presentation of the briefs and rejoinders.

Norm 21

The judge will render his decision according to moral certitude generated by the prevailing weight of that evidence having a recognized value in law and jurisprudence.

Norm 22

Any instance of nullity as defined in positive law with regard to acts or processes is considered sanated by the sentence itself provided that it was not previously challenged.

A sentence is irremediably null only when: 1. Its presuppositions were lacking grounds; 2. the right of defense has been denied; 3. the judge was coerced either by violence or grave fear to render his decision; 4. the sentence fails to address itself to the controversy in question.

The nullity described in the paragraph above may be perpetually proposed either as an action or as an exception.

Norm 23

I. Once an appeal has been made to a higher Tribunal and the Tribunal itself has been constituted in accord with Norm 3, the citation of the parties and the joining of issues shall take place within one month.

At the time of the joining of issues, if further investigations are requested either by the parties or the defender of the bond or the Tribunal itself *ex officio*, the case shall be heard in the ordinary manner of second instance. This instance, however, should not if possible exceed the limit of six months.

If further investigations are not required, the judge will immediately decree the case concluded. Within a month from the date of this decree, the Tribunal, taking into account the briefs and animadversions of the advocate and defender of the bond, shall issue a new sentence according to the norm of the law.

II. In those exceptional cases where in the judgment of the defender of the bond and his Ordinary an appeal against an affirmative decision would clearly be superfluous, the Ordinary may himself request of the Episcopal Conference that in these individual cases the defender of the bond be dispensed from the obligation to appeal so that the sentence of the first instance may be executed immediately.

APOSTOLIC LETTER ISSUED "MOTU PROPRIO"

DETERMINING NORMS FOR MIXED MARRIAGES

POPE PAUL VI

Mixed marriages, that is to say marriages in which one party is a Catholic and the other a non-Catholic, whether baptized or not, have always been given careful attention by the Church in pursuance of her duty. Today the Church is constrained to give even greater attention to them, owing to the conditions of present times. In the past Catholics were separated from members of other Christian confessions and from non-Christians, by their situation in their community or even by physical boundaries. In more recent times, however, not only has this separation been reduced, but communication between men of different regions and religions has greatly developed, and as a result there has been a great increase in the number of mixed marriages. Also a great influence in this regard has been exercised by the growth and spread of civilization and industry, urbanization and consequent rural depopulation, migrations in great numbers and the increase in numbers of exiles of every kind.

The Church is indeed aware that mixed marriages, precisely because they admit differences of religion and are a consequence of the division among Christians, do not, except in some cases, help in re-establishing unity among

Christians. There are many difficulties inherent in a mixed marriage, since a certain division is introduced into the living cell of the Church, as the Christian family is rightly called, and in the family itself the fulfillment of the gospel teachings is more difficult because of diversities in matters of religion, especially with regard to those matters which concern Christian worship and the education of the children.

For these reasons the Church, conscious of her duty, discourages the contracting of mixed marriages, for she is most desirous that Catholics be able in matrimony to attain to perfect union of mind and full communion of life. However, since man has the natural right to marry and beget children, the Church, by her laws, which clearly show her pastoral concern, makes such arrangements that on the one hand the principles of Divine law be scrupulously observed and that on the other the said right to contract marriage be respected.

The Church vigilantly concerns itself with the education of the young and their fitness to undertake their duties with a sense of responsibility and to perform their obligations as members of the Church, and she shows this both in preparing for marriage those who intend to contract a mixed marriage and in caring for those who have already contracted such a marriage. Although in the case of baptized persons of different religious confessions, there is less risk of religious indifferentism, it can be more easily avoided if both husband and wife have a sound knowledge of the Christian nature of marital partnership, and if they are properly helped by their respective Church authorities. Even difficulties arising in marriage between a Catholic and an unbaptized person can be overcome through pastoral watchfulness and skill.

Neither in doctrine nor in law does the Church place on the same level a marriage between a Catholic and a baptized non-Catholic, and one between a Catholic and an unbaptized person; for, as the Second Vatican Council declared, men, who, though they are not Catholics, "believe in Christ and have been properly baptized are brought into a certain,

though imperfect, communion with the Catholic Church." [1]
Moreover, although Eastern Christians who have been baptized outside the Catholic Church are separated from communion with us, they possess true sacraments, above all the Priesthood and the Eucharist, whereby they are joined to us in a very close relationship.[2] Undoubtedly there exists in a marriage between baptized persons, since such a marriage is a true sacrament, a certain communion of spiritual benefits which is lacking in a marriage entered into by a baptized person and one who is not baptized.

Nevertheless, one cannot ignore the difficulties inherent even in mixed marriages between baptized persons. There is often a difference of opinion on the sacramental nature of matrimony, on the special significance of marriage celebrated within the Church, on the interpretation of certain moral principles pertaining to marriage and the family, on the extent to which obedience is due to the Catholic Church, and on the competence that belongs to ecclesiastical authority. From this it is clear that difficult questions of this kind can only be fully resolved when Christian unity is restored.

The faithful must therefore be taught that, although the Church somewhat relaxes ecclesiastical discipline in particular cases, she can never remove the obligation of the Catholic party, which, by divine law, namely by the plan of salvation instituted through Christ, is imposed according to the various situations.

The faithful should therefore be reminded that the Catholic party to a marriage has the duty of preserving his or her own faith; nor is it ever permitted to expose oneself to a proximate danger of losing it.

Furthermore, the Catholic partner in a mixed marriage is obliged, not only to remain steadfast in the faith, but also, as far as possible, to see to it that the children be baptized and brought up in that same faith and receive all those aids

1. Decree on Ecumenism *Unitatis Redintegratio,* 3, AAS 57, 1965, p. 93; Cf. Dogmatic Constitution on the Church *Lumen Gentium,* AAS 57, 1965, pp. 19-20.

2. Cf. Second Vatican Council: Decree on Ecumenism *Unitatis Redintegratio,* pp. 13-18, *l. c.* pp. 100-104.

to eternal salvation which the Catholic Church provides for her sons and daughters.

The problem of the children's education is a particularly difficult one, in view of the fact that both husband and wife are bound by that responsibility and may by no means ignore it or any of the obligations connected with it. However the Church endeavors to meet this problem, just as she does the others, by her legislation and pastoral care.

With all this in mind, no one will be really surprised to find that even the canonical discipline on mixed marriages cannot be uniform and that it must be adapted to the various cases in what pertains to the juridical form of contracting marriage, its liturgical celebration, and, finally, the pastoral care to be given to the married people, and the children of the marriage, according to the distinct circumstances of the married couple and the differing degrees of their ecclesiastical communion.

It was altogether fitting that so important a question should receive the attention of the Second Vatican Council. This occurred several times as occasion arose. Indeed, in the third session the Council Fathers voted to entrust the question to us in its entirety.

To meet their desire, the Sacred Congregation for the Doctrine of the Faith, on the 18th March, 1966, promulgated an Instruction on mixed marriages, entitled *Matrimonii Sacramentum,*[3] which provided that, if the norms laid down therein stood the test of experience, they should be introduced in a definite and precise form into the Code of Canon Law which is now being revised.[4]

When certain questions on mixed marriages were raised in the first General Meeting of the Synod of Bishops, held in October 1967[5] and many useful observations had been made upon them by the Fathers, we decided to submit those questions to examination by a special Commission of Cardi-

---

3. Cf AAS 58, 1966, pp. 235-239.

4. Cf. *ibid.,* p. 237.

5. Cf. *Argumenta de quibus disceptabitur in primo generali coetu Synodi Episcoporum, pars altera,* Typis Polyglottis Vaticanis, 1967, pp. 27-37.

nals which after diligent consideration, presented us with its conclusions.

At the outset we state that Eastern Catholics contracting marriage with baptized non-Catholics or with unbaptized persons are not subject to the norms established by this Letter. With regard to the marriage of Catholics of whatsoever rite with Eastern non-Catholic Christians, the Church has recently issued certain norms,[6] which we wish to remain in force.

Accordingly, in order that ecclesiastical discipline on mixed marriages be more perfectly formulated and that, without violating divine law, canonical law should have regard for the differing circumstances of married couples, in accordance with the mind of the Second Vatican Council expressed especially in the Decree *Unitatis Redintegratio*[7] and in the Declaration *Dignitatis Humanae*,[8] and also in careful consideration of the wishes expressed in the Synod of Bishops, we, by our own authority, and after mature deliberation, establish and decree the following norms:

1. A marriage between two baptized persons, of whom one is a Catholic, while the other is a non-Catholic, may not licitly be contracted without the previous dispensation of the local Ordinary, since such a marriage is by its nature an obstacle to the full spiritual communion of the married parties.

2. A marriage between two persons, of whom one has been baptized in the Catholic Church or received into it, while the other is unbaptized, entered into without previous dispensation by the local Ordinary, is invalid.

3. The Church, taking into account the nature and circumstances of times, places and persons, is prepared to dispense from both impediments provided there is a just cause.

4. To obtain from the local Ordinary dispensation from

6. Cf. Decree on Eastern Catholic Churches *Orientalium Ecclesiarum*, 18, AAS 57, 1965, p. 82; Sacred Congregation for the Eastern Churches: Decree *Crescens Matrimoniorum*, AAS 59, 1967, pp. 165-166.

7. AAS 57, 1965, pp. 90-112.

8. AAS 58, 1966, pp. 929-946.

an impediment, the Catholic party shall declare that he is ready to remove dangers of falling away from the faith. He is also gravely bound to make a sincere promise to do all in his power to have all the children baptized and brought up in the Catholic Church.

5. At an opportune time the non-Catholic party must be informed of these promises which the Catholic party has to make, so that it is clear that he is cognizant of the promise and obligation on the part of the Catholic.

6. Both parties are to be clearly instructed on the ends and essential properties of marriage, not to be excluded by either party.

7. Within its own territorial competence, it is for the Bishops' Conference to determine the way in which these declarations and promises, which are always required, shall be made: whether by word of mouth alone, in writing, or before witnesses; and also to determine what proof of them there should be in the external forum, and how they are to be brought to the knowledge of the non-Catholic party, as well as to lay down whatever other requirements may be opportune.

8. The canonical form is to be used for contracting mixed marriages, and is required for validity, without prejudice, however, to the provisions of the Decree *Crescens Matrimoniorum* published by the Sacred Congregation for the Eastern Churches on 22nd February, 1967.[9]

9. If serious difficulties stand in the way of observing the canonical form, local Ordinaries have the right to dispense from the canonical form in any mixed marriage; but the Bishops' Conference is to determine norms according to which the said dispensation may be granted licitly and uniformly within the region or territory of the Conference, with the provision that there should always be some public form of ceremony.

10. Arrangements must be made that all validly contracted marriages be diligently entered in the books prescribed by canon law. Priests responsible should make sure

9. AAS 59, 1967, p. 166.

that non-Catholic ministers also assist in recording in their own books the fact of a marriage with a Catholic.

Episcopal Conferences are to issue regulations determining, for their region or territory, a uniform method by which a marriage that has been publicly contracted after a dispensation from the canonical form was obtained, is registered in the books prescribed by canon law.

11. With regard to the liturgical form of the celebration of a mixed marriage, if it is to be taken from the Roman Ritual, use must be made of the ceremonies in the *Rite of Celebration of Marriage* promulgated by our authority, whether it is a question of a marriage between a Catholic and a baptized non-Catholic (39-54) or of a marriage between a Catholic and an unbaptized person (55-66). If, however, the circumstances justify it, a marriage between a Catholic and a baptized non-Catholic can be celebrated, subject to the local Ordinary's consent, according to the rites for the celebration of marriage within Mass (19-38), while respecting the prescription of general law with regard to Eucharistic Communion.

12. The Episcopal Conferences shall inform the Apostolic See of all decisions which, within their competence, they make concerning mixed marriages.

13. The celebration of marriage before a Catholic priest or deacon and a non-Catholic minister, performing their respective rites together, is forbidden; nor is it permitted to have another religious marriage ceremony before or after the Catholic ceremony, for the purpose of giving or renewing matrimonial consent.

14. Local Ordinaries and parish priests shall see to it that the Catholic husband or wife and the children born of a mixed marriage do not lack spiritual assistance in fulfilling their duties of conscience. They shall encourage the Catholic husband or wife to keep ever in mind the divine gift of the Catholic faith and to bear witness to it with gentleness and reverence, and with a clear conscience.[10] They are to aid the married couple to foster the unity of their con-

10. 1 Peter 3:16.

jugal and family life, a unity which, in the case of Christians, is based on their baptism too. To these ends it is to be desired that those pastors should establish relationships of sincere openness and enlightened confidence with ministers of other religious communities.

15. The penalties decreed by Canon 2319 of the Code of Canon Law are all abrogated. For those who have incurred them the effects of those penalties cease, without prejudice to the obligations mentioned in number 4 of these norms.

16. The local Ordinary is able to give a *sanatio in radice* of a mixed marriage when the conditions spoken of in numbers 4 and 5 of these norms have been fulfilled, and provided that the conditions of law are observed.

17. In the case of a particular difficulty or doubt with regard to the application of these norms, recourse is to be made to the Holy See.

We order that what we have decreed in this Letter, given in the form of "Motu Proprio," be regarded as established and ratified, notwithstanding any measure to the contrary, and is to take effect from the first day of October of this year.

Given at Rome, at St. Peter's the thirty-first day of March in the year 1970, the seventh of our pontificate.

PAULUS PP. VI

ROMAN CATHOLIC — ORTHODOX MARRIAGE DECREE

The Sacred Congregation for the Oriental Church issued this decree on mixed marriages between Latin Rite Catholics and the Orthodox, Feb. 22, 1967.

The increasing frequency of mixed marriages between Oriental Catholics and non-Catholic Oriental Christians in the eastern patriarchates and eparchies as well as in the Latin dioceses themselves and the necessity of coping with the inconveniences resulting from this, were the reasons why the Second Vatican Ecumenical Council decreed: "When Oriental Catholics enter into marriage with baptized non-Catholic Orientals the canonical form for the celebration of such marriages obliges only for lawfulness: for their validity, the presence of a sacred minister suffices, as long as the other requirements of the law are observed" (Decree on the Eastern Catholic Churches, n. 18).

In the exceptional circumstances of today, mixed marriages between the Catholic faithful of the Latin rite and non-Catholic Oriental faithful are taking place and the variety in canonical disciplines has brought about many grave difficulties both in the East and the West. For this reason petitions from various regions have been addressed to the Supreme Pontiff asking that he be pleased to unify canonical discipline in this matter by also permitting to Catholics of the Latin rite what has been decreed for Catholics of the Eastern rite.

His Holiness, our Lord Paul VI, by divine providence Pope, after mature reflection and diligent investigation, has resolved to agree to the petitions and desires addressed to him and, as a means of preventing invalid marriages between the faithful of the Latin rite and the non-Catholic Christian faithful of the Oriental rites, of showing proper regard for the permanence and sanctity of marriages, and of promoting charity between the Catholic faithful and the non-Catholic Oriental faithful, he has kindly granted that, when Catholics, whether they be Orientals or Latins, contract marriage with non-Catholic Oriental faithful, the canonical form for the celebration of these marriages obliges only for lawfulness; for validity the presence of a sacred minister suffices, as long as the other requirements of law are observed.

All care should be taken that, under the guidance of the pastor such marriages be carefully entered into the prescribed registers as soon as possible; this prescription also holds when Catholic Orientals enter marriage with baptized non-Catholic Orientals according to the norm of the conciliar decree "On the Catholic Oriental Churches."

In conformity with the holiness of marriage itself, non-Catholic ministers are reverently and earnestly requested to cooperate in the task of registering marriages in the books of the Catholic party, whether of the Latin or Oriental rite.

Ordinaries of the place, who grant the dispensation from the impediment of mixed religion, are likewise given the faculty of dispensing from the obligation of observing canonical form for lawfulness if there exist difficulties which, according to their prudent judgment, require this dispensation.

The same Supreme Pontiff has ordered the Sacred Congregation for the Oriental Church, of which he himself is the prefect, to make known to all this resolution and concession. Wherefore, the same sacred congregation, after also consulting the Sacred Doctrinal Congregation, at the order of His Holiness, has composed the present decree to be published in the Acta Apostolicae Sedis.

Meanwhile, in order that his new statute may be brought to the attention of those whom it concerns, whether they be Catholics of any rite whatever or Orthodox, the present decree will go into effect beginning from March 25, 1967, feast of the Annunciation of the Blessed Virgin Mary.

Notwithstanding anything which in any way may be to the contrary.

EPISCOPAL FACULTIES

The most important single faculty granted to bishops is that described in the motu proprio *De Episcoporum Muneribus* (June 15, 1966). The Latin text is found in the Acta Apostolicae Sedis, LVIII (1966), 467-472. An English translation is in the *Canon Law Digest,* 1966 Supplement, under Canon 329. This faculty, based on the Decree *Christus Dominus* of the council (Vatican II), gives to the diocesan bishops the faculty to dispense their faithful in particular cases from the general laws of the Church whenever they judge that it would be for their spiritual good, unless a special reservation has been made by the Supreme authority. For each new case that arises all that will be necessary is to consult this motu proprio to determine whether the particular faculty is there. A Handbook on all these faculties had been prepared by a special committee of the Canon Law Society of America. Copies can be obtained by writing to the headquarters of the CLS.

MOTU PROPRIO "MATRIMONIA MIXTA"
"Provisional Norms" for Application in Canada

1. Formulated by the Canadian Catholic Conference June 5-6, 1970 and became effective August 1, 1970.
2. Approved by the Holy See.

I. THE CANONICAL FORM

General principle: A Catholic should normally contract marriage in and before the Catholic Church (cf. note 1).

A. The Ordinary of the Catholic party, or the Ordinary of the place where the marriage is to be celebrated, may dispense from the canonical form.
In cases where the marriage is celebrated in a diocese other than that of the Catholic party, the "nihil obstat" of the Ordinary of the place where the marriage is to be celebrated, should be given.

B. In order for the dispensations to be granted legitimately, the reasons for doing so should concern *in an important way* the good of the parties, especially their spiritual well-being and the tranquillity and peace of their personal and family relationships (cf. note 2).

II. PROMISES TO BE MADE BY THE CATHOLIC PARTY

A. The promises to be made by the Catholic party will be made orally (not in written form), and the presence of a witness is not necessary; the priest who prepared the couple for their marriage will certify to the Ordinary that these promises were sincerely made, and that he is morally certain that the Catholic party will be faithful to them.

(Cf. Annex "B").

B. The celebration of a mixed marriage will not be authorized in those cases where

a. it is clearly evident that the Catholic party is not sincere in making the promises;

b. the Catholic party refuses to promise to do his or her best to safeguard the Catholic faith and to see to the Catholic baptism and education of children to be born from the marriage.

III. PREPARATION OF THE NON-CATHOLIC PARTY

The priest who prepares the couple for marriage will inform the non-Catholic party of the promises made by the Catholic party and will certify to the Ordinary that this has been done. He will see to it that the couple accept the ends and essential properties of Christian matrimony. He can make use of the formula given in Annex "B" for this purpose.

IV. ANNOTATION OF THE MARRIAGE

A marriage celebrated with dispensation from the canonical form will be recorded at the place where the marriage was celebrated (v.g., church, court house, etc.).

A marginal annotation will be made in the baptismal records of the place where the Catholic party was baptized (see Annex "A").

Record of the granting of the dispensation from the canonical form will be kept in the Chancery Office of the diocese granting the dispensation.

V. CELEBRATION OF THE MARRIAGE

A. The celebration of a mixed marriage in the Catholic Church should be presided by the Catholic priest. It is desirable that the non-Catholic minister be invited to take part in the ceremony in some way, according to norms to be drawn up in an Ecumenical Directory.

B. The celebration of a mixed marriage outside the Catholic Church—with dispensation from the canonical form— should be presided by the non-Catholic minister. It is desirable that the Catholic priest be invited to take part in the ceremony in some way.

C. Thus, the celebration of the marriage of a Catholic with a non-Catholic will be accompanied by various sacred rites; this will depend on whether the non-Catholic party belongs to a given Church, ecclesial community, or religion, and on the personal religious convictions of the parties.

The marriage could be celebrated during Mass, or within a Liturgy of the Word, or simply by fulfilling the rites of the ceremony itself, but always *according to certain principles,* such as those of "Matrimonia mixta" which allows the celebration of Mass only when the marriage is taking place between two Christians.

D. In each case, it is the priest who will decide, after having consulted the couple, and in accordance with the directives given in Annex "C."

VI. MARRIAGE BANNS

In order to ensure greater cooperation between the ministers of both Churches, it is recommended that the practice be introduced of publishing the marriage banns in both Churches (Catholic and non-Catholic); this applies in places where it is customary to have such publications.

VII. WITNESSES

Non-Catholics may be invited to act as witnesses to such a marriage or to assist the spouses in some other capacity.

NOTES

1. Reasons in favor of maintaining or using the canonical form for mixed marriages:

a) greater facility in ensuring that appropriate instructions have been given for the preparation of the marriage;

b) possibility of avoiding the celebration of premature and hasty marriages;

c) greater order in parish records.

2. Among the many reasons for which the Holy See has granted dispensations from the canonical form since 1966, are the following:

a) to keep the non-Catholic partner from breaking with his/her Church or religious body;

b) to avoid the danger of having an invalid or illicit marriage celebrated outside the Church;

c) promotion of better relations between the two families so that both may offer better support for the newly-married couple;

d) *active* participation of the non-Catholic party in the life of his or her Church; for example, if the party were a Sunday School Teacher, Warden, Trustee, etc.

e) local customs (v.g., in Canada the marriage is traditionally celebrated in the bride's parish).

The other canonical reasons previously recognized in law for the dispensation from the impediments of mixed religion and disparity of worship (canon 1061) also apply in certain cases.

Concerning the procedure to be followed for the celebration of a marriage with dispensation from the canonical form, see Annex "A."

3. *Notation in the Marriage Register*

The following considerations seem to justify the proposed procedure:

a) avoid unnecessary administrative work;

b) the Catholic priest cannot attend to a marriage which took place elsewhere;

c) the registration of all dispensations in the Chancery office which grants the dispensation and assigns a protocol number to it;

d) the plural used in the Latin text of the Motu Proprio is to be interpreted according to the general rules of Canon Law and, in certain cases, applies only to baptismal registers.

Annex "A"

PROCEDURE FOR THE CELEBRATION

OF A MIXED MARRIAGE

WITH A DISPENSATION FROM THE CANONICAL FORM

1. The pastor (or the curate) of the Catholic party makes the prenuptial inquiry and completes the dossier which remains in the archives of the parish.

2. Using Form "V," the pastor or curate of the Catholic party requests from the Ordinary the dispensations required for a mixed marriage (mixed religion or disparity of worship, as the case may be), dispensation from the form, the nihil obstat, and, if necessary, the dispensation from other impediments. He indicates on the reverse side of Form "V," along with the reasons for requesting the other dispensations, the reasons for which he requests a dispensation from the canonical form, and mentions before what Church or civil institution the marriage is to be celebrated.

3. The pastor receives the regular rescript from the Chancery Office together with two copies of a document authorizing the celebration of the marriage outside the Catholic Church. The rescript is placed in the dossier, together with one copy of the authorization.

4. When advising the Catholic party that the dispensation has been granted, the pastor gives him or her one copy of the document authorizing the celebration of marriage before a minister other than a Catholic priest. The Catholic party

is requested to forward a certificate of marriage as soon as possible after the ceremony.

5. When the marriage certificate is received, the pastor will advise the parish where the Catholic party was baptized. The following text may be used:

X.................................., a Catholic baptized on
.... in ....Church,
..................................married Y...................
on.........................19........... in ....
(Church, temple, Courthouse) after receiving a dispensation from the canonical form of marriage (Prot. No _____)

Please make this annotation in your Baptismal Register and return this notice, certifying that the annotation has been made as requested.

Annex "B"

DECLARATION CONCERNING THE PREPARATION

OF THE PARTIES TO A MIXED MARRIAGE

(This form must be filled out by the priest who conducts the prenuptial inquiry. One copy is sufficient. It is to be sent to the Chancery Office with the petition for the nihil obstat, and will be returned to the parish to be included in the dossier.)

Names of the parties:
The Catholic party..
The non-Catholic party.....................................
Member of..
(Name Church)

YES
1. *Promise of the Catholic party*
   The Catholic party has been carefully instructed concerning his responsibility to live according to his faith, to give

witness to his faith, to avoid anything that could weaken his faith, and to do his best to have the children who will be born of his marriage baptized and educated in the Catholic faith. The Catholic party has explicitly promised to be faithful to these responsibilities.

YES

2. *Preparation of the non-Catholic party*
The non-Catholic party has been instructed on the doctrine of the Catholic Church with regard to Christian marriage and recognizes that the marriage he wishes to contract is to be one and indissoluble. The non-Catholic party is aware of the responsibilities of the Catholic party with regard to religious practice and to the Catholic baptism and education of the children.

Describe briefly the non-Catholic party's attitude:

YES

3. *Preparation for marriage*
Both parties have been adequately prepared for their forthcoming marriage.

YES

4. *Opinion of the priest*
I am morally certain that the Catholic party will be faithful to these obligations.

Date

Signature of the priest

Annex "C"

LITURGICAL CELEBRATION

General principles

1. For all marriages celebrated in the Catholic Church, it is normal that the exchange of consent should be accompanied by sacred rites which help the spouses to turn their minds and hearts to God, to discover God's love in their mutual love and to give thanks to Him.

2. However, no matter how keen our desire to share with non-Catholics the Church's means of grace, participation in the same sacred actions must always be respectful of truth. To avoid any ambiguity unworthy of an action which is directed to God and unbecoming of the persons who perform that action, the words, the acts, the chants and the responses of the ceremony must be in accord with the religious beliefs of both spouses. This respect for truth and for the convictions of the persons involved in *communicatio in sacris* is a primordial principle of ecumenism.

   Though it may be painful to the spouses that the divergence of their respective convictions appear at a time when they join together in marriage, they should be invited by the priest to acknowledge in humility this distressing reality and to accept the suffering that it brings instead of seeking to cover it up with false pretences.

3. No one should be surprised that the Catholic Church should consider itself closer to one Church than to another and that, as a consequence, it should invite certain Christians to participate more fully in its worship. This difference of attitude does not stem from a judgment on persons but rather from the fact of a greater unity in faith and sacramental life.

   The marriage of a Catholic with a non-Catholic will therefore be differently accompanied by sacred rites depending on what Church, what community, what religion, the non-Catholic partner belongs to, as well as upon the personal religious dispositions of those who are contracting marriage. This marriage could be celebrated within the Holy Sacrifice or even in the framework of the Celebration of the Word, or simply using the rites for marriage alone.

This decision will be made for reasons in the religious or pastoral order and not for reasons foreign to faith or to the spiritual good of the persons such as, for example, the desire of underlining the celebration of a marriage celebration or of following social conveniences.

In some cases it will be necessary to recall that the sacred rites are not favors and consequently the decision to not accompany the marriage with a Mass is not because of an intention of penalizing those contracting a mixed marriage.

Catholic and Orthodox

A marriage of a Catholic to a Christian of an Oriental Church separated from the Roman Catholic Church may be celebrated within Mass; in this particular circumstance, the Orthodox Christian may, if he has the required dispositions and *his own Church has no objections*, take part with the Catholic partner in the blessed Eucharist.

Catholic and Protestant

The differences in doctrine and the sacrament of life which exist between the Catholic Church and the churches and church communities in the West, generally lead one to celebrate the marriage of a Catholic with a Christian Protestant outside the ceremonies of Mass. Since Christian fiancees have nevertheless in common their faith in the Word of God, their marriage naturally fits into the framework of a Celebration of the Word.

Nevertheless it may sometimes be desirable that the marriage of a Catholic with a Protestant Christian be celebrated within Mass. This would particularly be the case when the spouses have requested it for motives which flow from a living and educated faith. The non-Catholic spouse nevertheless is not permitted to receive communion at this Mass and the priest will take care to inform the non-Catholic partner of this disposition and if necessary during the preparatory meetings for the marriage indicate the reasons for such a law.

SOURCES OF NULLITY

What are some of the sources or grounds upon which a marriage can be declared null?

1.	Insincere prenuptial promises	C. 1061
2.	Want of age	C. 1067
3.	Impotency	C. 1068
4.	Former Bond of Marriage	C. 1069
5.	Disparity of Cult	C. 1070
6.	Sacred Orders (Deacon-Subdeacon)	C. 1072
7.	Solemn Religious Vows	C. 1073
8.	Abduction	C. 1074
9.	Crime	C. 1075
10.	Consanguinity	C. 1076
11.	Affinity	C. 1077
12.	Public Propriety	C. 1078
13.	Spiritual Relationship	C. 1079
14.	Legal Relationship	C. 1080
15.	Insanity	C. 1081
16.	Ignorance or Error	C. 1082 & C. 1083
17.	Simulation	C. 1085, p. 1

THE CHURCH WEDDING

Wedding Procession

It is customary in some places to have a wedding procession to give dignity to the marriage ceremony. The minimum required for a valid marriage is the pastor and two witnesses. In the United States, the latter are called the matron-of-honor and the best man. The law states *two witnesses,* and as such these could be two men or two women. It is a custom in some countries to have two men as witnesses (Italy).

Due to the difficulties that may arise in some parish churches regarding the procession, it will facilitate matters for the priest who has the rehearsal before the wedding to follow definite rules and regulations, otherwise there will be just as many ways for the procession as there are people in the bridal party. Some churches have their own custom which is followed at all times. However, the following is the general method which is used in most church weddings.

First of all, the Catholic Church is known for its liturgy and rubrics. It is always concerned about the proper decorum and etiquette in its churches and ceremonies. However, since there is no canonical or liturgical rule for a wedding procession, the following regulations are suggested:

Regulation I

A.

1. The Ushers
2. The Bridesmaids
3. The Matron-of-honor
4. The Flower Girl or Girls
5. Bride and the Bride's Father or his substitute

B.

The Groom and Best Man stand between the pews and the altar rail.

```
┌─────────────────────────────────────┐
│              ALTAR                   │
├─────────────────────────────────────┤
│                  ↑                   │
│   Ushers — — — — | — — — —Ushers     │
│                                      │
│   Bride's— — — — | — — — —Maids      │
│                                      │
│   Matron— — — — —|— — — —of Honor    │
│                                      │
│   Flower Girl— — —|— — — Ring Bearer │
│                                      │
│   BRIDE — — — — —|— — — —FATHER of   │
│                          BRIDE       │
└─────────────────────────────────────┘
```

Position of the Bridal Party at the Altar

Priest

Maid-of-Honor   **Bride**   **Groom**   Best-Man

Flower Girl   **Ring Bearer**

Ushers	Brides-maids		Brides-maids	Ushers
	(or)			(or)
	All Bridesmaids			All Ushers
	Bride's Parents			Groom's Parents
	Bride's Relatives			Groom's Relatives
	Bride's Friends			Groom's Friends

Recessional

The procession goes in the reverse order, namely:

The Bride and Groom	The Bride and Groom
The Maid of Honor alone	The Maid of Honor with the Best Man
The Bridesmaids	The Bridesmaids with their Usher Escort
The Bride's Parents	The Bride's Parents
The Groom's Parents	The Groom's Parents

BIBLIOGRAPHY

AUGUSTINE, *Commentary on the Code of Canon Law*, 8 Vols. St. Louis, 1927.

AYRINHAC, H. A., LYDON, P. J., *Marriage Legislation*, New York, 1957.

ABATE, A., *The Dissolution of the Matrimonial Bond in Ecclesiastical Jurisprudence*, New York, 1962.

BASSET, William, *The Bond of Marriage*, Notre Dame Press, 1968.

BARRETT, J. D. M., *The Councils of Baltimore* and *The Code of Canon Law*, Washington, 1932.

BOUSCAREN, T. L., *Canon Law Digest*, 5 vols. Milwaukee, Wis. 1934-1963.

BOUSCAREN, T. L., *Canon Law, A Text and Commentary*, Milwaukee, Wisc., 1957.

BONZELET, H. J., MATHIS, M. J., MEYER, M. W., *The Pastoral Companion*, 12 Ed. Chicago, 1961.

BRIDE, A., *Le Pouvoir de Souverain Pontife sur le Mariage des Infideles*, Revue de Droit Canonique, Paris, 1960.

CAPPELLO, F. M., *De Matrimonio*, Romae, 1950.

CARBERRY, J. J., *Juridical Form of Marriage*, Washington, 1934.

CATHOLIC LAWYERS GUILD OF CHICAGO, (Ed) *Canon Law on Civil Action in Marriage Problems*, Chicago, 1944.

CAVANAUGH, J. R., M. D., *Fundamental Marriage Counseling*, Milwaukee, 1957.

CAVANAUGH, J. R., M. D., *Sexual Anomalies and the Law*, (The Catholic Lawyer) IX, New York, 1963.

CHATHAM, J. G., *Force and Fear as Invalidating Marriage*, Washington, 1950.

CATHOLIC CENTER, Ottawa, Canada, Ottawa University, *Mosaic*, 1970.

CLAYS-BOUAAERT, Simenon, *Manuale Jurio Canonici*, Gandae et Leodin.

CLOREN, O., *Previews and Practical Cases of Marriage*, Milwaukee, 1960.

CLARK, Contracts

CHARDON, *Histoire des Sacrement du Mariage*.

DILLON, R., *Common Law Marriage*, Washington, 1942.

DOHENY, W. J., *Canonical Procedure in Matrimonial Cases*, 2 Vols., Milwaukee, 1958.

DOHENY, W. J., *Practical Manual for Marriage Cases*, Milwaukee, 1953.

DUSKIE, J. A., *Canonical Status of the Orientals in the United States,* Washington, D. C., 1928.

DOWDELL, R. M., *The Celebration of Matrimony in Danger of Death,* Romae, 1944.

FRAENKEL, F., *Missing Persons,* New York, 1950.

FLEMING, T., *The Divorced Ones,* This Week Magazine, January, 1964.

GASPARRI - SEREDI, *Corpus Juris Canonici Fontes,* 9 Vols.

GASPARRI - SEREDI, *De Matrimonio,* 2 Vols., Romae, 1932.

GOLDSMITH, J. W., *The Competence of Church and State over Marriage,* Washington, 1944.

HARING, Bernard, *The Law of Christ,* Newman Press, 1966.

HERMAN, E., *Adnotationes, Periodica de Re Morali Canonica Liturgica,* Rome, 1949.

HERTEL, James R., *When Marriage Fails,* Paulist Press, N.J.

JOYCE, G. H., *Christian Marriage,* (An Historical and Doctrinal Study), London, 1948.

KAY, T. H., *The Prenuptial Investigation,* Washington, 19—.

KEARNEY, F. P., *Principles of Canon 1127,* Washington, 1942.

KELLY, G., *Medical-Moral Problems,* St. Louis, 1958.

KELLY, G., *Modern Youth and Chastity,* St. Louis, 1943.

KING, J. P., *Canonical Procedure in Separation Cases,* Washington, 1952.

KOEGEL, Otto, E., *Common Law Marriages,* Washington, 1922.

LONG, J., *A Treatise on the Law of Domestic Relations,* Indianapolis, 1948.

MACKEY, R. V., Mandell, I., *Law of Marriage and Divorce,* New York, 1955.

MAHONEY, E. J., *Marriage Preliminaries,* London, 1949. *Questions and Answers: The Sacraments,* London, 1946.

MARBACH, J. F., *Marriage Legislation for Catholics of the Oriental Rites in the United States and Canada,* Washington, 1946.

MARKELBACH, B. H., *Summa Theologiae Moralis,* 3 Vols., Paris, 1935-1938.

MONDEN, Louis, S.J., *Sin, Liberty and Law,* Sheed & Ward, N.Y. 1965.

MONTSERRAT, J., *The Abandoned Spouse,* Bruce, 1969.

MOORE, Thos., *Legal Reply,* Pennsylvania, 1955.

MARRIAGE CASES - Detroit Chancery, Michigan, 1960.

NAU, L. J., *Marriage Laws of the Code of Canon Law*, New York, 1934.

NOLDIN, H., SCHMITT, A., HEINZEL, G., *Summa Theologiae Moralis*, 3 Vols., Oeniponte.

NIEDERMEYER, A., M. D., BUONANNO, F., *Compendium of Pastoral Medicine*, New York, 1961.

OESTERLE, D. G., *Consultationes de Iure Matrimoniali*, Romae, 1942.

OMMEREN, V., *Mental Illness Affecting Matrimonial Consent*, Washington, 1961.

O'CONNOR, W. R., *The Indissolubility of a Ratified-Consummated Marriage*, Ephem. Theo. Loveniensis.

PIETRZYK, S., *A Practical Formulary in Accordance with the Code of Canon Law*, Little Rock, Ark., 1949.

POSPISHIL, V. J., *Interritual Canon Law Problems in the United States and Canada*, Chesapeake City, Md., 1955.

POSPISHIL, V. J., *Divorce and Remarriage*, Herder & Herder, N. Y., 1967.

PRUMMER, D. M., *Manuale Juris Canonici*, Friburgi, Brisgoviae, 1933.

POPE PIUS XII, *Allocution to the Roman Rota*, AAS XXXIV (1942).

RAMSTEIN, M., *A Manual of Canon Law*, Hoboken, N. J., 1947.

RICE, P. W., *Proof of Death in Prenuptial Investigations*, Washington, 1940.

ROBERTS, R. P., *Matrimonial Legislation in Latin - Oriental Canon Law* (A Comparative Study, Westminster, Md., 1961.

SNEE, J., CLARK, J. D., *Diocesan Faculties in the United States*, Woodstock, 1948.

SULLIVAN, B. O., *Legislation and Requirements for Permissible Cohabitation in Invalid Marriages*, Washington, 1954.

VERMEERSCH, A., CREUSEN, *Epitome Juris Canonici*, 3 Vols., Rome, 1956.

VERMEERSCH, A., BOUSCAREN, T. L., *What is Marriage?*, New York, 1952.

VROMONT, G., *De Matrimonio*, Paris, 1952.

WERNZ, F. X., VIDAL, P., *Jus Canonicum*, 7 Vols., Rome, 1927-1946. *Jus Matrimoniale*, Rome, 1946.

WINSLOW, F. S., *The Pauline Privilege* & *The Constitution of Canon 1125*, New York, 1942.

WOYWOOD, S., SMITH, C., *Practical Commentary on the Code of Canon Law*, New York, 1958.

WRENN, Lawrence G., *Annulments*, C. L. S. A., Washington, D. C. 1970.

WRZASZCZAK, C. F., *The Betrothal Contract in the Code of Canon Law*, Washington, 1954.

Acta Apostolicae Sedis, Romae, 1909.
Acta et Decreta Concilii Plenarii Baltimorensis Tertii, Baltimore.
Codex Iuris Canonici, Pius X, Rome, 1917.
The Jurist, Catholic University, Washington, D. C.
N.C.W.C., News Service.

Periodicals:
    America, N.Y.
    Bulletin of Guild of Catholic Psychiatrists, 1960
    Catholic Theological Society Proceedings, 1967
    Chicago Studies, 1963
    Commonweal, 1967
    Concilium, N.Y., 1967
    Irish Theological Quarterly, 1968
    Jubilee, 1966
    Marriage, 1966

Decrees of Vatican Council II
    Studia Canonica, Canada, 1970

INDEX